Managing for Results 2002

The PricewaterhouseCoopers Endowment for
The Business of Government

THE PRICEWATERHOUSECOOPERS ENDOWMENT SERIES ON THE BUSINESS OF GOVERNMENT

Series Editors: Mark A. Abramson and Paul R. Lawrence

The PricewaterhouseCoopers Endowment Series on The Business of Government explores new approaches to improving the effectiveness of government at the federal, state, and local levels. The Series is aimed at providing cutting-edge knowledge to government leaders, academics, and students about the management of government in the 21st century.

Publications in the series will include:

2001
Transforming Organizations, *edited by Mark A. Abramson and Paul R. Lawrence*
E-Government 2001, *edited by Mark A. Abramson and Grady E. Means*

2002
Leadership
Financial Management
Human Capital
Innovation

Managing for Results 2002

EDITED BY

MARK A. ABRAMSON
THE PRICEWATERHOUSECOOPERS ENDOWMENT
FOR THE BUSINESS OF GOVERNMENT
and
JOHN M. KAMENSKY
PRICEWATERHOUSECOOPERS

ROWMAN & LITTLEFIELD PUBLISHERS, INC.
Lanham • Boulder • New York • Oxford

ROWMAN & LITTLEFIELD PUBLISHERS, INC.

Published in the United States of America
by Rowman & Littlefield Publishers, Inc.
4720 Boston Way, Lanham, Maryland 20706
www.rowmanlittlefield.com

12 Hid's Copse Road
Cumnor Hill, Oxford OX2 9JJ, England

British Library Cataloguing in Publication Information Available

Library of Congress Cataloging-in-Publication Data Available

0-7425-1351-3 (alk. paper)
0-7425-1352-1 (pbk.: alk. paper)

Printed in the United States of America

∞™ The paper used in this publication meets the minimum requirements of American National Standard for Information Sciences—Permanence of Paper for Printed Library Materials, ANSI/NISO Z39.48-1992.

To

Ellen K. Abramson

Jeanne M. Kamensky

TABLE OF CONTENTS

PART I

Getting Ready to Manage for Results

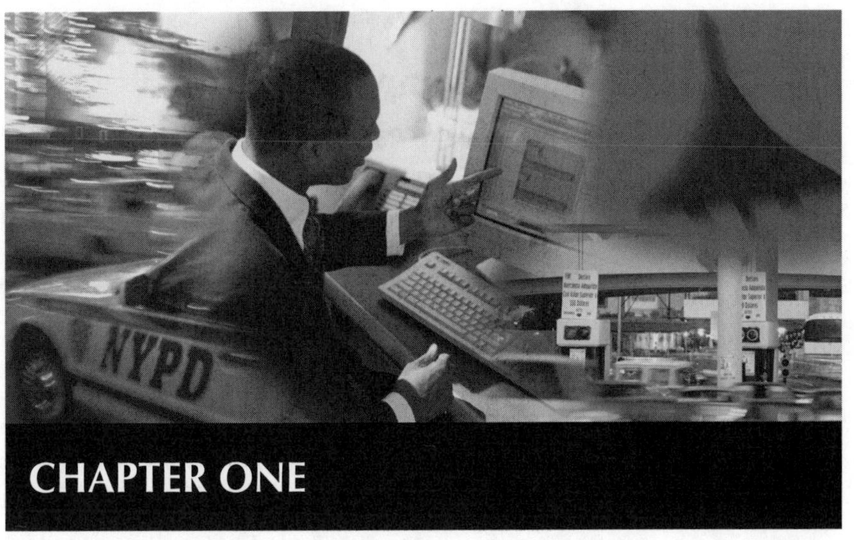

CHAPTER ONE

Managing for Results: Cutting-Edge Challenges Facing Government Leaders in 2002

John M. Kamensky
Director, Managing for Results Practice
PricewaterhouseCoopers

Mark A. Abramson
Executive Director
The PricewaterhouseCoopers Endowment
for The Business of Government

Why Is It Important to Manage for Results Now?

The time has come for public leaders to manage for results. The public demands it. A statutory framework is now in place at the federal level, as well as in many state governments. The state of the art has matured dramatically. And, huge advances in technology during the past decade make it possible. The key ingredient, as always in any major organizational culture change, is the will to do it. And that is growing across the public sector as leaders see that managing for results gets results.

A 1999 study of why citizens distrust government concludes that "the government's perceived performance failures significantly undermine trust."[1] This is echoed by author Jonathan Walters, who says, "citizens are getting testy about insisting on a bottom-line look at what government is producing.... [They] want government to deliver quality services that yield good results (and do it without raising taxes)."[2]

According to the General Accounting Office (GAO), "There has been a groundswell movement in recent years toward performance-based management in public sector organizations.... Governments have implemented reform agendas that have tended to include a common recognition that improved management was a critical part of the answer to meeting demands.... A part of this common recognition was the widespread acceptance of the need to shift the focus of government decision making and accountability away from a preoccupation with the activities that are undertaken—as grants or inspections made—to a focus on the results of those activities—such as real gains in employability, safety, responsiveness, or program quality."[3]

In chapter four, Kathryn Newcomer and Mary Ann Scheirer reinforce this observation with a list of factors pressing federal agencies to focus on performance reporting, and include success stories from states, localities, and other countries. They note that at the federal level, this has been reflected in a series of management reform laws over the past decade, including the Government Performance and Results Act (GPRA), the Chief Financial Officers Act, and the Clinger-Cohen Act reforming the use of technology.

Newcomer and Scheirer also note that technologies evolving in the past decade have greatly enhanced the potential uses of performance measurement. The "use of graphics capabilities in modern analytic software helps to communicate evaluation and performance results in 'user-friendly' formats." This includes the use of Geographic Information Systems and integrated management information systems.

However, the biggest reason that government leaders are increasingly using a managing for results approach is that it works. In chapter five,

Peter Frumkin describes how the state of Oklahoma's Milestone Contracting approach cut waiting times in half for job applicants, paperwork by one-third, and cost-per-case-closed by 25 percent. In one case, for example, Goodwill in Tulsa was able to train twice as many people, with no increase in resources. In chapter six, Paul O'Connell tells the story of New York City's CompStat system, where the police department cut the city's murder, burglary, and robbery rates by two-thirds over an eight-year period. As a result, this approach is spreading. For example, Baltimore's CitiStat system is "the first time that a major American city has attempted to coordinate all of its major services and to formalize the process of interagency cooperation through the stat system," says O'Connell. Most striking, though, this system helped reduce Baltimore's homicide rate to a 10-year low.

The following chapters in this book provide a glimpse of this rapidly changing environment, and how managing for results can make a difference in all organizations.

What Is Managing for Results?

Managing for results is shorthand for a conceptual framework that reflects a fundamental change in the management culture of governments across the globe. It is a culture that is fact-based, results-oriented, open, and accountable. As the Canadian auditor general observes, "Managing for results allows managers to make changes once they know what is working and what is not. It represents a significant difference in the way government programs are managed. Managers can then pay more attention to finding out whether programs are meeting their objectives and less to only carrying out activities or setting up structures and processes."[4]

A managing for results framework is comprised of two major dimensions: building the basic infrastructure—and then using it.

Building a Managing for Results Infrastructure

The basic infrastructure for a managing for results system includes:

- an organization's multiyear strategic plan,
- the development of metrics and the basic data collection system,
- data validity and verification procedures,
- an annual operating plan,
- an annual performance report, and
- performance evaluation.

In and of itself, this dimension often takes years to put in place and goes through at least a couple cycles to shake out the kinks. At the federal level, the construction of this infrastructure is still underway even though agencies put together their first strategic plans in 1997 and issued their first performance reports in early 2000.

The next three chapters highlight insights and lessons learned related to the planning, measuring, and evaluation components of this first dimension.

In chapter two, Colin Campbell describes the U.S. Air Force's corporate strategic planning process. Developed in 1996, Air Force Chief of Staff Ronald Fogleman's approach challenged Air Force leaders to look 25 years down the road as a way of reassessing conventional wisdom. He concludes that the only way General Fogleman was able to create a credible planning process was to create a collaborative process—not to focus on the resulting vision. General Fogleman believed that "historically the Air Force adapted to new challenges best through broad canvassing of views, which, apart from encouraging innovative perspectives, improved 'buy-in' once programmatic commitments were made." Campbell also observes that one weakness of the Air Force approach was that, while it did a good job in involving internal stakeholders, involving external stakeholders was "a key ingredient to successful corporate strategic planning."

In chapter three, Patrick Murphy and John Carnevale go beyond the experience of creating a plan that measures for a single agency and describe the development of a common plan that measures the country's antidrug efforts. They tell how the U.S. Office of National Drug Control Policy (ONDCP) created a collaborative effort, reaching to develop buy-in around common metrics, targets, and strategies to wage the war on illegal drugs. The effort was organized around a logic model that shows the interaction among five goals, 31 objectives, 97 performance targets, and 127 measures.

While ONDCP's cross-agency, results-oriented measurement effort is uncommon at the federal level, most significant policy outcomes in government cannot be achieved by any single agency. Collaboration, networks, and partnership are keys to successfully managing for results. Consequently, the ONDCP case study may serve as an important set of lessons for future collaborative efforts.

And in chapter four, Newcomer and Scheirer assess the capacity and progress of federal agencies' use of program evaluation as a tool for making program improvement decisions and strengthening performance management. Performance measures can tell managers *what* is happening. Only by investing in evaluation will they find the answer to *why* something is happening (or not happening!).

Concurrent with building the basic managing for results infrastructure, leaders and managers need to align and integrate other existing management systems so that they reinforce their organization's intended program results. For example, the Occupational Safety and Health Administration (OSHA) changed its strategic approach for achieving programmatic results in the mid-1990s. It shifted from an adversarial stance that relied on fines and sanctions to gain compliance with workplace safety rules, to a partnership strategy where it worked collaboratively with businesses and employees to reduce injuries in the workplace. However, it quickly recognized that the performance appraisal system for its field investigators still rewarded the number and amount of fines levied. So while its Washington-based leaders reoriented the agency's strategic plan, behavior in the field did not change until the performance appraisal system was revamped.

In addition to aligning the individual performance management systems, other systems that need to be realigned around an organization's intended program results include:

- the budget structure in both the legislative and executive branches, which reinforces outcome-oriented thinking when policymakers and agency staff consider resource allocations;
- the financial management system, which needs to be able to generate current cost information so managers can use financial information to make informed decisions and set priorities; and
- the human capital system, which needs to support overall goals by ensuring the availability of critical workforce competencies to accomplish the organization's mission, necessary training, succession planning, and performance management incentives tied to organizational goals.

Finally, the overall organizational structure should be framed around customers and intended results, not around organizational processes and functions. Examples of federal agencies that are in the process of organizing around customers include the Office of Student Financial Assistance, the Internal Revenue Service, and the Centers for Medicare and Medicaid Services.

Using Information to Manage for Results

The basic managing for results infrastructure creates the ability to manage for results. However, to be effective, managers must then link intended performance results to their day-to-day operational management. Regarding the ONDCP performance measurement process, Patrick Tarr, a senior policy advisor in the U.S. Department of Justice, observes that the "... real goal is not just to write a report, but establish a process that is used."

Does information affect day-to-day behaviors and conversations by managers and employees? Several tools to transform an organization's culture to be more results-oriented and performance-based include:

- personal accountability of the agency's top leadership for specific, measurable results;
- the use of organizational and individual balanced scorecards to link targets to results;
- the availability of live, transparent performance data to everyone in the organization; and
- the use of written individual and team performance agreements tied to an incentive system.

The remaining three chapters in the book provide real examples of these tools in use.

In chapter five, Frumkin tackles the challenge of getting public sector results when using nonprofit groups, while respecting their need for autonomy through the use of written performance contracts. He describes the state of Oklahoma's Milestone Contracting system, which pays providers for a series of collaboratively defined distinct achievements, rather than the traditional fee-for-service reimbursement. This approach simultaneously achieves accountability and autonomy in that state's jobs programs for developmentally disabled individuals.

In chapter six, O'Connell tells the story of how the New York City Police Department developed "CompStat," a computer-based management system that is credited for helping cut the city's crime rate by nearly two-thirds. This approach uses live, transparent data, stresses personal accountability of top leaders, and uses scorecards to keep track of performance. He also describes how this system is now being applied in other areas, such as the parks, the health department, and the prison system.

And finally, in chapter seven, David Frederickson assesses the potential of the Government Performance and Results Act as a tool to influence state and local governmental priorities to support national outcomes. He examines five agencies within the U.S. Department of Health and Human Services that have a wide range of responsibilities and use different policy tools (e.g., grants, regulations) to influence their intended outcomes. He concludes that while GPRA has created new lines of communication among a wide range of stakeholders, it is hard to develop common measures and outcomes. But this is becoming easier with the advent of live, Geographic Information Systems with customer-centric, transparent data available to an entire network, and with the use of techniques such as logic models and CompStat systems.

Frederickson also observes that, for now, performance measurement systems tend to be more useful for managers. Success, according to many observers, is the eventual linking of intended results to decision-making cycles, such as budget, policy, and management. Performance budgeting links expected results to spending decisions. This can be done within an agency, by the Office of Management and Budget, and by Congress. The Bush administration has committed to submitting performance budgets to Congress starting in 2002. Policy decision making—changing the service delivery methods, rethinking the programs used to reach intended goals, or rethinking the appropriate roles of the federal government in meeting a national goal—often requires a longer time-series of performance information in order to make informed judgments. This often implies the use of evaluation to understand the whats and the whys of a particular intended policy outcome. And the use of performance information in making management decisions within an agency often helps determine how the organization should be doing something.

Four Cutting-Edge Challenges

Much has been written in the past decade about both dimensions of managing for results. But more has been written about the basic managing for results infrastructure than about the use of such a system to get results. The case studies in this book, however, are a snapshot of innovative approaches and thoughtful reflections on better ways to manage for results that bridge the two dimensions. They reflect the cutting edge of the challenges facing those committed to managing for results in the coming year. These challenges include:

- involving customers, stakeholders, and employees;
- increasing the use of performance information to get results;
- achieving crosscutting outcomes; and
- changing the fundamental jobs of individuals, organizations, and institutions.

Challenge Number One: Involve Customers, Stakeholders, and Employees

One common theme in this book is the imperative to involve customers, stakeholders, and employees in the design and implementation of any managing for results system. Not engaging all three can result in problems for an organization. One federal agency, noted for its state-of-the-art performance system, has been roundly criticized by its stakeholders for poor performance. This criticism baffled employees and customers. They were engaged; the stakeholders were not. Campbell makes a similar observation about the Air Force's corporate strategic planning efforts, "If you do not have buy-in, you do not have a plan."

Jim McEntire, director of the Department of Transportation's widely recognized performance planning system, says that the different stakeholders—the Congress, the White House, department leaders, and bureau heads—all have different, yet legitimate, "systems of rationality." He observes that this is why a "defined performance framework is so valuable, it provides an important way of communicating." The key is to involve all parties to give them a common forum for communicating their unique points of view—ones based on their different systems. His observations are reinforced by the authors in this book. For example, Frederickson found that "GPRA has resulted in new lines of results-oriented communication and improved cooperation with the third parties that agencies rely on to carry out their missions."

There are four logical points in the managing for results framework to engage customers, stakeholders, and employees:

- when defining overall outcomes,
- when developing measures and targets,
- when creating the technical capacity to gather and use performance information, and
- when using the information for implementation and accountability.

Involvement in Defining Overall Outcomes

One of the key lessons learned in the Oklahoma Milestone Contracting system was that "good communication between public and nonprofit managers early in the contracting design process is essential." Frumkin observes, "Collaboration will go a long way toward both assuring nonprofit support for change and the selection of meaningful and appropriate measures of progress."

Involvement in Developing Measures and Targets

If there ever was a place where "the devil is in the details," it's when specific measures and targets are developed. This is the core message of the ONDCP story. As Murphy and Carnevale observed, "The countless small issues that will emerge during the implementation and operationalization of the system can derail strategic planning efforts." That's why ONDCP attempted to create a credible process. Because the ONDCP effort was seen as something that would take years before it would become fully operational, "to sustain such an effort, it was important to secure a genuine commitment from the many participants early on in the development process." Murphy and Carnevale concluded, "The process of constructing the system secured a commitment from one group of critical stakeholders: mid-level policy officials in Washington, D.C." Carnevale added his observation that "By being inclusive, starting from first principles, and asking the 'should' question, the ONDCP and the agency participants managed to produce a system of measuring performance that is credible."

Frederickson found Murphy and Carnevale's observations had a broader application: "The results orientation of GPRA coupled with the development of performance indicators to measure agencies' success in achieving these results have required a level of communication and coordination with third parties that did not exist in most agencies prior to GPRA's passage."

Involvement in Creating the Capacity to Gather and Use Performance Information

Agreeing on measures is different than actually collecting the data. This is a thread through the ONDCP, the CompStat, and the Oklahoma Milestone Contracting stories. Most agencies historically report performance around existing measures—because they already exist, not because they are the best metrics. O'Connell concludes that some of the key lessons behind the success of the CompStat model is collection of accurate and timely information, meaningful data analysis and the dissemination of results to all levels of the organization, and relentless follow-up and assessment.

Also, technology is not only making it easier to collect data, but it is also making it far easier to understand it. Newcomer and Scheirer say, "... another innovative tool is the use of Geographic Information Systems to examine the co-occurrence of programmatic and other indicators." Making current data available in easy-to-use formats, like geographic displays, is transforming management, as is the case with the New York CompStat system.

Involvement in Ensuring Implementation and Accountability

The importance of implementation and accountability is O'Connell's core message, "CompStat has quite simply resulted in more communication taking place within the organization." He summarizes the four basic principles of the CompStat model—accurate and timely intelligence, rapid deployment, effective strategies, and relentless follow-up. This, however, assumes constant, ongoing dialogues with frontline police officers, departmental staffs, staff from other agencies, as well as nonprofits in the community.

While O'Connell describes a system that creates day-to-day focus, Newcomer and Scheirer say evaluation and research results are essential to the longer view. They say evaluation "can also help agencies to set realistic targets" and communicate to key stakeholders "a realistic view of what is achievable within a short period in moving toward the long-term desired results." As an example, they describe how the Coast Guard used evaluation to better understand the root causes of marine accidents over a period of years, and then used these evaluation insights to redesign their strategies, which, in turn, affected day-to-day activities. Again, this process involves talking directly with the customers, in this case the tugboat operators and sailors.

Challenge Number Two: Increase the Use of Performance Information to Get Results

A common lament among many performance measurement devotees in Washington these days is that while the performance system envisioned by GPRA is largely in place, it's not being used. But the question is, "Who should be using it?" As Newcomer and Scheirer observe, "GPRA has required agencies to measure performance, but the law cannot make managers use the performance data to improve their programs." Frederickson posits that, "While performance information has not proven useful for appropriators, it has shown some promise for management decisions." And that's okay for now. The O'Connell chapter on CompStat is a powerful story about using performance information to make day-to-day management decisions. However, performance and results information are increasingly being used in policy and budget decisions as well as in agency and program oversight.

Using Performance Information to Instill a Results-Based Orientation into Day-to-Day Management

The CompStat story shows that leaders can transform day-to-day management behavior in a large organization. Prior to 1994, O'Connell says, "In accordance with classic bureaucratic structure, the overall orientation of managers within the department was downward rather than outward.... Precinct commanders 'did not see crime reduction as their foremost responsibility.'"

When CompStat was introduced, it was a "computer-driven program that helps ensure executive accountability." But it was more than that. The people are the same, the budget is the same, and they come to work in the same building, yet everything is different. In sum, O'Connell found that "CompStat provides a holistic approach to administration.... [It] has opened existing lines of communication within the organization but, perhaps more importantly, has also created new ones." He concludes, "Perhaps the most significant feature of CompStat is the fact that information is not just meticulously compiled, it is used. It is openly shared for the express purpose of collaboration and the development of effective new strategies."

Using Performance Information to Inform Policymaking and to Reshape Programs

Newcomer and Scheirer assess the current capacities for and uses of program evaluation to support performance and management. They find that more is going on at the federal level than previously thought and that "many stakeholders are now asking good, hard questions about performance."

Performance evaluation can help support strategic and program planning, improve program delivery, support accountability, and better link intended results to agency programs. For example, the use of "logic models" maps the chain of results between an organization's concrete activities and its long-term goals or purposes. Program evaluation helps define and quantify the significance of the links in the chain.

And there is a performance payoff. For example, an evaluation of the Department of Transportation's seat belt use campaign demonstrated a strong link between increased seat belt use and the reduction in highway deaths that resulted from the department's campaign.

Using Performance Information to Link Budget Decisions to Performance Consequences

While not addressed directly by any of the authors, linking resources to results is a hot topic in Washington. The Bush administration has committed to making resource allocations for a number of programs in fiscal year 2003 on the basis of performance-based budgets. Although there is no agreed upon definition, the GAO says, "performance budgeting is an evolving concept that cannot be viewed in simple mechanistic terms. The process of budgeting is inherently an exercise in political choice—allocating scarce resources among competing needs and priorities—in which performance information can be one, but not the only, factor underlying decisions.... The risk lies in expecting too much too soon.... GPRA holds the potential to more explicitly infuse performance information into budgetary deliberations, thereby changing the terms of debate from simple inputs to expected and actual results."[5] In fact, Murphy and Carnevale conclude that if the ONDCP system is to "become the management tool that some envision, it will have to be integrated with the budget process."

Using Performance Information to Inform Program Oversight When Delivering Services Via Someone Else

Both Frumkin and Frederickson tackle the special challenge of achieving results in environments where the accountable agency has little control over what happens. While many observers see this challenge as hopeless, they offer some hope. Frumkin describes an innovative tool for how government and nonprofit organizations can work together to deliver quality services in a way that respects nonprofits' need for autonomy in defining and pursuing their missions, while, at the same time, responding to the public sector's need for accountability. He says Milestone Contracting "allows government and nonprofits to simultaneously maximize both the accountability and autonomy dimensions" and that it allows government to "move away from process measures inherent in traditional fee-for-service arrangements and toward a system geared to outcomes."

Frederickson, while describing a number of challenges federal agencies face in enlisting state and local partners to achieve national goals, concludes that "GPRA can lead to improvements in the relationship between federal agencies and the third parties they oversee or with whom they collaborate to produce public services."

Challenge Number Three: Achieve Crosscutting Outcomes

One of the looming challenges of managing for results is achieving outcomes that reach across agencies and levels of government. All really important results do. But government is not now institutionally capable of thinking in those terms. It is divided into agencies, programs, congressional committees, and geographical-political boundaries. Air pollution, for example, knows none of these boundaries. Neither does poverty nor the lack of health care.

The Murphy and Carnevale story of ONDCP's approach to the war on drugs is the closest the federal government has come to comprehensively spanning these kinds of boundaries in a major policy arena. Their chapter describes how ONDCP developed a crosscutting strategic plan and collaborative approach across 50 agencies to define common measures and strategies. They are now in the process of extending this effort to partners in state governments. Likewise, the CompStat system also shows promise as a boundary-spanning approach for achieving outcomes. O'Connell tells how different kinds of local government agencies now use this approach to drive change and get results, and how it could be used in the federal government. Tacitly, both of these stories confirm that, ultimately, technology, and not some massive organizational reform, will create the bridges needed to achieve results reaching across the federal, state, local, and nonprofit sectors.

Crosscutting Outcomes Among Federal Agencies

There are no institutional structures at the federal level to encourage the pursuit or achievement of crosscutting results. Murphy observes, "The measurement of performance for crosscutting programs falls outside of the GPRA provisions." In fact, several federal laws explicitly discourage agency collaboration. However, there are some exceptions. Buoyed by the momentum generated by GPRA, the ONDCP used its unique legislative authority to create a system that gauges the effectiveness of national antidrug efforts and uses performance measurement to "hold other executive agencies accountable for their contributions to the crosscutting effort."

Crosscutting Outcomes That Reach across Levels of Government and the Nonprofit Sector

The real challenge, according to Frederickson, is that "GPRA requires agencies to set goals at the federal level for programs for which they do not have the final authority in many crucial areas." Increasingly, however, there is a more sophisticated assessment of how states, localities, and nonprofits can collaborate with the federal government and each other to achieve common goals. These will be described in future Endowment reports.

Challenge Number Four: Change the Jobs of Individuals, Organizations, and Institutions

Adopting a managing for results approach implies that over time there will be significant changes in the jobs of individuals, organizations, and, ultimately, institutions such as Congress and the White House.

Changing the Jobs of Individuals

After reviewing the effects of the Oklahoma Milestone Contracts system, Frumkin concludes, "Outcome measurement requires new skills, including participative planning, negotiated rules, quantitative and qualitative yardsticks, valid and reliable data collection, and a system for feeding information back into strategic planning systems." As a specific example, Frumkin says, "The job coach is really the linchpin of the whole process." These are the people who work directly with clients to help them develop job skills. Frumkin says they seem to have "a better understanding of what would be expected from them under the new system than the managers did." One job coach told Frumkin, "We went from being caretakers to being coaches."

While the effects of the Oklahoma system on recasting the jobs of front-line workers are encouraging, the federal government seems to have a long way to go. A 2001 GAO report found that less than half of managers in 11 of the 28 largest agencies in the government saw a commitment by their agencies' leaders to achieve results. Also, only about one-third of senior executives see their performance—and their rewards—as being tied to their agency's performance. This will change with the increased emphasis on performance, as has occurred in Oklahoma, and will also be described in future Endowment publications.

Changing the Jobs of Organizations

O'Connell saw the New York Police Department being transformed as it became more results-oriented due to its use of CompStat: "An ambitious reengineering effort shifted the department from being a centralized, functional organization to a decentralized, geographic organization.... This resulted in greater empowerment and participation in decision-making, and more open, less hierarchical communications within the organization." He concludes, "What began as an innovative and effective police management model has rapidly developed into one of the most promising new tools for unleashing the creativity of managers at all levels of government."

Similarly, Frumkin sees a significant change by the nonprofits in Oklahoma: "As long as the nonprofits meet the conditions of their contract... they have complete freedom in determining the best way to do it.... An organization without strong management may soon be out of business, because the freedom given to nonprofits can be used to innovate or it can be an excuse to flounder." He finds that the biggest obstacle to success of Milestone Contracting was the mindset of the nonprofits. Managing the process under the fee-for-service approach was easy. All they had to do was keep track and bill the agency for every minute of the workday. This approach, however, distorted the process, causing poor performance and inefficiencies. But Milestone Contracting offers the nonprofits an interesting bargain, "If the nonprofits do a better job of putting their clients to work, the state will leave it to the nonprofits to figure out the best way to achieve this goal."

Changing the Jobs of Key Institutions

Ultimately, the managing for results approach has to culminate in job changes for larger institutions of governance, including the White House and Congress. Today, both are rewarded largely for launching new initiatives. But President Bush says he wants to do business differently: "Good beginnings are not the measure of success, in government or any other pursuit. What matters in the end is performance. Not just making promises, but in making good on promises." His budget director, Mitch Daniels, recently said a key Bush administration effort in the coming year will be "to create the incentives to enhance effectiveness."

The case studies that follow hold promise in this regard. Expanding the use of Milestone Contracting, CompStat, and ONDCP's cross-agency logic models, for example, would help transform the jobs of both Congress and the White House to be focused more on the bigger picture of getting results Americans care about—and restoring citizens' trust in government.

Endnotes

1. Kohut, Andrew (1998). *Deconstructing Distrust: How Americans View Government.* Washington, D.C.: Pew Research Center for the People and the Press, p. 10.

2. Walters, Jonathan (1998). *Measuring Up: Governing's Guide to Performance Measurement for Geniuses (and Other Public Managers).* Washington, D.C.: Governing Books, pp. 6, 7.

3. U.S. General Accounting Office (1997b). *Managing for Results: The Statutory Framework for Improving Federal Management and Effectiveness.* (GAO/T-GGD/AIMD-97-144) Washington, D.C.: U.S. Government Printing Office, p. 1.

4. Office of the Auditor General (2000). *Report of the Auditor General of Canada, 2000,* Chapter 20: "Managing Departments for Results and Managing Horizontal Issues for Results," pp. 20-25.

5. U.S. General Accounting Office (1997a) *Performance Budgeting: Past Initiatives Offer Insights for GPRA Implementation.* (GAO/AIMD-97-46) Washington, D.C.: U.S. Government Printing Office, p. 4.

Bibliography

Kohut, Andrew (1998). *Deconstructing Distrust: How Americans View Government.* Washington, D.C.: Pew Research Center for the People and the Press.

Office of the Auditor General (2000). *Report of the Auditor General of Canada, 2000,* Chapter 20: "Managing Departments for Results and Managing Horizontal Issues for Results."

U.S. General Accounting Office (1997a). *Performance Budgeting: Past Initiatives Offer Insights for GPRA Implementation.* (GAO/AIMD-97-46) Washington, D.C.: U.S. Government Printing Office.

___________ (1997b). *Managing for Results: The Statutory Framework for Improving Federal Management and Effectiveness.* (GAO/T-GGD/AIMD-97-144) Washington, D.C.: U.S. Government Printing Office.

___________ (2001). *Managing for Results: Federal Managers' Views on Key Management Issues Vary Widely Across Agencies.* (GAO-01-592) Washington, D.C.: U.S. Government Printing Office.

Walters, Jonathan (1998). *Measuring Up: Governing's Guide to Performance Measurement for Geniuses (and Other Public Managers).* Washington, D.C.: Governing Books.

PART II

Creating an Infrastructure to Manage for Results

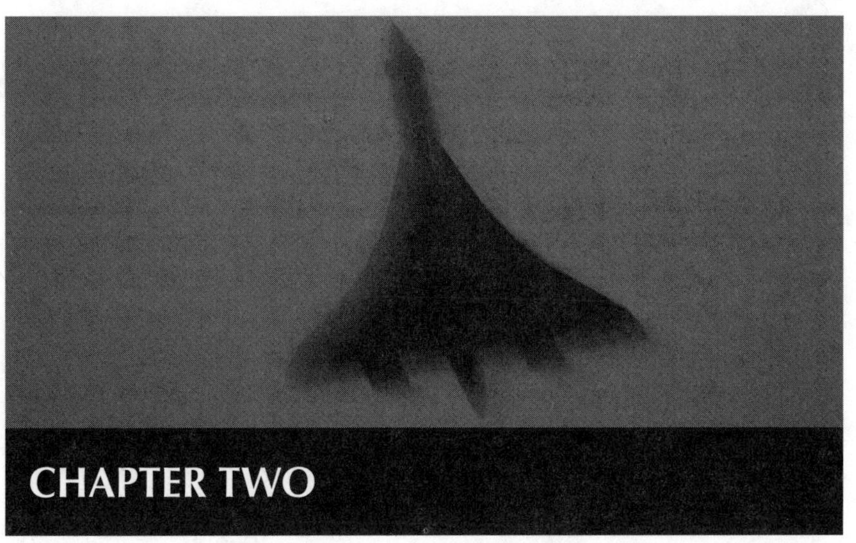

Corporate Strategic Planning in Government: Lessons from the United States Air Force

Colin Campbell
University Professor of Public Policy
Georgetown University

Introduction

Why the Air Force Needed to Vision and Plan for the Long-Range Future

The time frame for Air Force long-range planning, upwards of 25 years, might strike those more familiar with domestic agencies as stretched extraordinarily far beyond the visible horizon. However, one could certainly see the benefit of applying this discipline to such domestic programs as Social Security or Medicare, in which economic and actuarial imponderables often lead to decisional paralysis. One might even find support for a study of long-range planning of the type pursued by the Air Force in areas that have received less attention in the domestic policy arena. For instance, as the National Park Service wrestles with mounting traffic problems, we might assume that some members of that agency have nightmares about national parks turning into parking lots sometime around 2025.

Regarding the need for clarity in the objectives of strategic visioning and planning, Barzelay and I argue elsewhere that strategic planning might well prove an oxymoron in most public service organizations (2001). One must grapple with the inherent limitations in government of reconciling the standards of a "plan"—namely, a detailed formulation of a program of action—with "strategy." In bureaucracy, the latter usually falls short of detailed prescription both because of ambiguities in discerning the future public good and immense uncertainty about the degree to which stakeholders will align behind stated goals. We advocate the concept "metaplanning." This captures the degree to which corporate strategic planners in public sector organizations discern and target inchoate futures that achieve poignancy only to the extent that they wrench stakeholders from incremental adaptations of the status quo.

Advocacy of metaplanning implies two things. First, while organizations cannot discern with certitude the futures that they might face, they can improve their performance by anticipating environmental change that will challenge them beyond the capabilities provided by the status quo projected "x" years out. Second, incremental change based on piecemeal modifications of the status quo inevitably will leave the organization falling short of requirements sometime in the future to a degree that its failure to adapt will endanger its institutional viability. A collateral issue emerges under this rubric as adaptive failure of a government organization could appreciably harm the public good just as a similar lapse in a key industrial concern could harm the competitiveness of a country in the world economy.

General Ronald Fogleman brought two concerns with him when he became chief in 1994. He believed that the Air Force had lost its innovative edge by falling into the habit of basing modernization plans on projections of existing programs into the future. His second concern really constituted the first writ large. He believed that the Air Force will transition very significantly by 2025 from an overwhelmingly fixed-wing aircraft culture to one in which many more of its missions would be done from space. He found little evidence that his fellow four-stars had attuned their commands to the strong likelihood that the Air Force would migrate first to an Air and Space Force and eventually, he believed, to a Space and Air Force.

Since the completion of the Fogleman process in spring 1997, one can see some discernible changes in the Air Force's corporate strategy toward a greater focus on space and some concomitant investments have emerged. However, Fogleman's objectives went beyond the programmatic consequences of the 1996-97 exercise. Fogleman also wanted to leave an institutional legacy whereby the Air Force would more consistently engage in future visioning and collective evaluation of programmatic requirements in light of this. He stressed collective processes due to his belief that historically the Air Force adapted to new challenges best through broad canvassing of views, which, apart from encouraging innovative perspectives, improved "buy-in" once programmatic commitments were made. To sustain the collective corporate process that he sought, Fogleman instituted consultative machinery.

It is at this point that General Michael Ryan's contribution comes to the fore. Under Fogleman, three annual meetings of four-stars and monthly meetings of their vice commanders (three-stars) had provided the institutional buttress for a collective process from which the 1996 vision and the 1997 long-range plan emerged. After Fogleman's departure, the apparatus—especially the pivotal role of vice commanders' meetings in preparing issues for four-stars—began to atrophy. Four problems prompted Ryan to re-engage the process. First, Ryan came to believe that the concept of the Air Force migrating ultimately to a Space and Air Force still bore separatist overtones. Thus, Ryan devised and sought to implement the notion that the Air Force aspired to become an "Aerospace" Force integrating the best of what space platforms and fixed-wing aircraft have to offer. Second, after some initial successes, it became clear that the 1997 long-range plan was exerting less than the desired effect on programmatic commitments. Third, contemporary geopolitical demands for a highly mobile, inter-service capacity to respond to crises led Ryan in January 1998 to initiate a very substantial reconfiguration of existing Air Force resources under the umbrella of the Expeditionary Air Force. Fourth, Ryan, very much as Fogleman did when he conceived of the 1996 vision process, sought to position the Air Force optimally for responding to the Quadrennial Defense Review (QDR) required by Congress at the onset of each new presidential term.

Through analysis of materials from an extensive series of interviews with participants, this chapter probes a number of issues surrounding the

Fogleman and Ryan iterations of corporate strategic planning. To what degree has the constellation of issues confronting the Air Force—including both the positive and negative demonstration effects of its success in the Kosovo conflict—changed its view of its future? Are the Air Force's efforts at "back-casting" credible? That is, has the Air Force engaged a process whereby its leadership strikes a realistic balance between comprehensive efforts to enshrine the visioned future programmatically and selective, even incremental, commitments designed to position the Air Force future opportunities? Did Fogleman leave an operable institutional legacy? That is, has the machinery he devised proven adaptive to the leadership style of his successor and effective in adjusting the Air Force's vision and corporate strategic plan to altered circumstances?

The Air Force Experience as a Case Study

The Fogleman Round

General Ronald Fogleman

Responding to the Signs of the Times

As noted above, the nature of the Air Force's core businesses requires that it look further into the future when planning than would most private and public sector organizations. The time frame, thus, puts a huge premium on visioning. However, unlike many private sector organizations, the Air Force does not function monocratically. So it is not simply a matter of the chief of staff going up to the mount and returning with sacred tablets. And, even if he did, he would still have to reconcile the holy writ with skeptical and, more important, powerful external stakeholders.

Key players in the Air Force visioning and planning processes have become acutely aware of this paradox. That is, they wrestle with the need for clear guidance about the future but must deal with conditions of governance that limit the capacity of the chief or, for that matter, the secretary to fix the organization on a specific vision. The question arises then, why bother with visioning at all? The answer rests in the culture of the Air Force whereby the key players consider themselves patriots and in a vocational sense worry about the Air Force's future viability in sustaining national security. Even in comparison to other services, the Air Force tradition—which, of course, has a much shorter period than the Army, Navy and Marines—

The Fogleman Round Report, 1996

United States Air Force 1996 Corporate Strategic Plan—*Global Engagement: A Vision for the 21st Century Air Force*

Air Force Mission:
To defend the United States through control and exploitation of air and space

Air Force Vision Statement:
Air Force people building the world's most respected Air and Space force ... global power and reach for America

Air Force Core Competencies:
Our nation's Air Force develops, trains, sustains and integrates the elements of air and space power to produce:

- Air and space superiority
- Global attack
- Rapid global mobility
- Precision engagement
- Information superiority
- Agile combat support

Speed, flexibility and the global nature of its reach and perspective distinguish the Air Force's execution of its core competencies.

Air Force Core Values:

- Integrity First
- Service Before Self
- Excellence In All We Do

has tended to place relatively greater emphasis on strategic planning. This might owe to the tortuous metamorphosis of the Air Force from the Army Air Corps, which finally quickened when strategic air warfare came of age during World War II (Gropman 1984). In other words, the Air Force had to justify its evolution each step of the way.

Notwithstanding a fairly strong innovative culture, planning itself usually functioned incrementally—although it did go through cycles in which it experienced spurts. The development of the controversial F-22 fighter as a replacement of the aging F-15 serves as an example of incremental planning. A more revolutionary possibility would have been an examination of whether a space maneuvering system might prove technologically feasible in time to fill the F-15's shoes. One encounters a wide range of views about the efficacy of such metaplanning that, by definition, requires assent to a visionary view of capabilities and operations.

A stark proposition such as "the function of the F-15 might be performed from space," thus, will provoke skepticism among the bulk of key players in plotting the Air Force's future. Many of the participants in the Fogleman and Ryan planning rounds have believed looking even 15 years into the future amounts to gazing into a crystal ball. Alternatively, they have spoken of devising a range of futures so as to hedge bets. But such an approach would prove prohibitively expensive if it translated into investments in a multiplicity of options. With dramatic advances in futurist technology, perhaps planners will soon find it easier to allay skepticism. In this respect, the Air Force has operated since 1996 under a "demand and supply" construct. This emphasizes a range of envisioned demands on national security more than specific scenarios in identifying desirable directions in force structure. In the meantime, the counsel that stresses the need for continual revisiting of visions will probably prove the wisest. Here conceptualization and implementation of core programmatic commitments would become less subject to inertia and incrementalism.

Having noted the reserve, if not skepticism, about visioning and planning in the top leadership of the Air Force, one still found support for such processes from the standpoint of positioning for opportunities. At the end of the day, however, participants remained chary of investments in the future that would leave the Air Force short-changed in terms of current capabilities. Some participants even registered the practical concern that many units lacked the time and resources with which to satisfy seemingly insatiable demands for information provoked by some approaches to planning. Others worried about the constituency for visions and plans as the Air Force's political leadership often focuses mainly on day-to-day issues and the Office of the Secretary of Defense has traditionally revealed little ken for corporate strategic issues in the services.

Scenario building and war games can add cogency to voices among the top leadership exhorting greater concern for the future. If we look at the

What the Nation Will Need from Its Military in 2025

(From *Global Engagement: A Vision for the 21st Century Air Force*)

What?

Protect the nation's interests, wherever and however they are threatened
Respond to the new challenges and new missions
Hedge against surprises
Support national information needs
Provide strategic and operational choices
Respond to changing science and technology

Where?

In non-traditional environments
In the shadow of nuclear, biological or chemical weapons, or after the use of nuclear, biological or chemical weapons
Increasingly from the Continental U.S.
Global infosphere

How?

To win the nation's wars decisively by dominating the battlespace
With minimal collateral damage
With reasonable demands on the nation's resources
In accordance with the nation's values
As partners in joint-combined and regional operations

When?

Immediately, when called upon

time in which General Fogleman led the Air Force, however, reality itself seemed to be bearing down on the organization. In the first place, the outside world had begun to debate openly the issue of whether the Air Force's neglect of space warranted the creation of a separate Space Force. Obviously, this prospect evoked a strong reaction from the top leadership of the Air Force, but one that did take on board the need to redefine the role of space in its mission. As well, deep concerns had arisen about the integration of command and control in the Air Force, which seemed to have fallen way behind potential technological innovation.

Most compellingly, Air Force doctrine was undergoing a metashift just as Fogleman was taking office. Here, actual engagement rather than war games had provided the stimulus. Historically, Army doctrine had governed the use of the Air Force in combat. As one respondent put it, the doctrine had the Air Force bombing an opponent until the Army reached the theater in overwhelming numbers and marshaled itself according to its fastidious standards for preparedness. Then, "the two opposing ground forces would meet as if there had not been any air warfare."

In 1991, Desert Storm had put a doubt in this doctrine. By the time the Army engaged Iraqi troops, the latter had been sapped, not only by air attacks on Iraqi battle lines, but also by highly effective assaults at command and control systems right to the heart of the regime in Baghdad. This provoked Major General Charles "Chuck" Link to press for a reconsideration of the so-called "halt phase" doctrine and advocate that in some cases air power alone could stop aggression. Link left the Air Force early—in order, some believe, to advocate his views more freely. However, this did not take away the nettlesome problem. The other services became defensive about the Air Force challenging the "little league" definition of jointness—which in the view of one respondent meant "everybody's here, everybody's on the team and everybody plays."

Recapturing the Air Force Consultative Tradition

General Fogleman's predecessor, General Merrill A. "Tony" McPeak, had centered most of his energies on implementing quickly the resource and personnel "draw down" necessitated by the pressures for a post-Cold-War peace dividend. He believed that a quick implementation of the draw down would protect a higher proportion of funds for modernization and leave remaining units with sufficient resources to operate effectively. McPeak, thus, almost embraced the politics of constraint. Further, within this framework, he functioned exceptionally monocratically. Significantly, McPeak's singular operating style caused problems with the other services insofar as he did not mince words when articulating in higher Pentagon councils the evolving view that the Air Force should play a role beyond providing fire for ground forces.

Fogleman, who had taught history at the Air Force Academy as a young officer, brought a historical perspective to the threat the Air Force faced in the possibility of a separate Space Force. He believed that the Air Force could avoid the mistakes the Army made in the 1930s—when it failed to accommodate the requirements of air combat capability—if it geared up culturally and programmatically for greater emphasis on space. Indeed, he soon took to styling the transition facing the Air Force as a migration to an Air and Space Force on the way to a Space and Air Force.

A voracious reader, Fogleman developed his ideas through a thorough canvassing of the literature on information warfare and how it melded with Air Force strengths such as range, flexibility, and speed. What he found steeled his resolve to get his colleagues thinking out of the box. A legendary episode drove this home. Fogleman was receiving a briefing from the Air Combat Command (ACC) in which a "follow-on" Airborne Warning and Control System (AWACS) that would require funding around 2015 received

Chronology of the Fogleman Round

1994 General Ronald Fogleman becomes Chief of Staff, United States Air Force.

1996 (Spring and Summer) Board of Directors (BoD) prepares issues for Fogleman and Four Stars (CORONA).

(Fall) CORONA meets for entire week
— develops vision presented in *Global Engagement.*

1997 (Winter 1996-97) Air Force Staff develops detailed long-range plan.

(August) Fogleman retires early due to conflicts with administration over personnel issues.

passing mention. In response to Fogleman's probe about the reference, the briefer said that ACC probably would take the latest Boeing aircraft and put a dome on top of it. The Air Force had done precisely this when it developed the current AWACS, which went into service in 1977. Fogleman grabbed the chance to drive home his view of the future of the Air Force. He challenged his briefers to consider whether the AWACS mission might more effectively function from space given the year 2015. Such incidents convinced Fogleman that the Air Force was not going to rise to the challenges of the future without rigorous strategic planning.

Predictably, tension arose between Fogleman and most of his four-star colleagues about how far in the future to aim. Fogleman wanted to stretch as far as possible—setting 2025, or at the time nearly 30 years, as the outer limit. He expected his colleagues to contemplate futuristically: "I want you to go into low earth orbit in a satellite and sit up there at 2025 and look down at the world as it is in 2025 and try to figure out what the Air Force should be contributing to national defense." Fogleman himself eventually realized that he had set the time frame too ambitiously. He scaled down to the year 2020 and urged his colleagues to come up with a believable future that even the average airman could understand and visualize.

One especially savvy participant with a deep knowledge of Air Force politics credits Fogleman and his vice-chief, General Thomas Moorman, with an "exquisite performance of leadership to effect change without being the person who says, 'this is step two, this is step three....'" A well-placed political appointee attributed Fogleman's successes to a "peculiar combination of weak leadership on the part of the secretary and very powerful direction from the chief—his departure left a void." Fogleman, thus, combined a highly visionary view of the future, an aura of collegiality, and a determination to rise to the challenges faced by the Air Force. Knowing he had not been the first choice of his fellow four-stars for chief, he did not believe he was bound by an internal mandate. His first agenda item was moving heaven and earth to alter thinking about the future in the Air Force. His second was to institutionalize long-range planning so that visioning would occur continually and link more directly to programmatic commitments.

Devising and Operating a Process

General Fogleman recognized that a hugely ambitious effort at corporate strategic planning required coordinative machinery. Air Force four-star generals met three times annually in several day sessions called CORONA. Fogleman assigned the task of developing the vision to CORONA and set aside an entire week—its fall 1996 meeting—for this work. He also shared with the four-stars his intention to block out his calendar in the weeks just before the fall meeting to read through the briefing materials and isolate key issues. This telegraphed to other four-stars that they should show up for CORONA prepared for meaningful discussion. As fall approached several four-stars on an individual basis discussed with Fogleman some of their ideas, largely to test them out before presenting them to the entire CORONA.

Almost invariably in such processes, principals such as the four-stars working through a collective process like CORONA find staff preparation for their deliberations to be essential. However, developing a staff system can pose paradoxical challenges. Often, the first-among-equals, in this case the chief, can make the mistake of assigning staff support excessively to a central coordinating unit. Under such circumstances, the operational units of an organization—in this instance the major commands (MAJCOMs)—might come to the conclusion that the center—in this case the Air Force Staff located in the Pentagon—might rig principals' deliberations by limiting the agenda and narrowing the issues briefed. On the other hand, an effort as momentous as the fall 1996 CORONA can hardly operate off the backs of envelopes.

Fogleman tried to strike a balance between principals' input and Pentagon staffing through creation of a Board of Directors (BoD). This body, which General Moorman chaired on Fogleman's behalf, consisted originally of the vice-commanders of the MAJCOMs and the deputy chiefs on the Air Force Staff, all of whom were three-star generals. As the theory went, the BoD would prepare issues for CORONA in dialogue back to their commanders, who as CORONA principals would be able to track the progress of the debate. Moorman did an excellent job of leading the BoD to identification of issues which Fogleman could select as foci for the fall CORONA. However, the loop from BoD through vices to commanders and back worked unevenly. Thus, after Fogleman selected from the BoD list 16 CORONA issues, Moorman established four committees, each of which developed papers preparing four CORONA issues. Here, one chairman, Lieutenant General Lawrence Farrell, the vice-commander of the Air Force Materiel Command, played an especially significant ring-mastering role.

Chance had provided an effective good-cop, bad-cop duo in the staff as direct support for Moorman and eventually Fogleman. Major General David McIlvoy led the staff strategic planning team. His gracious manner meant that disgruntled four-stars believed they at least had an even-handed broker in the planning team. McIlvoy's deputy, Clark Murdock—a former aide of President Clinton's first defense secretary, Les Aspin—had caught Fogleman's attention soon after the latter had become chief. Murdock continually tested the boundaries for a civilian appointee working in a Senior Executive Service position in the Air Force. Indeed, he played a crucial role in prodding both the Fogleman and Ryan rounds of visioning and planning. A perfectionist with a penchant for comprehensive approaches to linking plans and programs, Murdock had sparked Fogleman's interest through the latter's passion for reading. Soon after he took over as chief, Fogleman read a journal article by Murdock on long-range planning in the Pentagon (1994/95). Murdock made an appointment with Fogleman in response to a hand-written note on the article, and the two developed a strong intellectual bond.

Internally, the Air Force culture benefited both from the 1996 CORONA visioning process and development of long-range plans through the winter of 1996-97. The preparations for the CORONA had energized the MAJCOMs toward a more thoroughgoing consideration of the future. The intensive BoD sessions had proven useful, especially in bringing non-space commands to a discussion of the future role of space in the Air Force. Even the CORONA, especially because of its unusual length and the time commitment for participation, left the four-stars with a new sense of collegiate direction. Perhaps more important from the standpoint of institutionalization, Fogleman decided to reconfigure the Air Force staff so that programmers and planners would report to the same deputy chief. He chose as the first deputy chief for plans and programs Lt. General Farrell, who had distinguished himself in the preparations for CORONA.

Problems with Implementing the Vision

Where the process fell down most clearly was on the implementation side. Even the development of the long-range plan up to its completion in March 1997 proved hasty and poorly coordinated. The Federal Benchmarking Consortium Study Report notes that many private sector organizations complete their vision and then leave development of long-range plans to individual business units rather than working up an encompassing planning document (FBC 1997, 164). However, General McPeak had devolved significantly authority over resources to MAJCOMs. So, one can see how the staff found it tempting to develop a long-range plan aimed at improving the alignment of resource commitments to priorities throughout the Air Force. Clark Murdock had wanted to get a three-hour wedge in each CORONA that would step back and track implementation of the vision. But, the long-range planning process had worn out the planning staff and the BoD too appeared exhausted. Who would prepare issues?

Most significantly, a succession of difficult personnel issues had led Fogleman to reconsider his timing for retirement. He had fought William Cohen, the defense secretary, over whether Kelly Flinn, a female officer who had been involved in a relationship with the husband of an enlisted airwoman not under her command, should be discharged honorably. Following upon this, Cohen issued a negative report on the Khobar Towers bombing in Saudi Arabia that had killed 19 airmen. The report singled out the commanding officer, Brigadier General Terryl Schwalier, and recommended that he not advance to major general. This was the last straw for Fogleman. He viewed the assessment as an effort at scapegoating and decided to resign early. The Fogleman round came to an end in August 1997.

Handing over the Baton

Any reader tempted to conclude from this section that the Fogleman round failed should remember that this current analysis has tried to limit its compass to an assessment of the process. It will leave to a subsequent work a detailed treatment of the consequences of the Fogleman round. Suffice it to say, however, that the Air Force proved exemplary in the degree to which it rose to the challenge of identifying and defining "stretch goals," contemplated future scenarios as part of its organizational view, acknowledged the timeliness of General Fogleman's approach to leadership, and engaged in deliberative dynamics that fostered consensus about future directions.

Apart from some efforts to garner expert advice on futuristic issues and some vetting of ideas with think tanks, the Air Force exercised caution in consultation of external stakeholders. Yet, this approach comported with the realpolitik of most agencies in the federal government. It was the immediate follow-through from the vision to the planning stage, therefore, which proved less than satisfactory. Fogleman became distracted by personnel issues and ultimately resigned his post early. However, the entire Air Force leadership and the support elements that had immersed themselves in the Fogleman process by spring 1997 displayed palpable signs of visioning and planning fatigue. In the fall, Fogleman handed the baton to General Michael Ryan.

The Ryan/Peters Round

General Michael Ryan

Secretary of the Air Force F. Whitten Peters

Some Modest Progress to Build Upon

Notwithstanding hiccups associated with fatigue and Fogleman's distraction and eventual departure, the Air Force had taken significant steps toward its new vision. It created a new umbrella unit in the staff that, among other functions, brigaded together under a deputy chief of staff both planning and programming. Under this unified direction, the office, XP, each year develops Annual Planning and Programming Guidance (APPG) that keeps track of the resource commitments required to implement the 1997 long-range plan. The APPG, for a number of reasons associated with continued disconnects between the exigencies of planning, programming, and budgeting, remains an indicative rather than prescriptive document. The core competencies enunciated in the 1996 vision began to shape debate over capabilities and requirements. Even though different MAJCOMs would adduce conflicting interpretations of the holy writ, they would find that some passages compelled sympathetic responses because they had attained corporate legitimacy. Lieutenant colonels and majors in MAJCOMs can cite with page numbers passages of the vision favorable to their mission. Unlike the vision, the 1997 plan did not spawn such vehicles for reform. It had not been integrated properly and was overly complex.

However slowly, resources began to follow rhetoric. More money was going into space and research and development, unmanned aerial vehicles, and training of young officers in aerospace concepts. Doctrine too was shifting. Embraced in CORONA, "agile combat support"—a just-in-time concept that greatly reduces the front-end supply requirements for transporting combat units to theaters—became Air Force doctrine. Even before the Kosovo campaign, the debates surrounding capabilities during the visioning process had deepened acceptance in the Air Force of Major General Link's view that air power should play a dominant rather than support role in many engagements. Finally, on the organizational level, a new

The Ryan/Peters Round Report, 2000

United States Air Force 2000 Corporate Strategic Plan—*America's Air Force: Vision 2020*

Core Competencies

- **Aerospace Superiority:** The ability to control what moves through air and space ensures freedom of action
- **Information Superiority:** The ability to control and exploit information to our nation's advantage ensures decision dominance
- **Global Attack:** The ability to engage adversary targets anywhere, anytime holds any adversary at risk
- **Precision Engagement:** The ability to deliver desired effects with minimal risk and collateral damage
- **Rapid Global Mobility:** The ability to rapidly position forces anywhere in the world ensures unprecedented responsiveness
- **Agile Combat Support:** The ability to sustain flexible and efficient combat operations is the foundation of success

agency—led at the two-star level and lodged in the Air Combat Command—assumed responsibility for integrating the Air Force's highly fragmented information, intelligence, and command and controls systems. This move addressed a concern that had operated at the core of Fogleman's unease about the Air Force's ability to keep up with the demands of information warfare.

Notwithstanding such progress, General Ryan still had inherited an unfinished process. Two impulses competed with one another for his attention. One, which we will not dwell on here, sought to achieve a high degree of granularity in the relationship between the 1997 plan and programs. This standard would satisfy Fogleman's desire that the Air Force back-cast from its vision with sufficient robustness that it greatly enhance adjustment of programmatic commitments to future challenges. Back-casting continues to function as a driving force behind efforts to relate planning and programming. However, it did not serve as the rationale for revisiting the vision.

Different Circumstances

General Ryan brought to his new position about as good an Air Force pedigree as a person could have—his father had served as chief. Unlike General Fogleman, he was a consensus choice among the four-stars. Indeed, even Fogleman preferred Ryan as a successor—recognizing that a different style of chief could steadily move the implementation process forward as the players recovered from overexertion in the first round. As already noted, General Ryan from the outset made it clear to all that he viewed the 1996 vision and the 1997 plan as the Air Force's and corrected anyone who referred to them as Fogleman's.

The second impulse, thus, played a more critical role. It stemmed from the view that the most immediate challenges faced by the Air Force had shifted. First, it had become clear to many participants that Fogleman's concept of the Air Force transforming itself into an Air and Space Force and eventually into a Space and Air Force came across as overly sectional. It needlessly injected a sense of winners and losers to what consisted essentially of cultural re-socialization and organizational adjustment. Second, the endless pressure upon the Air Force to respond to multiple crises around the world was wearing out personnel and equipment. In response, General Ryan became a champion of the Expeditionary Air Force concept whereby combat units would take missions on rotation and for relatively short intervals. Implementing this doctrine required thoroughgoing review by CORONA. Finally, Ryan and many close to him became absorbed with the impending change of defense secretaries and the accompanying Quadrennial Defense Review that would follow. It was felt that the previous visioning process had placed the Air Force well for the 1997 QDR. Such

Chronology of the Ryan/Peters Round

1997 (August) General Michael Ryan succeeds General Ronald Fogleman as Chief of Staff, United States Air Force.

1998 Ryan focuses most of his attention on development of the Expeditionary Air Force.

(Fall) Acting Secretary F. Whitten Peters begins to prod Air Force Staff for more program-salient planning. Decision made to revise the 1996 vision in the fall 1999 CORONA.

1999 (Spring and Summer) BoD meetings intensify with a view to preparing issues for the fall CORONA.

(Fall) CORONA devotes four days to discussion of vision issues.

2000 (June) New vision issued.

positioning for opportunities, especially developing a reservoir of arguments for claims for additional resources, increasingly asserted itself as a core absorption in the 1999 visioning process.

Contrasting Leadership Styles

General Ryan's Approach

Many participants in the 1999 process noted that General Ryan's approach contrasted sharply with General Fogleman's. They viewed Ryan as quite considerably less visionary than Fogleman. As well, some noted that Fogleman's concept of buy-in had ossified into an overly formalistic approach to consultation. Ironically, understanding of future challenges, if anything, broadened and deepened within the Air Force leadership. Occurring right in the midst of the preparations for the fall 1999 CORONA, the Kosovo war drove home the singularity of the Air Force's ability to halt aggression with minimal danger to U.S. personnel—the latter operating as a crucial condition given public neuralgia about casualties. As well, development of future demand constructs, if not full-blown scenario building, and war-gaming took huge strides in the period between the two visioning exercises. In a unit located under the director for strategic planning, annual war games projected 20 to 22 years out played two crucial roles. They gave key MAJCOM representatives direct exposure to likely exigencies far into the future. They also provided a wealth of information that helped brief key members of the staff, the BoD, and CORONA on a common vision of the types of challenges the Air Force would face in the future. While General Ryan would prove a less charismatic and visionary leader than Fogleman, and the processes geared to buy-in had become routinized, the sense of urgency surrounding the need for adjustment of programmatic commitments to future challenges had intensified.

Within this frame, Ryan brought an element of pragmatism to both visioning and planning. Viewing much of what had been envisioned in the space domain as "science fiction," he opted for more realistic parameters. These, he believed, would still fit within the confines of earth-orbiting vehicles and, therefore, the compass of aerospace. He believed that adaptations of programmatic commitments to future challenges would have to strike a balance between evolutionary and revolutionary approaches. As an example of the latter, he cited the decision under General McPeak to disestablish the Strategic Air Command—by merging bombers with fighters in the Air Combat Command—on the grounds that targets, not weapons, are strategic or tactical. He believed that maintaining capability imposed the greatest restraint to such dramatic adjustments.

The Political Executive Enters the Equation

As noted above, a degree of ambiguity entered into General Ryan's leadership role through the greater involvement of the secretary of the Air Force than had pertained under Fogleman. The secretary during the Fogleman round, Sheila Widnall, had played a passive role until issues surrounding the possibility of weapons in space emerged in the fall 1996 CORONA. Her successor, F. Whitten Peters, had served for a lengthy period in an acting capacity due to an eventually abortive process in which a nominee for the position failed to obtain congressional confirmation. The uncertainty did not deter Peters from asserting himself as the Air Force struggled with the disjunction between planning and programming. A tension emerged between Peters and Ryan. The latter's view of planning tended to be project oriented—centered on the Expeditionary Air Force and preparation for the next Quadrennial Defense Review. The secretary sought more granular guidance for budgeting and acquisitions battles that he had to fight on a day-to-day basis. He believed that the best way to prepare for the next QDR was to have a budget for 2002 that worked off a vision for the Air Force that would win the day with key players in the next administration and Congress. Notwithstanding these contrasting views, the secretary and the chief actually worked closely with one another and developed a degree of synergy around two shared values—passionate concern that visioning come across as realistic and striking a functional mix between dramatic and incremental adjustment.

When Peters and Ryan agreed to a major effort to revise the vision in a fall 1999 CORONA, the Board of Directors (BoD) reactivated and assumed responsibility for preparing issues for discussion by the four-stars. However, it failed to operate effectively through most of the preparatory period. Even under Fogleman, concerns had arisen among political appointees and the Air Force staff that BoD should include assistant-secretary-level officials in the Pentagon and not simply vice-commanders of MAJCOMs and three stars in the Air Force Staff.

Personalities Make a Difference in the Process

The eventual inclusion of a wider circle of participants had two effects. The group dynamics of BoD changed due to size as participants became cautious of airing their views in such a diverse assembly. As well, the diversity of the group clouded the linkage role of BoD between the staff and MAJCOMs. Thus, commanders took less interest in its proceedings, and this compromised the capacity of vice-commanders to communicate views each way between the MAJCOMs and BoD. (General John Handy, the current vice-chief, now limits BoD membership to MAJCOM vice-commanders.) To further complicate matters, many participants believed that the vice-chief who chaired BoD until summer 1999, General Ralph Eberhart, did not place a high value on BoD as an instrument of a corporate process for preparing for CORONA. General Lester Lyles, who succeeded General Eberhart, adopted a more expansive view of the role of BoD. However, this left little time for the group to engage to a degree sufficient for it to assist in the preparation of issues for CORONA. At the end of the day, the strategic planning directorate under XP filled the gap. However, staffing can never fully compensate for collective processes that underachieve.

At this writing, the paint has not dried on the outputs from the fall 1999 CORONA. The Air Force's development of its Posture Statement for 2000—the rationale it provides in congressional testimony for its annual budget requests—delayed the generation of a vision document from the CORONA until June 2000. The CORONA did come to terms with the types of enhancements of resources that would enable it to pursue its vision of an integrated aerospace force. This accomplishment owes both to the dynamic which developed in the meeting and the quality of the briefing on strategic issues. It amounts to the Air Force taking a much more direct tack in communicating to Congress the implications of competing force structure commitments in terms of meeting envisioned future demands. The vision will drive the identification of issues. However, the Air Force will try to center discussion within a tighter and, presumably, more comprehensible time frame—focusing 20 years into the future.

A Significant Step Toward Fogleman's Dream: Institutionalization

The Ryan/Peters round provides some evidence of further institutionalization of Fogleman's approach to visioning and planning. The emergence of a number of new issues or difficulties with addressing matters identified in the 1996 CORONA rather than provoking an abandonment of the 1996 vision fostered a commitment to reengaging the Fogleman process. Significantly, participants believed that the 1996 process had helped the Air Force in the 1997 QDR. Thus, this served as an added motive for pursuing another round. The investment the Air Force had made in developing envisioned demand constructs and war-gaming far into the future had paid off. It had given participants a shared sense of urgency over the need for the Air Force to align itself programmatically with future challenges. The engagement of the secretary made direction of the process more complex than under General Fogleman. However, the secretary and the chief did develop a positive working relationship in guiding the process. The BoD did not work well in preparing issues for the CORONA. This constitutes a significant failure for which the staff partially compensated. Had Fogleman not made the investments in the strategic planning unit of XP and Ryan not maintained them, one certainly would have anticipated a less auspicious outcome.

Assessment of the Fogleman and Ryan/Peters Rounds

The Air Force through two cycles now has effectively deployed corporate strategic planning, with the proviso that the separation of powers constricts the art of the possible. The Air Force has devised "stretch goals" which increasingly form the basis for internal and external dialogue on its future. Envisioning of future demands and war-gaming have given fidelity to claims that the leadership should share a sense of urgency about gearing for its future. The top leadership has engaged in a sustained realization process. This constitutes a major accomplishment given significant differences between Generals Fogleman and Ryan in their stylistic approaches and views of how far out visioning should go, and the relationships the chiefs developed with Secretaries Widnall and Peters, respectively. A round-tabling norm has prevailed among decision-makers even though the use of specific consultative forums has ebbed and flowed. The brigading of the Programming and Strategic Planning directorates under the same deputy chief has added robustness to the interaction between the two domains. This, in turn, has allowed Strategic Planning to proffer advice to CORONA and the BoD, which serves up on a continual and systematic basis issues surrounding efforts to narrow the gap between planning and programming.

The Air Force followed strong architectonics in designing its process for a corporate strategic plan. However, it did make errors in implementation. General Fogleman probably did some damage to the initial process by setting his sights outward nearly 30 years. Tighter time frames make it easier for participants to see the salience of visioning to the present. However, they should not be so close that they fail to take participants out of their comfort zones. It probably would not have been possible for General Fogleman to engage Secretary Widnall more fully in the 1996 process, the latter seeming to have lacked a pro-active view of engagement with her department. However, notwithstanding its labor-intensive nature, the dialogic character of the 1999 process suggests a more serviceable approach as it provided a fulcrum for the reconciliation of political responsiveness and corporate strategic intent. However, this same dynamic preordained that BoD would become overly large and poorly bounding in corporate terms. While the fall 1999 CORONA proved successful in many respects, the Air Force must resolve the question of how issues are integrated before presentation to the four-stars. The Strategic Planning Directorate cannot sustain for long the role it currently must play in preparing issues for CORONA without more corporately coherent engagement on the part of BoD. As noted above, the current vice-chief, General John Handy, has limited BoD membership to the vice-commanders of MAJCOMs. This decision offers the potential for clearer corporate direction should the committee continue to take the lead in strategic planning issues for CORONA.

Observations About Corporate Strategic Planning in Government

Difficult in Most Systems but a Huge Challenge in the U.S.

Corporate strategic planning does not come naturally to organizations within the U.S. federal government. When we look at other countries, we find higher capacity for longer-range thinking. Although significantly driven by the need to renew their mandates, governments in parliamentary systems have often committed considerable energy to strategic thinking, taking them beyond the current legislative calendar. In these systems, career civil servants, largely because political appointees play only limited roles, have served as the oarsmen for devising how departments might face future challenges. Critically, two ingredients missing in the U.S. enter the equation. First, the government-of-the-day normally exerts sufficient control over the legislative branch to take initial steps toward a long-range strategic commitment once a consensus builds around it in the executive branch. This provides an incentive for career officials and a way for them to contribute to a legacy. Second, a strong, systemwide esprit de corps often prevails within these countries, which allows officials to detach themselves to some extent from the short-term interests within their units and departments.

Garnering commitments within U.S. governmental organizations often proves a tough sell because officials seldom see that their political masters can deliver on commitments to take the first steps toward change. Not unrelatedly, units within agencies can do a lot of damage to themselves by giving away hostages to opponents who belong to the same organization—even wear the same uniform—but imbibe a competing esprit.

Having noted the difficulty of engaging interest in corporate strategic planning in the U.S., one should observe as well that the conditions for this approach ebb and flow in other systems as well. The United Kingdom, Canada, and Australia, for instance, all made considerable efforts at comprehensive strategic direction in the mid-1970s that collapsed spectacularly. Broadly, the initiatives sought to prioritize demands for continued expansion of the welfare state notwithstanding the exceedingly daunting fiscal pressures associated with the economics of decline. In the end, fiscal realities won out and a politics of constraint emerged in which bold images of the future gave way to narrow-gauged concerns about efficiency and effectiveness of government programs. The latter foci spawned a very strong corporate—some have called it managerial—mind-set in many non-American public services. In the 1980s, public sector organizations of English-speaking countries other than the U.S. guided themselves through management boards. In these bodies, the heads of the principal businesses of government organizations would have to outline and justify their objectives and submit to reviews of their performance in terms of outputs and/or outcomes. One should note, however, that even with very substantial organizational commitments to such collective guidance, management boards inevitably encountered difficulty in installing and operating a feedback loop between corporate strategy and budgeting.

The Need for Government Organizations to Pursue Corporate Approaches

The Air Force process that we have examined here owes some lineage to the Planning-Programming-Budgeting System (PPBS) that emerged in the Department of Defense under Robert McNamara and ultimately won the imprimatur of Lyndon Johnson for implementation throughout the U.S. government. PPBS's architecture concerned itself with prioritization of long-range objectives so that decision-makers might align budgetary commitments more cogently (US General Accounting Office 1997, 5, 7).

Aaron Wildavsky, the most noted student of the budget process in the 20th century, had the last word on PPBS soon after the ink was dry on

Johnson's blueprint. Its promoters had failed to see that PPBS fell short of a one-size-fits-all proposition (1969, 190-192). Wildavsky did not perceive in domestic agencies the capacity for strategic planning that the Department of Defense had displayed in the 1960s. In implementing PPBS in the Pentagon, McNamara could tap a strong analytic legacy that dated back to the important role played by the RAND Corporation in generating first-rate analysis of defense policies after World War II.

Wildavsky held a very high standard for policy analysis as a capacity to transcend "the fire-house environment of day-to-day administration" and trace out "the consequences of innovative ideas" rather than "projecting the status quo" into the future. In words that could just as easily apply to the principal rationale behind the Fogleman and Ryan planning efforts as they did to McNamara's, Wildavsky notes that the originators of PPBS wanted to close the gap between planning and budgeting:

> ...they wanted to stop blue-sky planning and integrate planning and budgeting.... They wanted to use the program budget to bridge the gap between military planners, who cared about requirements but not about resources, and budget people, who were narrowly concerned with financial costs but not necessarily with effective policies.

Importantly, Wildavsky noted that, at least until the Vietnam War began to drain U.S. resources, McNamara's efforts to prioritize through PPBS did not meet stiff external resistance because defense budgets remained flush and contractors routinely amassed sizable backlogs.

Best Practices for Corporate Strategic Planning

Not only does the Air Force run an exceedingly diverse and complex bureaucratic system, but it also gobbles up nearly 4 percent of the annual budget of the federal government. To obtain a perspective on this figure, one need only reflect that the Air Force budget in FY00 reached $73 billion while the entire federal government of Australia budget in the same period exceeded this figure by less than one-third. The U.S. Air Force case, thus, presents a daunting challenge as the magnitude of corporate strategic planning in an organization of this size far exceeds the scale of any existing benchmarks. Before moving to conclusions and recommendations based on our case, however, we should take stock of available assessments of best practices in public sector concerns, albeit considerably smaller than the U.S. Air Force, which have distinguished themselves in strategic innovation.

Such an effort reveals five key elements to successful corporate strategic planning. First, the agency must devise a viable and convincing framework for visioning and planning. Second, processes centered far into the future will rely extensively upon scenario building and war-gaming. Third, the success of a process will depend substantially on the qualities of the organization's leadership and the extent to which they involve themselves in strategic planning. Fourth, collective processes will greatly enhance the buy-in among both the barons and rank-and-file of an organization. Finally, consultation with stakeholders comprises a crucial element to both visioning and planning.

The Need for Stretch Goals

The available literature suggests that organizations that succeed in corporate strategic planning more often than not have been able to wean themselves of incrementalism. For instance, Borins analyzed submissions from 217 semifinalists for the Ford Foundation's state and local Government Innovation Awards program between 1990 and 1994. He found that only 7 percent of the innovations emerged from organization-wide strategic planning (Borins 1998, 52). However, 59 percent of the reforms that emerged within discrete units of an umbrella organization developed from comprehensive efforts at redesign. Only 30 percent of the initiatives evolved from "groping" or incremental efforts to adapt to change (Borins cites Behn 1988).

Private and Public Sector Best Practices for Strategic Planning

1. Visioning identifies "stretch goals" that put an organization on a trajectory toward highly adaptive strategic plans.
2. Scenario building and role playing involving an organization's leaders prove invaluable to both specifying a vision and generating excitement and urgency toward fulfillment of strategic plans.
3. The top leadership—whether singular, as in the case of chief executive officers, or mutual, as in the case of the political executive coordinating with high-level officials—must personally lead the visioning process and communicate its results.
4. While they become exponentially more important under mutual leadership, consultative mechanisms prove crucial to attaining "buy-in" for any planning process.
5. While engaging external stakeholders may contribute greatly to the specification of a vision, many organizations—due to the sensitivity of planning issues—might have to consult vicariously rather than directly.

With respect to our current interest in corporate strategic planning in the U.S. Air Force, Borins' findings suggest also that comprehensive planning occurs most frequently among organizations that require large capital investments (Borins cites Golden 1990), programs that involve the coordination of a large number of organizations, and theory-driven programs (Borins 1998, 57, 64).

The 1997 Federal Benchmarking Consortium (FBC) promotes a view of corporate strategic planning that comports with the concept of metaplanning discussed at the outset of this chapter. Indeed, the FBC study—which examined best practices in the private sector, relating these to parallel developments in government agencies—stresses the fact that corporate strategic planning stands at the intersection of art and science (FBC 1997, 175). However, the study emphasized as well that visioning and planning far into the future most frequently occur in organizations with complex processes and/or very long-range programs (169-171). The report highlights the importance of future thinking to what I would term positioning for opportunities. Here an organization thinks out of the box and devises "stretch goals" that enable it "to recognize and capitalize on the events transpiring outside its span of control."

Galvanizing Attention through a Sense of Urgency

Scenario building and role playing can greatly assist an organization in devising the desired trajectory toward the future (FBC 1997, 165). Such approaches comprise the second key factor mentioned above. The FBC study reports that private corporations use this approach extensively, often even employing the term "war games." Obviously, the military brings to such a task immense experience with war games. However, these serve little purpose in visioning if they simply apply existing concepts of operation to the status quo projected "x" years out. In other words, stretch goals will not emerge unless the game itself forces thinking beyond conventional parameters. In any case, role playing through scenarios that invite a realistic grasp of future challenges can have immense bump-on effects in organizations. First, players develop through catharsis an appreciation of the need to prepare for uncertain futures. Second, when properly disseminated, the findings from war games can even work huge effects on non-players' views of possible organizational challenges. However deployed, war-gaming not only adds cogency to organizational visions, but also can inject a sense of urgency in the process of planning for the future.

We saw that General Fogleman considered visioning as relevant only if the Air Force "back-casted" so that expectations for the future actually guided changes in current programmatic commitments. The FBC study found that private corporations that prove most successful at strategic planning have achieved a similar discipline:

> After describing the vision of the vision of the future using standard techniques, the company leaders essentially move backward from the future state to identify how the company must look at a given point in time if the desired future is to materialize (FBC 1997, 175).

The inevitable gap between perceived future requirements and the likely capabilities in the status quo projected "x" years forward should galvanize the leadership's attention by creating "the urgency that spurs strategic action."

Leadership, Sine Qua Non

Another key factor to strategic planning, leadership, depends very much on the personal qualities of those in charge and their full engagement in the process. Borins found in his research a "trichotomy of innovation." Here politicians usually will lead innovation when an organization faces a major crisis; agency heads normally assert themselves most clearly when they first assume their responsibilities; and middle-level and front-line officials most often will probe creative options when faced with internal problems or technical opportunities (1998, 49). In the case of all three, the courage to lead agencies to innovation takes root in the integrity of those in charge—meaning they have not allowed crises to arise or deepen through neglect of warning signs or paralysis in the face of gridlock. In Borins' words, they bring to their work "the ability to recognize problems or opportunities in a proactive manner" (1998, 47).

The FBC report highlights the importance of "chief executives" taking an active part in a "strategic management group" along with the other top leaders of a "corporation" (1997, 164). It also stresses the need for the chief executive "personally" to "explain and cascade" the resulting strategic vision throughout an organization. Public service organizations do present ambiguity, however, along the lines identified by Borins. Who is the chief executive? Margaret Thatcher, for instance, wanted her ministers to actively manage their departments. Some did. In fact, a few participated directly in their ministries' management boards. Most ministers, however, remained aloof of managerial detail notwithstanding Thatcher's preferences. In such cases, the head career civil servant either was delegated or assumed the managerial mantel or the department shunned completely the corporate approach.

Ambiguity intrudes in the case of the U.S. Air Force in two ways. In the first round the political head of the Air Force, Secretary Sheila Widnall, took little interest in the strategic planning process. Therefore, General Fogleman found the way clear to act as a chief executive along the lines suggested by Borins and the FBC report. This fit the preference for "blue suits" to run the business end of the Air Force. However, ambiguity entered the equation because, by its nature, governmental corporate strategic planning takes an organization into a stratum of policy commitments that ultimately will require authoritative sanction by the political leadership. In the second round, the new secretary of the Air Force, F. Whitten Peters, assumed an active role in the process. This, in turn, introduced a dynamic whereby the private-sector model of principal executive authority being clearly vested in one individual did not pertain.

The ambiguity that appeared in the first round emerged because of weak political leadership that allowed General Fogleman to follow the stylistic preferences of "blue suits." That which emerged during the second round took root in the entrenched ambiguity of the U.S. executive-bureaucratic system. That is, the separation of powers makes it hard for federal government organizations to plan like private corporations. For the purposes of institutional survival, chief operating officers must weigh issues such as their departmental secretary's standing in the administration and the ability of the administration to get its positions through Congress.

Thus, the relationship between a secretary and a chief proves much less hierarchical than that between a chairman of the board and a chief operating officer or even a British cabinet minister and his permanent secretary. If departmental secretaries in the U.S. choose to engage in corporate strategic planning, they must, by the nature of the system, enter a dialogue with permanent officials. Officials, thus, will find it hard to bring authoritative corporate change if their political appointees have not participated in the process. Similarly, political appointees, who can change policies against the will of their permanent officials so long as the president and Congress approve, cannot change their organizations corporately unless they have worked with them dialogically.

The Need for a Collective Process

The non-hierarchical character of executive-bureaucratic relations in the U.S. finds amplification in the lack of horizontal integration within agencies. We will see that this presents very serious obstacles for corporate strategic planning in the U.S. The literature suggests that collective processes prove key to obtaining sufficient buy-in so that a consensus emerges among leaders about future directions and the rank-and-file understand and support these. The FBC report states emphatically that, if you do not have buy-in, you do not have a plan (1997, 167). It also makes it clear that chief executives cannot devise visions and plans singularly; they must work closely with other corporate leaders (1997, 164). As a Canadian examining innovation in U.S. public service organizations, Borins presumably brings a bias in favor of collective processes. These take on special significance north of the border due to the constitutional conventions of cabinet government and federal-provincial diplomacy. Whatever his bias, Borins makes a strong, empirically based case that holistic innovation in organizations most frequently takes place when the process has been supported by central staffs and the agencies' leaderships have interacted regularly through formal coordinative mechanisms (1998, 97-102). Borins concludes, "Collaboration across organizational boundaries does not happen naturally, it must be made to happen" (1998, 102).

Bringing Stakeholders Along

The literature strongly prescribes external consultation with stakeholders as a key ingredient to successful corporate strategic planning. This presents problems for any federal government agency. However, the secrecy surrounding many of the weapons systems and concepts of operations envisioned for the future sets even tighter limits to the Air Force pursuing external consultations. Space serves as a clear example. Even though it became a central absorption of General Fogleman's planning process, most of it lived in the "black" domain, meaning that it was top secret.

In the adversarial politics associated with the separation of powers, the planner does not want to give away hostages to congressmen, congressional staff, and contractors who just as readily as not will betray confidences if they conclude their positions will not prevail. In the circumstances, Popovich's exhortation that early external consultation allows planners to take an inventory of whom to involve in their process might backfire in a federal agency (1998, 60). Of course, Popovich speaks much more from the experience of agencies at the state and local levels, where often less adversarial dynamics guide the interaction of stakeholders in planning processes. However, the FBC report, which focuses on the applicability of best practice in private sector concerns to planning in federal agencies, also highlights the importance of external consultation (1997, 160, 166). Yet, the report speaks almost entirely with reference to the "marketplace" and "customers," which suggests that it especially pertains to agencies that provide goods and services to specific individuals and groups. Such commercial analogues fail for the Air Force because the market, even including other military services, does not offer substitutes for most of what it provides. Further, it usually cannot discriminate between the citizens who will receive its benefits.

Liaison with Congress would certainly constitute for the Air Force the most important form of external consultation. However, the General Accounting Office (GAO), in canvassing the likely dynamics for dialogue between agencies and Congress on strategic plans produced in compliance with the Government Performance and Results Act, underscores the difficulty of the two working in tandem. Although the act specifically requires such consultation, the GAO report anticipates significant difficulties. Legislative staff concentrate on their "oversight roles and stress near-term program performance" whereas agency officials stress "long-term goals, adaptability to changing needs, and flexibility in execution" (GAO 1997, 3).

The cultural divide, the report suggests, leaves agency heads "skeptical that consensus on strategic goals could be reached, especially given the often conflicting views among agencies multiple congressional stakeholders" (GAO 1997, 11). Patrick Wolf, through an analysis of 170 cases of federal agency reform from 1890 to the present time, has found that organizations operating with a relatively high degree of autonomy from direct political control prove the most innovative (1997, 377). For the Air Force, this might suggest that it simulate this condition as much as possible by low profile corporate strategic planning. It then can enter the marketplace of policy ideas with more elaborately honed arguments that demonstrate the consequences of Congress supporting the continued funding of programs that have become "pet rocks" at the expense of future investments.

Recommendations

This chapter has stressed the difficulty of pursuing corporate strategic planning within federal government agencies. As a case, the Air Force experience since 1996 offers several encouraging signs. These, along with an assessment of best practices in other government agencies, provide the basis for a number of recommendations:

Goals Must Truly Stretch but Fit as Well Within Optimal Timing Parameters

Agencies face a considerable challenge just in deciding how far into the future to vision. Their answer to this question will depend very much on the nature of their core businesses. Those who face long lead times for programmatic adaptation will inevitably find themselves pulled toward metaplanning—that is, attempting to discern largely inchoate futures. Still, the corporate leadership cannot embrace such a futuristic view that it requires monumental suspension of disbelief among those who did not accompany them to the mountaintop. This does not mean that metaplanning finds no role in institutions with tighter time frames for programmatic development. For instance, radical changes in information technology occur at an exceptionally rapid rate. Thus, agencies or businesses within them that could profit from enhanced use of cybernetics run the risk of habitually implementing yesterday's solutions—ones that cannot even cope with today's challenges much less tomorrow's. This type of problematic seems to argue for much greater up-front investments in visioning technological developments and changes in requirements between the time that equipment and systems will come on line and their likely obsolescence. Paradoxically, the leaders of organizations facing extremely volatile conditions will encounter difficulty in shifting their corporate culture from short-term fixes to long-term solutions.

Scenario Building and Role Playing Can Quicken a Sense of Urgency

We have seen that the literature emphasizes the importance of scenario building and role playing in engaging key players in corporate strategic planning. Actual events, especially nascent pressures for a separate Space Force and reconsideration of the "halt phase" doctrine for the use of air power, conveyed urgency in their own right. However, future war games have contributed significantly as well. In this regard, the decision to emphasize ranges of future envisioned demands rather than fix upon specific scenarios constitutes a major contribution on the part of strategic theorists in the Air Force—one which appears highly worthy of emulation by other agencies. The innovation specifically attempted to move the emphasis from threat-based to opportunity-oriented planning. It employed two avenues toward this cultural shift. The first gave players, principally sub-general officers, exposure to the difference that certain capabilities will make in addressing various plausible futures. The second provided the Air Force leadership in the Staff and MAJCOMs, through analysis of data from the games, systematic input about the benefits of pursuing new programmatic opportunities and shedding old commitments in a timely fashion. Two lessons emerge for other federal agencies. First, agencies actually can pull themselves out of cognitive ruts—for instance, an over-emphasis on threats—by adopting more open-ended and dialogical views of how to relate scenarios and demands. Second, agencies that pursue future gaming, notwithstanding the unavailability of over-scheduled top leaders, can reap the benefits of consciousness raising below the top management echelon and increased systematic input for senior decision makers.

Leadership Must Engage and Be Engaging

As the contrast between Generals Fogleman and Ryan drives home, leaders can vary immensely in their approach to corporate strategic planning. However, a more important issue emerges in the U.S. In most other bureaucratic systems, we find an apex of power whereby one top career official serves as the organizational fulcrum for relations between the permanent civil service and the political leadership. Something comparable to this apex exists in the Air Force—although only Secretary Peters actually engaged it and chiefs share the same rank with other "four-stars." The latter fact means that chiefs must function more collegially than would the career heads of departments in other systems. Cabinet-level departments in the U.S. will not likely embark on corporate strategic planning exercises with the spontaneity of the Air Force. That is, one would not expect the upper echelons of the career cadre to instigate on their own initiative the sweeping process that Fogleman advanced. The absence of an apex figure and the placement of the top echelon of career officials at least five levels down in department hierarchies preordain this expectation. Thus, domestic departments will rely much more on their secretaries and other top political appointees to move forward efforts at corporate strategic planning. However, sub-cabinet agencies might prove much more amenable to the type of dynamics that prevailed in the Air Force case—largely because fewer layers separate political appointees and career officials in such organizations. Still, corporate strategic planning at this level would likely prove most successful when both sides form a dialogical partnership as occurred between Secretary Peters and General Ryan.

Collective Processes Tailored for the Realpolitik of the Agency Are Essential

The importance of CORONA and the BoD to the Air Force case certainly reinforces the view that collective machinery must buttress corporate strategic planning. However, the experience also suggests that agencies must work hard in developing mechanisms that balance the need for consultation with economies of scale. CORONA has worked well at critical points because the legitimacy of its deliberating on behalf of the corporation founds itself on four-star collegiality. BoD has struggled at mirroring this legitimacy. At the end of the day, this raises the issue of whether the notion that four-stars represent the Air Force captures all the nuances of the corporate structure. BoD worked well in the Fogleman round when it simply included three-stars from the Staff and MAJCOMs. However, inclusion of political appointees from the Department of the Air Force during the Ryan/Peters round attempted to address the need for buy-in among the political leadership. In the event, the enormity of attaining buy-in both among the top general officers and the political leadership went far beyond the capacity of a BoD which had, in any case, become far too large for meaningful deliberations. This experience seems to be saying to other agencies that they must devise consultative mechanisms tailor-made both for the challenges faced by the organization and the corporate realities connected with constituting consultative bodies that balance legitimation and efficient deliberation.

The Agency Must Devise a Politically Viable Method for Consulting Stakeholders and/or Anticipating Their Responses

While the Air Force process stressed greatly consultation of internal stakeholders, it eschewed involvement of external stakeholders. This tack owes both to the political sensitivity of the issues it faced and the secrecy that enshrouds any military organization. However, one clear side product of sustained corporate strategic planning has manifested itself in the past year or so. The Air Force has begun to recognize that failure to identify and communicate to the political executive and Congress sensitive but vital issues could amount to a self-denying ordinance for an organization devoted to national security. There is no question that visioning and future gaming quickened this process of realization. A sizable irony presents itself here. Corporate strategic planning rarely connects as robustly in programmatic terms in U.S. federal agencies, largely due to the powerful effects of the separation of powers. However, the Air Force case indicates that corporate strategic planning might prove indispensable even as organizations position themselves for opportunities to achieve sub-optimal adaptation.

Bibliography

Barzelay, Michael and Colin Campbell. 2001. *Planning Corporately in Government: Envisioning and Crafting the US Air Force's Future*. Washington, D.C.: The Brookings Institution.

Behn, Robert. 1988. "Managing by Groping Along." *Journal of Policy Analysis and Management* 7: 643-663.

Borins, Sandford. 1998. *Innovation with Integrity: How Local Heroes Are Transforming American Government*. Washington, D.C.: Georgetown University Press.

Federal Benchmarking Consortium (FBC). 1997. "Serving the American Public: Best Practices in Customer-Driven Strategic Planning." Study Report. February.

Golden, Olivia. 1990. "Innovation in Public Sector Human Services Programs: The Implications of Innovation by 'Groping Along.'" *Journal of Policy Analysis and Management* 9: 219-248.

Gropman, Col. Alan L. 1984. "Air Force Planning and the Technological Development Planning Process in the Post-World War II Air Force—The First Decade (1945-1955)." In *Military Planning in the Twentieth Century*, ed. Col. Harry R. Borowski. Washington, D.C.: Office of Air Force History.

Murdock, Clark A. 1994/95. "Mission-Pull and Long-Range Planning." *Joint Forces Quarterly* No. 6: 28-35.

Peters, Thomas J. and Robert H. Waterman. 1982. *In Search of Excellence*. New York: Warner Books.

Popovich, Mark G. ed. 1998. *Creating High-Performance Government Organizations: A Practical Guide for Public Managers*. San Francisco: Jossey-Bass.

United States General Accounting Office (GAO). 1997. "Performance Budgeting: Past Initiatives Offer Insights for GPRA." Report to Congressional Committees. March.

Wildavsky, Aaron. 1969. "Rescuing Policy Analysis from PPBS." *Public Administration* Review 29: 189-202.

Wolf, Patrick J. 1997. "Why Must We Reinvent the Federal Government? Putting Historical Development Claims to the Test." *Journal of Public Administration Research and Theory* 7: 353-388.

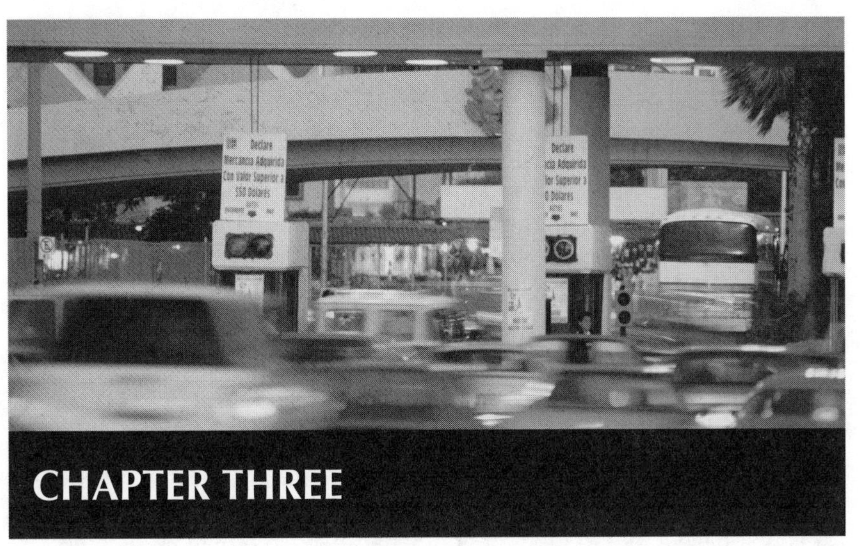

CHAPTER THREE

The Challenge of Developing Cross-Agency Measures: A Case Study of the Office of National Drug Control Policy

Patrick J. Murphy
Assistant Professor
Department of Politics
University of San Francisco

John Carnevale
President
Carnevale Associates

Introduction

How do elected officials and public managers hold programs accountable for their activities and achieve intended results? Absent some scale against which progress toward a program's goals can be measured, it is difficult to assess how effective a given government program may be. Performance measurement has long been seen as the key to holding public agencies responsible for their programs and for ensuring they deliver expected outcomes.

The 1993 Government Performance and Results Act (GPRA) took this concept of performance and public reporting and put it into statute as a set of tasks to increase accountability and better manage for results. GPRA requires federal departments to develop performance measures for their programs and report on their progress relative to those indicators. The intent is clear. Once fully implemented, the Congress and executive branch managers will have a tool to monitor and better manage program outcomes. In turn, they will be able to hold individual programs accountable for the impact, or lack thereof, that they have on the problems they were designed to address. Perhaps as important, the institution of performance measurement systems should enable the public to see whether their taxpayer dollars produce any results.

GPRA's emphasis on monitoring program outcomes clearly advances the goal of making government more accountable and results-oriented. Its focus on individual departments as its unit of analysis, though, can be misleading relative to causes and effects. Concentrating on individual departments implies that a single government program would be responsible for any change in the measure. The relationship, unfortunately, often is not so clear-cut. In addition to a variety of external factors, programs in other departments often attempt to address related facets of the same problem. For example, few would hold the Department of Housing and Urban Development (HUD) solely responsible for improving the plight of the homeless. HUD's role may be critical in addressing this issue. Homelessness, however, is a problem with dimensions that extend well beyond HUD's authority. The problem's overlap with issues such as substance abuse, mental health, job training, and domestic violence are well documented. The federal government's response to the problem of homelessness, consequently, cuts across several different departments, programs, and levels of government.

The measurement of performance for *crosscutting* programs falls outside of the GPRA provisions. Indeed, some observers already have noted the lack of crosscutting analysis to be something of a blind spot in the effort to improve accountability of federal programs (O'Neill, 2001). The problem of illicit drug use is an example of such a crosscutting issue. What is unique about the drug issue, however, is the fact that the federal government established the Office of National Drug Control Policy (ONDCP) to manage the nation's anti-drug efforts. Created by the Congress in 1988, the ONDCP was charged with coordinating drug policy and establishing priorities government-wide. As the policy office began to mature in the mid-1990s, and buoyed by the momentum generated by GPRA, the ONDCP began the process of creating a system to gauge the efficacy of anti-drug efforts. It would prove to be a daunting task.

Complicating the effort is the fact that what constitutes *the* drug problem is really a broad set of issues that range from health and education concerns to criminal justice issues. Not surprisingly, the government response has been equally expansive. At the federal level, over 50 federal agencies claim some role in efforts to reduce the use of illicit drugs. The federal drug control budget totals over $19 billion. Simply cataloging these wide-ranging activities presents a significant challenge. The development of a performance measurement system to manage these programs and monitor their progress would require a considerable investment in terms of time and staff resources. Despite these difficulties, the ONDCP embarked on a process to bring 50 different agencies together to develop joint measures and strategies to both drive and monitor the performance of the government's anti-drug efforts. From that process would emerge the ONDCP Performance Measurement and Evaluation System (PME) in 1997. By most accounts, the PME system has been deemed an impressive and credible attempt to introduce accountability into the management of federal drug policy.

Acronyms

DoJ	Department of Justice
GAO	U.S. General Accounting Office
GPRA	Government Performance and Results Act of 1993
HHS	Department of Health and Human Services
HUD	Department of Housing and Urban Development
IWG	Interagency Working Groups
NAPA	National Academy of Public Administration
OMB	Office of Management and Budget
ONDCP	Office of National Drug Control Policy
PME	Performance Measurement and Evaluation System

That the ONDCP was able to create the PME system is a success story. The difficulties in developing meaningful performance measures are well documented. The ONDCP, however, faced the additional obstacles of trying to develop performance measures for programs that cut across many organizational lines. In addition, the ONDCP had to contend with its own limited authority. As a policy office, the ONDCP office has few formal powers. Despite these obstacles, it managed to produce an impressive set of goals, objectives, and performance measures intended to improve management of federal drug control efforts. In fact, the PME system represents the most extensive and systematic attempt to date at measuring performance for a crosscutting issue at the federal level. Just as important, the system is a credible one and, for the most part, has been bought into by key stakeholders in the federal drug control agencies.

This chapter describes the evolution of the PME system as a case study to illustrate how one agency coped with the difficulty of measuring performance for programs that span organizational boundaries. Illicit drug use is not the only crosscutting problem with which the government must cope. The list of these issues is lengthy and includes such critical concerns as terrorism, AIDS, and the environment. For managers working with other crosscutting issues who are seeking to develop performance measurements, the case of the ONDCP PME system offers an example of one method of approaching the task. At a minimum, it should prove instructive in identifying the factors that facilitated the project as well as those elements that hindered the effort.

The chapter begins with a discussion of the more general challenges of measuring performance as well as the specific obstacles that the ONDCP faced. It then describes the collaborative process that produced the PME system, and how the ONDCP organized the over 250 individuals representing about 50 agencies who participated in the process. Drawing on the experiences of the ONDCP personnel and federal agency officials who participated in the process, the chapter identifies the elements that contributed to the endeavor and those factors that threatened its success. Given that the PME system is still in the early stages of implementation, this chapter also assesses what the future holds for the PME system and singles out the factors that will prove critical as the process begins to move forward. Finally, the chapter discusses the general lessons that can be distilled from the ONDCP experience. These lessons should be of interest to those administrators seeking to measure the performance of drug control efforts in state and local government as well as managers faced with the challenge of administering programs that cut across organizational lines.

The Challenge of Measuring Performance

Public management scholars have long maintained the need for performance measurement and accountability in the administration of public programs (e.g., Wholey, 1979; Wholey and Hatry, 1992; Hatry, 1999). The rationale for such effort is simple. Public organizations, using public resources, should be able to demonstrate that their programs are making progress toward their stated objectives.

Performance measurement encapsulates sound management and accountability in aligning the operation of an organization with the realization of a defined set of outcomes or end states. In the federal government, performance measurement is presenting managers with a new paradigm to rationalize programs and resources. Programs and the resources to support them are being justified in a strategic context. Rather than attempting to maximize bureaucracy by expanding resources (inputs), managers must now articulate resource needs in relation to their contribution to desirable outcomes.

Despite its straightforward reasoning, widespread interest in holding government agencies accountable for their performance emerged relatively recently over the past decade. Osborne and Gaebler (1992) call for "reinventing" government focused on freeing administrators from their rule-bound environment while holding them responsible for results. The Clinton administration was quick to embrace these concepts as evidenced by the National Performance Review (Gore, 1993). The Congress then codified the notion of accountability in the form of GPRA.

It is not possible to hold agencies accountable without some standard against which their performance can be gauged. Consequently, implementation of GPRA required federal departments to develop plans for performance measurement. It should be noted that the management benefits of such a system could extend well beyond the need to comply with a statutory requirement. In addition to providing support for accountability, performance measurement systems can also assist in improving program delivery overall as well as forcing an agency to clarify and focus its long-range strategic planning efforts (Newcomer and Scheirer, 2001). Though the implementation of GPRA is still in its early stages, there has been some evidence that the type of data produced by performance measurement efforts can contribute to understanding the impact of an agency's programs and provide an avenue for accountability (GAO, 2000b).

The potential benefits of systematically monitoring performance, then, are clearly appealing. Managers should be able to develop reasonable approaches on how best to achieve goals and objectives using measurement to document progress toward those goals and objectives. Managers are, in effect, using measurement to manage programs for results.

Developing a process that enables an organization to realize these benefits, however, can be an extremely difficult task. One of the most basic challenges is to identify outcome measures as opposed to merely tallying program outputs. Measures of program activity are relatively easy to find. Identifying a metric or metrics that begin to quantify a program's impact on a particular problem is much more difficult. Once measures are identified, managers face the problem of determining what are acceptable performance levels (Wholey and Hatry, 1992). A third obstacle to the institution of performance reviews is the possible cost involved. The development and monitoring of a performance measurement system can be a labor-intensive exercise. And, if appropriate outcome measures do not currently exist, the cost of developing new data collection instruments can be considerable. Finally, and perhaps most importantly, officials seeking to implement performance measurement must secure the cooperation and participation of the administrators responsible for the program. Absent a sincere *buy-in* from these individuals, efforts to create performance monitoring systems run the risk of merely becoming a paper exercise.

Though these problems are significant, an impressive volume of material has been produced to provide guidance for those willing to take on the challenge. There have been numerous publications that offer practical advice on all aspects of the process of measuring performance (see, for example, Hatry, 1999; Keehley, et al, 1997; Walters, 1998). The National Academy of Public Administration (NAPA) has established a federal performance consortium to assist federal agencies in the implementation of performance measurement systems. It stands out as an organization that has systematically addressed GPRA implementation issues within the federal community. Unlike the General Accounting Office (GAO), its role has been to facilitate rather than review agency progress in implementing GPRA. Over the past few years, NAPA has written guides on how to align program and budgets with outcomes, how to incorporate GPRA into agency planning mechanisms, measurement, and understanding the language of performance measurement (NAPA, 1998a-1998d).

Despite the considerable degree of information and technical assistance available, the early experience of federal agencies with implementing performance measures can be described as mixed, at best. Some promising examples have emerged, notably the Department of Labor's efforts to measure performance in its Job Training Partnership Act programs (Uhalde, 1991; Barnow, 2000). Other efforts have been less successful. An early GAO review of efforts to implement GPRA revealed that the obstacles administrators faced in developing performance measures were formidable. Managers cited difficulty in translating long-range strategic goals into annual objectives and then identifying specific performance measures to gauge the progress. Perhaps more troubling, the GAO investigators found that several officials did not distinguish between output and outcome measures. Not surprisingly, the implementation process in many of the programs examined was moving relatively slowly (GAO, 1997). A later examination of the first round of federal agency performance measure plans concluded that they did not provide a clear picture of the organization's intended performance, and they were not credible (U.S. GAO, 1998a). In short, the challenge of constructing performance measures already has proven to be a significant one for federal agencies.

Crosscutting Performance and Accountability

It is against this backdrop, then, that the ONDCP set out to develop a performance measurement system. In addition to the systemic problems of building performance and accountability systems, however, the office had the additional challenge of constructing a system that cut across traditional organizational and functional lines in the federal government. Accountability in this context means that programmatic responsibility extends beyond departmental lines. (This is an important distinction from GPRA, which focuses on the departments, holding them accountable only for the programs that fall under their purview). In trying to hold anti-drug programs accountable, the federal drug office must address a collection of activities of tremendous breadth, cutting across organizational lines, over which it has little formal authority, in a highly politicized environment.

First, the absolute breadth of what constitutes the federal drug control effort is impressive, complicating efforts to measure performance. Federal drug control policy is a conglomeration of agency programs in several functional areas (treatment, prevention, domestic law enforcement, international, and interdiction), for which many different agencies are responsible. Included under the rubric of drug control are law enforcement programs designed to investigate, arrest, prosecute, and incarcerate individuals violating drug laws. Federal programs also involve a substantial collection of activities overseas that are designed to assist foreign governments in reducing the production of drugs destined for the United States. At the other end of the spectrum are health and education-based activities that seek to prevent drug use and/or treat individuals addicted to illicit substances.

To implement this collection of programs, federal anti-drug activities involve over 50 different federal organizational entities (see Appendix I). Twelve of the 14 Cabinet departments are represented as well as two independent federal agencies. Though other crosscutting examples exist (e.g., AIDS, terrorism, the environment), it is difficult to identify one that entails coordinating the activities of as many organizations and involving such a variety of activities.

A second factor making the task of performance measurement more difficult is that, despite its "czar" designation, the office possesses relatively little formal authority. The Congress has charged the ONDCP with drafting a strategy that establishes policy goals and priorities for the nation's drug control efforts. The office is also responsible for coordinating and overseeing the implementation of that strategy. To carry out these responsibilities, however, the office is granted rather limited authority (P.L. 105-277). The role of the ONDCP director in the formulation of a drug control budget is the most clearly defined of the office's powers. The ONDCP is required to *certify* agency budget requests as to their adequacy in support of the national drug control strategy. The director can also request the reprogramming of funds from one agency to another. Even with these budget powers, the most explicit in the office's authorizing statute, the ONDCP has had only limited success in realizing its funding priorities (Carnevale and Murphy, 1999). The problem is that the authority applies to the formulation of the president's budget request to the Congress for drug control. Congress ultimately is responsible for determining appropriations for drug control, and ONDCP is understandably not allowed under the law to certify congressional action.

A third element complicating the ONDCP's development of a performance measurement system stems from the fact that illicit drug control is a *national* program—that includes states, localities and nonprofit partners—that is relying upon a federal structure for much of the program implementation and service delivery. Drug control efforts are not unique in this regard, as many federal programs are structured similarly. Nevertheless, trying to assess the performance of government efforts over which federal control is limited serves to compound an already difficult problem (U.S. GAO, 1998b).

Finally, the political environment surrounding drug policy has been, at various times, highly charged. Congress has been quick to point the finger of blame at the executive branch. Consequently, it is difficult for political appointees to get enthusiastic about the prospect for a system that partisan opponents could later use to "beat them over the head." Indeed, early in the history of the ONDCP, when drug policy was higher on the policy agenda and a hot political topic, ONDCP officials went so far as to develop goals and objectives that were intentionally vague. On one level, the tactic was motivated by a desire to protect a Republican administration from a Congress controlled by the Democrats. On a more pragmatic level, ambiguous goals enabled the office to avoid accountability for a problem over which the office had limited control. Regardless, it illustrates how partisan political concerns can overshadow the desire for accountability.

Ironically, the motivation for the PME system grew out of these complicating factors, not a statutory requirement. Though the *spirit* of GPRA was embodied in the ONDCP's development of the PME system, it was not required under that legislation. GPRA focuses upon individual departments and agencies and does not include crosscutting programs in its reporting requirements. Instead, the ONDCP was motivated by the office's own desire to more effectively manage the programs under its purview. As is discussed later, subsequent to the development of the Performance Measurement System, Congress did add language that mandated that ONDCP report annually on its progress toward achieving the targets established by the Performance Measurement System.

That the ONDCP chose to develop the PME system of its own accord offers insight into both the merits of measuring performance as well as the policy office's development as an organization. To begin with, one typically views performance measurement as a way for the legislators and the public at large to hold executive branch agencies accountable for their efforts. The case of the ONDCP's PME system, however, offers an example of how an executive branch policy office was similarly motivated. In this case, the ONDCP sought to use performance measurement to hold other executive agencies accountable for their contributions to the crosscutting effort.

The decision to develop the PME system also suggests maturation on the part of the ONDCP as a policy office. In the office's early years, it was essentially used as a bully pulpit to champion various themes, often with an ideological tenor. The development of the PME system indicates a move beyond that role, as the office takes on the more difficult task of managing policy across organizations. The ONDCP made the decision to try to hold the drug control agencies accountable for their program contributions to desirable outcomes knowing full well that others would also use the system to hold the ONDCP responsible for the collective progress, or lack thereof, relative to the strategy's goals. The PME system, then, represents a self-imposed check on performance. Prior to the passage of GPRA, there were few examples of federal government organizations willing to expose themselves to the fallout that can result from such transparency.

Constructing the PME System

ONDCP by law must propose annually a strategy with long-term goals and short-term measurable objectives to *reduce* drug use and its consequences. The emphasis on the word *reduce* is important, as it means that ONDCP must propose a plan of action to ameliorate the drug situation. A simple maintenance strategy would not satisfy the law; the strategy must propose a course of action to reduce drug use and its consequences.

The statutory requirement that ONDCP develop a strategy to reduce the drug problem is worthy of momentary consideration. If the long-term trend for a particular illicit drug is up, then the strategy must propose demand and supply reduction activities to reverse this trend. Proposing a course of action that reduces the rate of growth, but allows for some, growth, is unacceptable in relation to ONDCP's statutory requirement to reduce drug use and its consequences. The statutory imperative, therefore, becomes the political reality for the formulation of drug policy. After all, if reducing the rate of growth in a long-term trend is the best one can reasonably expect, then the merit of any underlying performance management system is called into question. A strategy and supporting budget will not have credibility with the community of stakeholders; the supporting evaluation will fail to produce results in line with stated expectations.

The overall approach of the PME development process was to start with the strategy and its explicit goals, and, working through a logic model, connect those goals to specific objectives, performance targets, and measurements. Figure 3.1 lays out the basic structure of this plan.

Though relatively simple to describe, implementation of this plan would prove more difficult.

Figure 3.1: Performance Measurement Framework

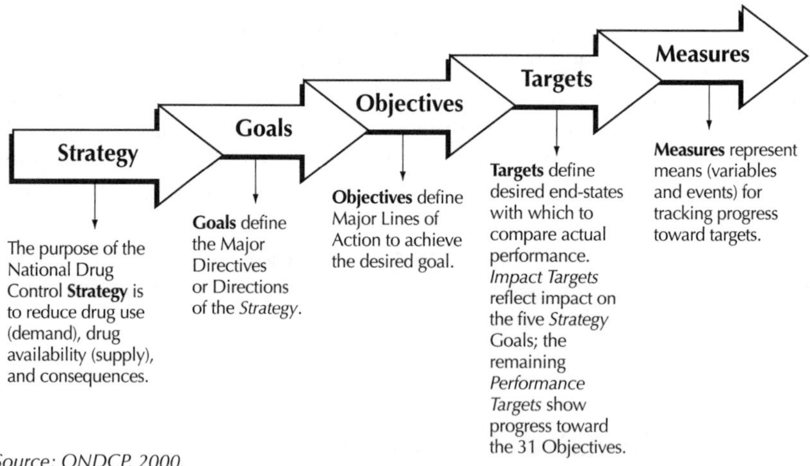

Source: ONDCP, 2000.

A Collaborative Effort

By statutory design, ONDCP is a policy office responsible for *coordinating* agency activities. It has very little direct line authority. With the power at its disposal limited, the office is not in a position to *order* agencies to develop their own drug-control specific performance measures in support of the strategy. Nor could the ONDCP develop its own performance measures and then unilaterally impose them on the agencies. Most likely, the agencies would simply reject or ignore such an attempt.

Cognizant of the literature stressing participation by stakeholders, and well aware of the limits of its own authority, the ONDCP embarked on a collaborative process to develop a performance measurement system designed to measure the efficacy of the goals and objectives of the strategy. It would require extensive coordination of the agencies involved in delivering key programs. Managing the consultative process was important for both organizational reasons as well as the need to get agency personnel to buy into the concept.

In the end, the process would use the input of over 250 people representing numerous government agencies and other organizations. To organize the effort, the ONDCP constructed a complex set of steering committees and working groups designed to address the specific tasks of developing a performance measurement system.

The process of managing this effort was difficult but key to the development of the performance measurement system. Handled badly, it could have resulted in the failure to get federal agencies and other stakeholders to buy into the national effort to achieve meaningful outcomes for national drug control policy.

ONDCP officials also understood that the performance measurement system would require a long-term effort. Owing to the crosscutting nature of the issue and the extensive number of federal agencies involved in drug control activities, they anticipated a process that would span years and might pass through several iterations before it could be reasonably expected to become fully operational. To sustain such an effort, it was important to secure a genuine commitment from the many participants early on in the development process.

The initial effort was presented to the federal agencies and others in the community of stakeholders as one requiring a few years, perhaps as many as three, before system development could be declared adequate to begin the business of bringing accountability to drug control. In fact, the development process did take three years. Year One began in 1997 and involved using working groups to identify performance targets and measures for the system. Year Two involved designing and implementing an information management system to handle the extensive federal agency data reporting requirements. It also involved continued refinement of the performance targets and measures. By 2000, the system became operational. While not entirely complete, enough of it was functioning to measure progress toward key performance targets.

Chronology of Events

1988	Congress creates the Office of National Drug Control Policy (ONDCP).
1989	
— March	ONDCP officially formed with confirmation of William Bennett as first director.
— September	First National Drug Control Strategy released.
1993	Congress passes the Government Performance and Results Act.
1996	
— February	National Strategy released with five goals that would be the starting point for the PME system.
— June	ONDCP hosts workshops for agencies on performance measurement.
— December	Internal work at ONDCP lays the foundation for the PME process.
1997	
— February	PME process formally begins. Steering and interagency working groups are formed.
— July	ONDCP proposes to "stretch" the performance measure targets.
— September	Interagency clearance process begins. Agencies and OMB register objections to PME system generally, and stretch targets in particular.
— December	Agencies sign off on the PME report.
1998	ONDCP issues *Performance Measures of Effectiveness*, the first PME report.
1999	ONDCP issues *Performance Measures of Effectiveness: Implementation and Findings*.
2000	ONDCP issues *Performance Measures of Effectiveness: Progress Report*.

Logic Models

In developing the performance measurement system, one tool that proved invaluable for keeping the development process on track was a logic model. Logic models have been around for many years and are used by policy and program managers to describe the causal structure relating program inputs to outcomes. Theory-based, they provide a tool for public managers to plot out causal relationships between programmatic actions and outcomes. They also provide a method to identify interrelated factors. Appendix II provides an additional discussion of logic models and performance management.

The ONDCP's national drug control strategy identifies five broad goals focused on reducing the use and consequences of illicit drugs. For the PME system, ONDCP staff constructed a logic model to link the strategy's five goals to 32 objectives. It is important to note that the ONDCP imposed the rule that strategic goals and objectives were not on the table during the development process. These would be treated as a given to the exercise of developing performance targets and measures. To permit discussion of the strategic goals and objectives, which had been developed through a multi-year interagency process, would have introduced too many variables into the exercise. It also would have reopened discussions and debates that, for some in the agencies, had never been fully resolved. Most participants accepted this constraint, and the logic model did provide a reasonable policy and program basis to the system.

The logic model, then, served as the foundation for much of the work that would follow. It served to focus the many participants with disparate perspectives on and interests in the task of identifying a common set of performance outcomes (reducing drug use, availability, or drug use consequences) for which they would be jointly accountable. This tool would also became a vehicle for getting the federal drug control agencies to link budget and evaluation through a strategic planning process (Millar, Simeone, and Carnevale, 2001).

To facilitate the process, ONDCP staff provided mini-workshops on the use of logic structures to working group participants with the assistance of outside experts. Beginning with the strategic goals and associated objectives, participants in the working groups clarified each objective and began to identify relevant performance measures. Eventually, these measurements would be used to establish performance targets. For example, one working group was tasked with developing performance targets for the objective under the strategy's drug prevention goal. The objective calls for federal program managers to "pursue a vigorous advertising and public communications program dealing with the dangers of illegal drugs, alcohol, and tobacco use by youth." The working group managers added clarity to this

The Original 5 Goals and 32 Objectives

Goal 1: Prevent Drug Use Among America's Youth
- Increase the Ability of Adults to Discourage Drug Use
- Pursue a Vigorous Media Campaign
- Promote Zero Tolerance Policies
- Provide Sound School-Based Prevention Programs
- Increase Mentoring
- Develop Community Coalitions
- Engage the Media
- Develop Principles of Prevention
- Conduct Research

Goal 2: Increase the Safety of America's Citizens
- Disrupt Drug Trafficking Organizations
- Strengthen High Intensity Drug Trafficking Areas (HIDTAs)
- Disrupt Money Laundering Organizations by Seizing Assets
- Treat Offenders
- Break the Cycle of Drug Abuse and Crime
- Conduct Research

Goal 3: Reduce the Health and Social Costs of Drug Use
- Support Effective and Accessible Treatment
- Reduce Health Problems
- Promote a Drug-Free Workplace
- Certify Drug Treatment Workers
- Develop Pharmaceutical Treatments
- Support Research
- Oppose Legalization of Schedule I Drugs

Goal 4: Shield America's Air, Land, and Sea Frontiers
- Reduce Drug Flow in the Transit and Arrival Zones
- Improve Coordination Among U.S. Agencies
- Improve Cooperation with Source and Transit Nations
- Conduct Research and Develop Technology

Goal 5: Break Foreign and Domestic Sources of Supply
- Reduce Production
- Disrupt Organizations
- Improve Source Country Capabilities
- Support Multilateral Initiatives
- Deter Money Laundering
- Conduct Research and Develop Technology

Source: ONDCP, 1998b.

objective by establishing performance targets pertaining to changing youth drug use attitudes about the dangers of drug use and how the media was to be engaged. They logically connected an objective target for more inputs (e.g., double the number of media messages) to a goal (e.g., changes in youth attitudes about the dangers of drug use) to a strategic outcome (reduced youth drug use).

Working through the Process

Initial work on the development of the performance measurement system began in February 1997. A total of 23 federal Interagency Working Groups (IWGs) comprised of federal career staff were formed to identify targets for each of the 32 objectives of the national drug control strategies. Each IWG was chaired by an agency representative and assisted by the ONDCP evaluation staff. The working groups consisted of agency program staff, line managers, and other drug program or data experts knowledgeable of drug control programs, policy, and research. Working group leaders were named and received the bulk of the training provided by ONDCP staff.

Interagency Steering Groups provided oversight for the IWGs. The steering groups were comprised of senior federal career (mostly Senior Executive Service members) policy officials. In addition to monitoring the IWGs, the steering group members served as the primary liaisons with the agencies. Well positioned to facilitate communications with parent agency senior policy and career staff, they provided assurance that individual agency concerns would be brought to the table and articulated clearly.

The working groups were instructed to identify targets that would signal success at reducing the nation's drug control problem 10 years into the future. The prior year, 1996, would serve as the baseline. ONDCP wanted the working groups to develop recommendations, without paying attention to resource constraints, for performance outcomes to reduce drug use, availability, and drug use consequences. Research had demonstrated that drug use can change over the long term, and ONDCP staff felt that the working groups would have an easier time thinking about establishing performance outcome targets for the distant future rather than in the immediate short term. Some performance targets were used to represent end states for the strategic plan. These targets—12 in total—were referred to as "impact targets" to distinguish them from those performance targets for the strategic goals and objectives. Table 3.1 shows the impact targets established for one of the impact targets, reducing drug use among hard-core users, and the progress to date. Taking cocaine as an example, the ONDCP reported 3.4 million hard-core cocaine users in 1996, the base year. The impact targets call for a 20 percent reduction by 2002 (to 2.7 million users) and a 50 percent reduction by 2007 (to 1.7 million). As the table suggests, progress appears to being made with regard to cocaine use, but the number of heroin addicts is clearly moving in the wrong direction. Table 3.2 presents similar data for the impact target focusing on raising the age at which users first try illegal drugs.

Table 3.1: Impact Target—Reduce the Number of Number of Chronic Drug Users
(number of hard-core drug users in thousands)

	1995	1996 Baseline	1997	1998	1999	2000	2001	2002 5-year Goal	2007 10-year Goal
Cocaine									
Target		3,410						2,728	1,705
Observed	3,555	3,410	3,162	3,045	3,103	3,103			
Heroin									
Target		917						724	459
Observed	855	917	935	980	977	977			

Source: ONDCP, personal communication.

Table 3.2: Impact Target—Increase the Average Age at First Use
(average age in years)

	1995	1996 Baseline	1997	1998	1999	2000	2001	2002 5-year Goal	2007 10-year Goal
Marijuana									
Target		17						18	20
Observed	16.9	17	17.2	17.3	*	*			
Cocaine									
Target		20.1						21.1	23.1
Observed	20.3	20.1	19.6	20.6	*	*			
Heroin									
Target		20.5						21.5	23.5
Observed	20.5	22.6	21.3	*	*	*			

** Data not yet available; there is a reporting lag time of 2-3 years for these measures.*
Source: ONDCP, personal communication.

Stretching the Outcome Targets

The next task was to get the working groups to identify five-year performance outcome targets that linked to the 10-year targets. This step gave each group three data points in a time trend (the baseline being 1996, a five-year target, and a 10-year target) to track the progress of the strategy's goals and objectives.

The working groups were also told to ignore existing data systems when considering candidate performance targets. Many federal data systems that contained drug-related information had been in place long before the drug strategy and were designed to serve particular agency program needs. While many of these had relevance for measurement of performance, not all of them did. Working groups were told not to develop performance targets to justify the continued use of existing measures, but to develop targets and measures from a normative standpoint. Once targets and measures were identified, ONDCP would look to the federal community to see what existing data systems could serve the system's needs. Data gaps would be identified and the challenge to ONDCP would be to obtain resources to fill these gaps. The intent was to construct a performance measurement system that was most relevant for the strategy. This stipulation proved critical and freed the working groups to look beyond currently available data.

With the more macro impact targets identified, the working groups set about the task of recommending specific performance targets and measures to correspond with each of the objectives. Each working group took responsibility for one or more strategy objectives. They met throughout the spring of 1997, eventually proposing 111 performance targets to track the strategy's efficacy.

During the summer, ONDCP staff and the steering committees reviewed the proposed targets and measures. It was at this time that the ONDCP sought to "stretch" the targets proposed by the interagency process. For example, an expert recommendation for a 10-year target to reduce overall drug use by 30 or 40 percent was changed to a 50 percent target under the notion that this represented a more desirable end state than what current trends might otherwise produce. The introduction of "stretch targets" would prove controversial among the agency participants, both substantively and procedurally.

The reaction of the IWGs to the stretch targets was swift and negative. Some participants complained that the new targets were simply unrealistic. Others argued that the stretch targets were unachievable given current funding levels. That line of reasoning led the Office of Management and Budget (OMB) to object to the targets in general, because they could be interpreted as committing the government to increasing funding for these programs in the future. Finally, most of the participants protested the fact that the stretch targets were being imposed by the ONDCP. Up to that point, the process had been functioning in a much more *bottom-up* fashion. The imposition of the stretch targets, however, broke from that pattern and threatened the goodwill and commitment to the process that had been cultivated to that point. Finally, some participants felt the stretch targets were politically motivated. The revisions represented a thinly veiled effort by a Democratic administration to demonstrate to a Republican Congress a level of seriousness about the drug problem.

To a certain degree, some of the criticisms were valid. The ONDCP was sensitive about forwarding performance targets to the Congress that were vulnerable to charges of being too timid or meek. Substantive concerns, however, also motivated the drug policy office. The initial targets had been the product of the IWG process. The ONDCP was worried that, at least in some cases, these working groups had produced conservative estimates of progress that agency representatives felt confident they could achieve. Guided by the literature[1], the ONDCP sought to avoid performance targets that were essentially the lowest common denominator of an interagency process. The stretch targets were designed to motivate the agencies to do more than maintain the current rate of progress; they challenged the community to look beyond the status quo.

The debate over stretch targets threatened to derail the entire PME process. It was eventually resolved when the ONDCP agreed to qualify the presentation of the system in a number of areas. First, to placate OMB, the drug policy office agreed that the PME system did not imply any commitment to funding increases in the future. It was not, in the words of the ONDCP director, "a budget document" (McCaffrey, 1998). Second, the ONDCP also acknowledged that the goals and targets identified in the PME system were national ones, as opposed to federal ones. Therefore, reaching particular targets was not solely the responsibility of federal agencies. State and local governments as well as a number of nongovernmental organizations also play important roles. In retrospect, the ONDCP introduces these two major accountability loopholes in exchange for the stretch targets in an effort to hold together the fragile collaborative process. And third, ONDCP included a discussion of the performance targets in its first performance measurement report that demonstrated that the out-year targets were analytically plausible. This analysis was research-based and demonstrated that the stretch targets were indeed plausible in that they had a reasonable probability of being achieved with an integrated effort and commitment of the federal government. It succeeded in quieting the critics.

In the fall of 1997, the ONDCP began the formal interagency clearance process for the draft report. The clearance process enabled each agency to formally review and comment on the proposed system and to recommend changes. Some congressional staff and members of nongovernmental organizations were also involved in the consultation process. Of the major departments, State and Defense signed off on the document with relatively little comment. Education provided a qualified approval, citing a concern over the relationship between the PME and the budget process. Both the Departments of Treasury and Health and Human Services echoed the concern about the budget, in addition to offering several specific suggested changes to the document, much of which were incorporated.

The Department of Justice (DoJ), the department with perhaps the most at stake, proved the most intractable in the clearance process. Despite participating broadly in the IWGs and on the steering committees, DoJ's leadership chose the clearance process to question the PME system generally and, in particular, the ONDCP's role in directing the process. The department's formal response also included 113 line-by-line comments, most critical of the report's contents (ONDCP, 1998a). The department eventually did sign off on the PME report, but only after it reached the most senior policy officials in DoJ and ONDCP. Clearance was obtained after ONDCP highlighted two things to the attorney general: that the development process included the substantial involvement of a substantial number of DoJ staff who were picked by DoJ's chief of staff, and that the system of performance measures applied to the nation and not necessarily to the department's programs and activities.

In February 1998—one year after the initial effort began—the ONDCP released a report to Congress presenting its proposed performance measurement system (ONDPC, 1998b). The congressional reaction was mixed. Some members complained vehemently that the policy office had not gone far enough with its performance targets. It was something of an ironic reaction since the agencies had just been arguing that the stretch targets were too ambitious. ONDCP's own oversight committees, however, expressed greater appreciation for what had been accomplished. The following language was included in the reauthorization bill passed later that year.

> It is the sense of Congress that the performance measurement system developed by the director [of ONDCP] is central to the national Drug Control Program targets, programs, and budgets: the Congress strongly endorses the performance measurement system. (ONDCP 1998 Reauthorization Act, P.L.105-227)

Since the introduction to the public of the performance measurement system, it continues to be refined to reflect stakeholder concerns. At this point in the process, the group of stakeholders has expanded beyond the federal agencies to include state and local governments, Congress, and those with expertise in drug control policy. The refinements included action plans designed to indicate the programmatic changes necessary to realize performance outcomes (ONDCP, 1999). A process to link the PME system to the budget certification process was also explored. By the end of its third year of development, attention shifted to filling the data gap and activating a management information system to meet the extensive data requirements (ONDCP, 2000). In the 2000 PME report, the ONDCP PME system is an imposing array of five goals, 31 objectives, 97 performance targets, and 127 measures (Figures 3.2a-3.2f).

Figure 3.2a: The National Drug Control Strategy

Supply	Demand
• Reduce availability of illicit drugs in the United States (Goal 2c) • Reduce the rate of shipment of illicit drugs from source zones (Goal 5a) • Reduce the rate of illicit drug flow through transit and arrival zones (Goal 4) • Reduce domestic cultivation and production of illicit drugs (Goal 5b) • Reduce the drug trafficker success rate in the United States (Goal 2b)	• Reduce the demand for illegal drugs in the United States (Goal 3b) • Reduce the prevalence of drug use among youth (Goal 1a) • Increase the average age of new users (Goal 1b) • Reduce the prevalence of drug use in the workplace (Goal 3c) • Reduce the number of chronic drug users (Goal 3d)
Consequences	
• Reduce the rate of crime associated with drug trafficking and use (Goal 2a)	• Reduce the health and social costs associated with illegal drug use (Goal 3a)

Source: ONDCP, 2000, Appendix B

Figure 3.2b: The National Drug Control Strategy Goal 1—Prevent Drug Use Among America's Youth

Pursue a Vigorous Media Campaign

- Increase the percentage of youth who perceive drug use as harmful (1.2.1)
- Increase the percentage of youth who disapprove of drug use (1.2.1)
- Double the number of viewing hours that provide anti-drug messages (1.2.3)

Engage the Media

- Establish partnerships with media organizations to avoid glamorizing drug use (1.7.1)

Increase the Ability of Adults to Discourage Drug Use

- Increase the proportion of adults who have the capacity to help youth reject drugs (1.1.1)
- Increase the proportion of adults who attempt to influence youth to reject drugs (1.1.2)
- Reduce the proportion of adults who regard drug use as acceptable (1.1.3)

Increase Mentoring

- Develop a national program for increasing the number of mentors and mentoring organizations (1.5.1)
- Increase the proportion of adults who are trained to serve as mentors (1.5.2)

Develop Community Coalitions

- Publish a national inventory of community-based coalitions and partnerships (1.6.1)
- Increase the number of communities with funded, comprehensive, anti-drug coalitions (1.6.2)

Provide Sound School-Based Prevention Programs

- Establish criteria for effective prevention programs and policies (1.4.1)
- Increase the proportion of schools that have implemented effective programs and policies (1.4.2)

Promote Zero Tolerance Policies

- Promote zero tolerance policies in all schools (1.3.1)
- Increase the proportion of communities with zero tolerance policies (1.3.2)

Develop Prevention Principles

- Develop principles for prevention models (1.8.1)
- Disseminate information on these principles (1.8.2)

Conduct Research

- Assess prevention research (1.9.1)
- Increase the proportion of research-based prevention products (1.9.2)

Source: ONDCP, 2000, Appendix B

Figure 3.2c: The National Drug Control Strategy Goal 2—Increase the Safety of America's Citizens

Disrupt Trafficking Organizations

- Reduce the rate of specified drug-related violent crimes (2.1.1)
- Disrupt domestic drug trafficking organizations (2.1.2)

Strengthen HIDTAs

- Ensure HIDTAs meet NDS (2.2.1)
- Disrupt drug trafficking organizations in HIDTAs (2.2.2)
- Reduce the rate of specified drug-related violent crimes in HIDTAs (2.2.3)

Disrupt Money Laundering Organizations by Seizing Assets

- Increase use of asset seizure policies and procedures (2.3.1)
- Ensure that all states enact drug-related asset seizure and forfeiture laws (2.3.2)
- Increase the cost of money laundering to drug traffickers (2.3.3)

Break the Cycle

- Develop standards for drug testing policies (2.4.1)
- Increase the proportion of drug-using offenders who receive treatment (2.4.2)
- Reduce inmate access to illicit drugs (2.4.3)
- Decrease the proportion of drug using offenders who are rearrested (2.4.4)

Conduct Research

- Identify and disseminate information on successful law enforcement and treatment initiatives (2.5.1)
- Increase the proportion of agencies that have implemented similar initiatives (2.5.2)

Source: ONDCP, 2000, Appendix B

Figure 3.2d: The National Drug Control Strategy Goal 3—Reduce the Health and Social Costs of Drug Use

Promote a Drug-Free Workplace

- Increase the proportion of businesses with drug-free workplace policies, drug abuse education and EAPs (3.3.1)

Certify People Who Work With Drug Users

- Develop nationally recognized competency standards for people who work with drug users (3.4.1)
- States adopt nationally recognized competency standards for prevention professionals (3.4.2)
- States adopt nationally recognized competency standards for treatment professionals (3.4.3)
- States adopt nationally recognized competency standards for other professionals (3.4.4)
- States adopt nationally recognized competency standards for treatment EAP professionals (3.4.5)

Reduce Health Problems

- Reduce the incidence of tuberculosis in drug users (3.2.1)
- Reduce the incidence of drug-related hepatitis B in drug users (3.2.2)
- Reduce the incidence of drug-related hepatitis C among drug users (3.2.3)
- Stabilize and then reduce the incidence of drug-related HIV infection (3.2.4)

Support Effective and Accessible Treatment

- Close the treatment gap (3.1.1)
- Increase the effectiveness of treatment (3.1.2)
- Decrease waiting time for treatment (3.1.3)
- Design and implement a national treatment outcome and monitoring system (3.1.4)
- Disseminate information on the best available treatment protocols (3.1.5)

Support Research

- Fund a "results-oriented" portfolio of federally funded research projects (3.6.1)
- Develop and implement a comprehensive set of federal epidemiologic measurement systems (3.6.2)
- Develop and implement a model to estimate the health and social costs of drug use (3.6.3)

Develop Pharmaceutical Treatments

- Develop a comprehensive research agenda for research on medications (3.5.1)

Oppose Legalization of Schedule I Drugs

- Develop an information package on pharmaceutical alternatives to marijuana and other drugs (3.7.1)
- Conduct nationwide dissemination of information on the adverse effects of marijuana and other drugs (3.7.2)
- Develop a plan to oppose the legalization of Schedule I drugs (3.7.3)
- Implement the plan to oppose the legalization of Schedule I drugs (3.7.4)

Source: ONDCP, 2000, Appendix B

Figure 3.2e: The National Drug Control Strategy Goal 4—Shield America's Air, Land, and Sea Frontiers

Improve Coordination Among U.S. Agencies

- Identify all existing U.S. interagency drug control relationships (4.2.1)
- Assess these relationships and develop a strategy to address identified gaps (4.2.2)
- Establish secure, interoperable communications capabilities (4.2.3)

Conduct Research and Develop Technology

- Develop and deploy technology to deny entry of illicit drugs through the Southwest border and maritime PEO (4.4.1)
- Develop and deploy tagging and tracking systems that allow real-time monitoring of carriers throughout the Western Hemisphere (4.4.2)
- Develop and deploy detection capability for "over-the-horizon" tracking (4.4.3)
- Develop and demonstrate high-risk technologies (4.4.4)

Reduce Drug Flow in the Transit and Arrival Zones

- Develop interagency drug flow models (4.1.1)
- Increase the proportion of cocaine seized, jettisoned, or destroyed in transit and arrival zones (4.1.2)
- Increase the proportion of heroin seized, jettisoned, or destroyed in transit and arrival zones (4.1.3)
- Increase the proportion of marijuana seized, jettisoned, or destroyed in transit and arrival zones (4.1.4)
- Increase the proportion of methamphetamine seized, jettisoned, or destroyed in transit and arrival zones (4.1.5)

Improve Cooperation with Source and Transit Nations

- Identify all existing bilateral and multilateral relationships (4.3.1)
- Assess these relationships and develop a strategy to address identified gaps (4.3.2)
- Establish bilateral and multilateral relationships (4.3.3)

Source: ONDCP, 2000, Appendix B

Figure 3.2f: The National Drug Control Strategy Goal 5—Break Foreign and Domestic Sources of Supply

Deter Money Laundering

- Ensure that priority countries ratify 1988 U.N. Convention (5.5.1)
- Ensure that priority countries adopt laws consistent with FATF (5.5.2)

Support Multilateral Initiatives

- Establish agreements for bilateral and multilateral action (5.4.1)
- Ensure that each major source country adopts a drug control strategy (5.4.2)
- Increase donor funding for counternarcotics goals (5.4.3)

Conduct Research and Develop Technology

- Develop a wide area airborne multi-sensor system to detect cocaine manufacturing facilities (5.6.1)
- Develop standoff methodology to detect illegal amounts of currency secreted on persons (5.6.2)
- Develop new technology to detect drug production and movement (5.6.3)

Disrupt Organizations

- Disrupt trafficking organizations (5.2.1)

Improve SC Capabilities

- Improve capability to conduct interdiction activities (5.3.1)
- Develop judicial institutions (5.3.2)

Reduce Production

- Reduce the worldwide cultivation of coca used in the illicit production of cocaine (5.1.1)
- Reduce the worldwide cultivation of opium poppies (5.1.2)
- Reduce the cultivation of marijuana in the Western Hemisphere (5.1.3)
- Reduce the production of methamphetamine (5.1.4)

Source: ONDCP, 2000, Appendix B

Developing a Credible PME System

The PME system that emerged out of this process, though by means not perfect, appears to be capable of holding federal drug control programs accountable for their performance. And, relative to other efforts in the federal government, the ONDCP appears to have been successful in developing a credible system. The fact that the ONDCP managed to produce a performance measurement plan that has integrity, and succeeded while working across organizational boundaries, is an impressive accomplishment—especially when, as one participant noted, constructing a performance measurement system for a crosscutting issue like drug control constituted an "unnatural act" for many department-loyal federal bureaucrats.

To understand how the ONDCP managed to overcome these obstacles, we interviewed individuals who participated in the process of creating the PME system. The respondents were current and former officials in the ONDCP, the Departments of Justice, Education, Treasury, and Health and Human Services (HHS). Most participated in the process from the very beginning in 1997; some remain their agency's point of contact for the PME system.

By asking these individuals to look back over the process, they were able to identify a number of elements that contribute to the successful development of the system, as well as features that they found to be detrimental to the effort. The participants also raised important questions about the process that have yet to be addressed. These factors are discussed below.

What Worked in the PME Process

Government officials who participated in the PME process generally agreed that the following elements helped the ONDCP overcome the various obstacles that one would associate with an interagency effort such as this one. These elements were also the ones most often cited as contributing to the system's credibility.

Inclusiveness

Almost all of the respondents noted that the ONDCP's efforts to include the agencies affected by the process contributed to the successful creation of the PME system. The problem of illicit drug use is multifaceted with a number of interconnected relationships. The result is that several different factors can contribute to a single outcome measure such as drug use by adolescents. Similarly, several different government programs are designed to mitigate those factors. For example, the Department of Education provides funds designed to aid school-based prevention programs; HHS oversees community-based prevention efforts targeting initiation and drug use; and the Department of Justice helps local areas offer high-risk youth activities as alternatives to drug use and selling. If the eventual goals are to develop an integrated strategy that cuts drug use and to develop meaningful measures to hold agencies accountable, the ONDCP realized they had to have all of the relevant federal organizations in the room.

Buy-In from Mid-Level Officials

The ONDCP not only got mid-level administrators "in the room," they were quite successful in getting them to buy into the process. Consequently, the participants felt that most of the officials involved genuinely tried to contribute to the final outcome as opposed to undermine the effort.

It is important to note, however, that participants were divided in describing what motivated their involvement. For some, they truly were committed to the concept of accountability and measuring performance in government. The PME process, for these individuals, was seen as an opportunity to put into practice an idea they supported in theory. For others, they were more skeptical of the overall benefit of ONDCP's PME system and similar GPRA-like activities. They did recognize, however, that the PME process was going to move forward with or without their participation. Taking part in the ONDCP effort was the best way to protect their agencies' interests.

Starting from First Principles

Asking the agency working groups to develop the logic models was perhaps the most important factor that enabled the process to move forward. As discussed earlier, the logic models were intended to connect the goals of the strategy to specific objectives and, finally, to quantifiable output measures. To do so necessitated the construction of causal relationships linking these elements. The ONDCP could have imposed a set of measurements on the agencies and merely convened their representatives to ask how they would be implemented. Instead, it chose the more difficult, time-consuming, and at times tedious path of developing the measurements through a collection of interagency working groups. In the end, the time was well spent. Once agency representatives agree on the causal relationships, the task of defining objectives and identifying appropriate measures was essentially bounded. As a result, the debates over these details were more focused than they otherwise might have been.

Working from "Big" to "Little"

The combined effect of having the main goals established and providing the agency representatives the latitude to start from first principles enabled the PME process to avoid getting bogged down in details. The countless small issues that will emerge during implementation and operationalization of the system often can derail strategic planning efforts. The ONDCP strove to keep the working groups focused on the relationship of the main goals and objectives to their individual programs, and then, once the big issues were agreed upon, move forward to address the associated details.

Asking the "Should" Question

To gauge progress relative to the stated objectives, ONDCP asked the agency representatives to identify the appropriate measures that *should* be included in such a system. By not limiting the selection of measures to available datasets, the ONDCP gained credibility for the system as well as improving its quality. Most government programs can easily put their hands on statistics measuring level of activity and, in some cases, program outputs. By not restricting the discussion to data currently being collected, the participants were given the freedom to identify *outcome* measures. The participants also identified a secondary benefit of this approach. They felt that this method demonstrated that the ONDCP was serious about measuring performance and not just seeking to develop a paper exercise consisting of numbers only loosely connected to the objectives.

Opportunity to "Think Outside of the Box"

The previous two factors led to an unintended but positive consequence. Some of the participants appreciated the intellectual challenge of the exercise. Though they could easily identify the aspects of the process that fell short of the ideal, they enjoyed the opportunity to step back from their immediate responsibilities and view the problem of illicit drug use in a broader perspective. The PME process also provided the participants with a chance to gain from the perspective of their colleagues in other agencies. The attractiveness of the opportunity to "think outside of the box" was an interpretation that was not universally shared; nor did it contribute directly to the development of the PME system. It did, however, appear to motivate some participants and help sustain their involvement in the process.

Sticking to Timetables and Deadlines

The scale of the effort, the number of participants, and general bureaucratic inertia could have combined to grind the construction of a PME system to a halt. The ONDCP staff, however, established a timetable early on and did their best to keep the process on schedule. The presence of a timetable and deadline also kept the agency participants engaged. The timetable assured them that the process would, at some point, come to closure. The presence of a final deadline also served as a reminder that a final report was going to be forwarded to the Congress. Either reason served to encourage the participants to stick with the effort.

What Did Not Work

The process set in motion by the ONDCP did produce a credible set of performance measures. It was not, however, without its shortcomings. The deficiencies of the process are discussed below. It should be noted, however, that some of the elements labeled problems in this section are correlated to the positive factors identified above.

Cumbersome, Time-Consuming

Though the ONDCP was applauded for its inclusiveness, the cost of broadly reaching out was a cumbersome structure and process. The effort was composed of 23 working groups and involved over 250 individuals. By one estimate, the Department of Justice and its bureaus had as many as 50 officials taking part. According to ONDCP documents, the working groups officially met 64 times. Assuming that the average working group was composed of 11 people, and each meeting lasted two hours during the development process, over 1,400 person-hours were spent in meetings alone. This would represent a conservative estimate of the time involved, as it does not include time devoted to the process in between meetings or securing final clearance. It is difficult to see how one could have as inclusive an effort without the unwieldy process. It is important to realize, however, the cost that comes with such an all-encompassing endeavor.

Not Enough Time

The ONDCP-imposed deadlines, some participants felt, restricted the process. On one level, participants felt the time frame was simply too short to address such an ambitious task. On another level, participants noted that the rigid deadlines led to necessary, but frustrating, compromises. The challenge put to the participants was to develop a logic model based on causal relationships supported by scientific research. But, as Patrick Bell, a former policy advisor for the undersecretary of the Treasury for enforcement, noted, there are gaps in the existing research. In some cases, the effort to identify science-based causal relationships merely served to highlight where basic research questions still needed to be asked. The ONDCP attempted to allay some of the frustration by noting that the PME system would be reviewed annually and that there would be some room for revision in the future. Despite that assurance, some participants felt the final product was "less than advertised" in terms of its scientific foundation.

Imposition of "Stretch" Targets

A universal criticism of the PME process focused on the pressure exerted by the ONDCP to "stretch" the performance targets beyond what agency officials felt was reasonable. In general, they felt that the working groups had established realistic targets and then the ONDCP came in and pushed them out further for political reasons. These targets were, from the agencies' perspectives, not achievable, particularly given current funding levels. The stretch targets also caused friction with OMB, when that office suggested that they might be interpreted as a future commitment of resources.

The issue of stretch targets was clearly the most critical point in the PME development process. On the one hand, the ONDCP wanted to push the agencies beyond the "lowest common denominator" targets produced by the working groups. On the other, the agencies were reluctant to sign off on targets that they were not certain they could meet. Not surprisingly, a compromise was struck. The ONDCP agreed to present the PME system and its performance targets as part of the *national* strategy. Responsibility for reaching the targets, therefore, would not fall solely on the federal agencies. Instead, state and local governments would have to cooperate as well if the objectives were to be realized. This realization, in fact, led to the ONDCP beginning to reach out to state and local governments in an attempt to more completely integrate their efforts. Consequently, the federal office formed *performance partnerships* with the states of Oregon and Maryland and the city of Houston. These partnerships focus on monitoring specific outcomes in these jurisdictions.

ONDCP's effort to push the performance targets beyond what the working groups had developed came at a significant cost. The agency participants felt manipulated by ONDCP, causing the office to lose some of the goodwill it had accumulated. Perhaps more significantly, the compromise blurred the lines of accountability in the future by expanding the scope of responsibility for achieving successful results to include states, localities, and nonprofits.

Questions Yet to Be Answered

The conversations with individuals who participated in the development of the PME system revealed more than just what did and did not work. They raised important procedural questions, but noted that it was too early in the process to assess the impact of these issues.

Connection to the Budget Process

As initially established, the PME system did not incorporate resource requirements. Indeed, the absence of established linkages with the budget process appears to be a characteristic shared by several performance measurement plans (U.S. GAO, 1999a). Early in 1999, the ONDCP took steps to begin to connect the PME system with the budget certification process.

Meetings were held with agency program and budget staff to identify the types of programs necessary to achieve performance targets. ONDCP led the discussion, which also included members of working groups who helped establish the performance targets. The idea was simple: ONDCP had to issue budget guidance to the federal agencies each spring to assist them in formulating their drug control requests, so why not base this guidance on the performance targets? Each year, the ONDCP director must certify the drug control portion of federal agencies' budgets as *adequate* to carry out the national drug control strategy. This certification is based on how well the agency budgets accord with the budget guidance issued by ONDCP each spring. Linking this guidance to the specific performance targets would obviously strengthen ONDCP's certification process and ensure the integrity of the strategic plan. Thus, ONDCP officials encouraged the agencies to use the PME system and its objectives as a blueprint for crafting their upcoming budget requests. It is difficult to ascertain the degree to which this guidance affected their submissions and eventually their congressional appropriations. But, for the PME system to become the management tool that some envision, it will have to be integrated with the budget process.

Additional Data Collection Needs

The blessing of being able to look beyond the available data to identify performance measures could also become a curse. Some of the 97 performance targets identified in the 2000 PME report did not have data currently being collected to measure progress. In fact, the 2000 report noted that a total of 20 measures were identified as requiring data systems (some simple, some complex) to be developed or modified (ONDCP, 2000). ONDCP had a mechanism in place to address the data gap. Its Subcommittee on Data, Evaluation, and Interagency Coordination was given the assignment of closing the data gap and has ensured that the federal budget process recognizes resource needs. Some measures are now being developed. But implementation of the data collection will require resources, which is subject to the annual appropriations process. Should the Congress decide not to fund certain new data systems, the integrity of the performance measurement system could be jeopardized. And "improving data collection" has a limited constituency among elected officials and political appointees. Politically, asking for additional agents or funding a certain number of drug treatment beds is a much easier sell.

Consequences for Not Reaching Targets

The main procedural issue that is, as of yet, unresolved is the process for dealing with failure. The interagency working group process focused on developing logical connections between the causes and effects of illicit drug use and identified meaningful goals to measure progress against the stated objectives. Absent from this discussion and subsequent policy documents, however, is a prescribed set of steps that would be taken if a target were not met. This question, of course, is the very crux of accountability. ONDCP did recognize that targets may not be met because of problems such as poor program management, external factors outside the control of the strategic plan, and inadequate and inefficient use of resources, or the underlying logic model might be faulty. It further identified the need for program evaluations rather than program terminations as the first line of attack whenever targets were not reached. However, it has yet to codify an approach, which is essential to a performance management system. How the ONDCP handles failure, both politically and procedurally, will be critical to the future of the PME process.

Prospects for the Future

Patrick Tarr, a senior policy advisor in the U.S. Department of Justice, observed that the "... real goal is not just to write a report, but establish a process that is used." The ONDCP has accomplished the first step and produced a system that is both comprehensive and credible. Whether it is capable of moving the PME system to the next level and having it institutionalized as a management tool remains to be seen. If history is any indicator, the ONDCP faces a considerable challenge. The list of these types of public management reforms that have failed is much longer than the list of those that have succeeded.

The future of the PME system will depend, in part, on how the ONDCP addresses the procedural questions raised in the previous section. Other factors, many of which are out of the control of the ONDCP, will also have a big impact. These elements are discussed below, sorting them into the aspects that may have a negative effect on the PME system and those that suggest that it may be possible to sustain the PME system.

Discouraging Signs

The sheer size and scale of the PME system may be one of its biggest liabilities. Composed of five goals and 31 objectives that are linked to 97 performance targets may simply be too much for any one agency to oversee. The ONDCP sought to design a comprehensive system. It succeeded, but the consequence may be too many priorities. In short, the PME system may fall of its own weight.

One way to avoid having the PME system collapse in on itself is to prioritize the priorities. Though the ONDCP should be applauded for its thoroughness, it may be prudent to identify key areas and concentrate its oversight energies and resources. The rationale for such an approach stems from the minimal authority the ONDCP possesses. Outside of the budget certification process, the ONDCP is limited in what it can direct the agencies to do. The significant power that the ONDCP director possesses is the power to persuade—the agencies, the President, the Congress and the American people. The true test of the PME system will come when a target is not achieved. At that time, the ONDCP will have to concentrate its political capital in seeking to remedy the situation.

A second threat to the PME system is the change in administration. How the PME system will fare under a new director appointed by President George W. Bush is unclear. The new director may not see any value in the effort and let it simply disappear. Or, a new administration may embrace the concept of measuring the performance of drug policy programs, but it might want to change the five goals established under Clinton-appointed General McCaffrey. The PME system, however, was based on a logic model linking the various goals, objectives, and targets. A change in one of the goals, then, would have a ripple effect throughout the system. Changing one or more of the goals, therefore, would require going back to square one in the construction of the system.

A third shortcoming of the PME system as one looks to the future surrounds the degree to which agencies have bought into the process relative to the degree of buy-in necessary for the system to be successful. The process of constructing the system secured a commitment from one group of critical stakeholders: mid-level policy officials in Washington, D.C. For the system to become a completed integrated management tool, however, that sense of acceptance will have to spread both *up* to political appointees, as well as *out* to the program managers.

Eventually, senior policy officials must embrace the PME system. Appointees in the Clinton administration endorsed the concept of measuring performance in drug policy, but they did not have to oversee its complete implementation. Without the support of the key individuals capable of changing agency priorities and willing to advocate for shifts in resources, it is difficult to see how the system can move forward.

Securing the support of program officers is equally important to the success of the PME system. As has been noted in other crosscutting efforts, the programs must be integrated in the effort and treated with respect, not merely tolerated (Radin, 2000). The development process involved program managers only to the extent that their agency representatives chose to consult with them. It would appear that very little of that type of consultation occurred. That program people were not involved in the process does not come as a great surprise. Just with mid-level policy officials, the process was cumbersome enough. Plus, the relatively constrained timeline limited how much intra-agency consultation could take place. The result is that program managers may now be held accountable to a system into which they had very little input.

The challenge of gaining the support of program people will vary across agencies and activities. For programs that primarily distribute grants, incorporating the objectives of the PME system and adjusting priorities may be a function of rewriting the regulations covering the allocation of those funds. For programs that directly deliver services, embracing the objectives of the PME system may require changes in policies and procedures.

A final discouraging aspect of the PME system is that the public will find it difficult to understand. The beauty of a well-designed performance measurement system is that it makes transparent the objectives of government and monitors progress toward those objectives. If an agency fails to realize its performance targets, the public will find out and hold its representatives accountable. The problem with the PME system is that, though transparent, its comprehensiveness makes it complex. As a result, it does not lend itself to a straightforward narrative that the media can report easily. Even the most attentive observers of drug policy will have to immerse themselves in the minutiae of the system to gauge progress toward the goals. The complexity of the system, then, diminishes the threat that ONDCP can leverage recalcitrant agencies with the threat of public exposure.

Encouraging Signs

Despite the external threats to the future of the PME system, the future is not entirely bleak. A combination of political and institutional factors may also contribute to its sustainability.

Perhaps the most significant factor that favors a continuation of the PME system is the fact that its existence, in some form, is guaranteed by statute. When the Congress reauthorized the ONDCP in 1998 (P.L. 105-277), it included among the various provisions a requirement that ONDCP use and report annually on the performance of the strategy's goals and objectives. It endorsed the system developed by ONDCP and its federal partners:

> It is the sense of Congress that—the performance measurement system developed by the director [of ONDCP] is central to the national Drug Control Program targets, programs, and budgets; the Congress strongly endorses the performance measurement system for establishing clear outcomes for reducing drug use nationwide … and the linkage of this system to all agency drug control programs and budgets.

The reauthorization required ONDCP to report to Congress each year on the following topics: 1) the performance targets and measures and any proposed changes to such; 2) the identification of programs and activities of drug control agencies that support the goals and objectives of the strategy; 3) the consistency between agency drug control budgets and the performance targets; and 4) the implementation of the national drug control data system to support the performance measurement system. Institutionalizing the system in this manner, as Congress did, provides some assurance that the ONDCP will have to continue to measure performance and report on progress.

From a political perspective, congressional support for holding agencies accountable for their performance appears to be sustained. Despite changes in the executive branch, the legislature appears to be as committed as ever to hold the executive branch responsible for what it does. Whether this general support for measuring performance will translate into a specific endorsement of the ONDCP PME system remains to be seen. It is hard to imagine a political climate more amenable to the concept, however.

Finally, perhaps the biggest asset that the PME system possesses in assessing its future is its integrity. This advantage is a direct result of the development process. By being inclusive, starting from first principles, and asking the "should" question, the ONDCP and the agency participants managed to produce a system of measuring performance that is credible. It is not a perfect construction, but as Tom Vischi, a senior advisor for drug policy in the Department of Health and Human Services described it, it may be a "pretty good first draft." From this starting point, the ONDCP and the agencies could work together to refine and adjust it as they move forward. The willingness of these mid-level policy officials to sustain their commitment to the system will rest on their assessment of its credibility. Maintaining the system's integrity also will be critical if these individuals are going to push for integration of the PME system upward to the senior policy officials, as well as outward to the program managers.

Recommendations

This chapter presents the results of a single case study, and therefore, the general applicability of the findings are limited by the nature of the challenges the ONDCP faced in developing their system. Though it represents a unique situation in the experience of measuring performance, it does suggest some useful lessons. Described below are recommendations for public managers looking to establish performance measures for other crosscutting issues, or those state and local drug policy administrators seeking to introduce an element of accountability into their own efforts.

Start with a Clear Sense of Mission

ONDCP was fortunate in that national legislation required that it develop a strategy to accomplish specific outcomes for drug policy: reduced drug use, availability, and the consequences of drug use. The office had been annually producing a national strategy since 1989. This document became the starting point and shaped the subsequent strategic planning that developed the performance targets. Establishing a clear sense of direction is essential for a program that cuts across organizational lines. Absent one, agencies representing a variety of missions and perspectives will have a very difficult time finding common ground to even begin the process.

Seek a Credible Process; It Is More Likely to Produce a Credible Product

Since buy-in from the affected agencies is critical to simply creating the system, let alone implementing it, the process must maintain its integrity. Inclusiveness and collaboration contributed significantly to the degree to which agency representatives were willing to commit to the process. Identify those who have a stake in the outcomes and include them in the process of setting performance targets and measures. The inclusion of stakeholders, however, must be substantive. They should not be expected to merely endorse objectives and measures produced by others. Instead, the stakeholders should be participating in the development of these metrics. Encouraging them to focus on what *should be* included in the system instead of what *can be* currently obtained will contribute to both the credibility and the substance of the system. The performance targets will define the direction of change, and it is critical that stakeholders contribute to setting targets and buy into that change.

Designate Someone to Drive the Process

Though a bottom-up process contributes to the credibility of the final product, someone still has to direct the effort. This is especially true in the development of a system that cuts across organizational lines. Most of the participants in the PME process were, from an organizational perspective, hierarchical equals. Absent ONDCP authority to convene the effort, as well as bring to closure the various steps, the PME system might never have been completed. The ONDCP provided the starting point for the effort by establishing the initial strategy goals and objectives as the organizing framework. It also stepped in with stretch targets at a critical point. Agency participants would have never taken these steps on their own.

Recommending that an inclusive, participative process also have someone drive it means that a balance will have to be struck. The process must involve substantive participation by the agencies while, at the same time, the process needs to move forward. Without the presence of a single organization or individual to lead the effort, there is a risk that the process will merely muddle along. The agency participants may recoil at the prospect of having some elements of the system imposed upon them. More dangerous, however, is if the agency representatives get frustrated and disillusioned if the working groups become forums to continually rehash the same debates.

Be Willing to Test Your Model

Embrace the use of evaluations to test the strength of the performance measurement's underlying logic structure. The causal relationships relating outcomes to inputs must be understood, evaluated, and, if necessary, refined. If results are not being realized even though resources have been provided, it may indicate flaws in the underlying logic structure. Much of ONDCP's success was due simply to the use of research and analysis to link programs (inputs) to desirable outcomes and to demonstrate the plausibility of performance targets. Its future utility, as well as its credibility, will depend on the ONDCP's willingness to continue to ask whether it has mapped the relationships between policy and outcomes.

Connect Objectives and Strategies to Budget

It is important to identify programs and funding to achieve outcomes. There are many reasons for programs not achieving their performance targets; adequate resources are one of the most critical elements. The ONDCP had only begun to align the budget process with the PME system, but the connection was an inevitable next step. By encouraging agencies to use the PME system to guide the identification of their budget priorities, the ONDCP began to link resources to performance. Budget formulation and the execution of appropriated funds must not be divorced from the design of the performance measurement system.

It should be noted that such a connection is merely a logical extension of the rationale underpinning the measurement of performance in the first place. The GPRA was passed in an attempt to hold agencies responsible for the performance of their programs. Motivating this legislation was the notion that if government is going to spend taxpayer dollars, it should have something to show for it. (Indeed, the act includes provisions for the piloting of performance budgeting.) Connecting performance measures to budgets merely brings this argument full circle, noting that if an agency is going to be held accountable for its performance relative to certain policy objectives, it should have the resources necessary to carry out those tasks.

Realize That the First Report Is Just That, a First Report

The development of any performance measurement system is going to require refinement as it moves forward in its implementation. For crosscutting programs of this scope, the need for an iterative process increases. And, for a performance system to be fully implemented, buy-in at the policy/planning level is just the beginning. Eventually, the commitment to measurement performance must spread up to senior policy officials and out to program officers.

Incorporate Performance Measurement into Overall Management Strategies

Though the institutionalization of performance measurements holds significant promise for accountability, the process of developing a system has the potential to facilitate the coordination of policy across organizational lines more generally. For example, the PME process eventually led to a systematic review of data collection efforts and the identification of important gaps in the available information. The process itself also appears to have contributed to stronger ties across agency lines and between the ONDCP and the agencies. Whether it was a product of shared misery, the cultivation of mutual respect, or a combination of both, participants in the PME process noted that it enabled them to expand and solidify their connections with professionals in other organizations beyond ONDCP. The building of those ties could prove advantageous to the coordinating of federal drug policy in the future, regardless of the fate of the PME system.

Build on This Effort

The change in administrations will, undoubtedly, be accompanied by changes in policies and priorities. While the PME system may not reflect these new emphases, it is certainly capable of accommodating them and incorporating them into its structure. It would be a great loss if the incoming administration were to scrap the PME effort. On one level it would be a rejection of one of the only credible efforts to measure performance across several agencies and the work that went into creating it. On another, and more important level, it could set back the effort to reduce the use of illicit drugs and the associated consequences.

Conclusion

The case of the PME system is an important one. The ONDCP managed to overcome obstacles, beyond the usual ones associated with the development of performance measures, to create a successful system. Policy officials eventually bought into the process, and the subsequent product of those efforts, even though it required a considerable investment of both patience and time. The fact that the Congress decided to write the system into the ONDCP's reauthorizing statute provides further evidence that even the PME system's most strident potential critics endorsed the effort. In short, the ONDCP produced a credible system of measuring performance for a crosscutting policy issue.

Some elements of the ONDCP's experience with the PME system may be unique to the illicit drug issue. Nevertheless, the case should be enlightening for public managers seeking to implement performance measurement in other policy areas. At the federal level, there already have been efforts to improve the coordination of programs for issues such as poverty, AIDS, and race relations. The Congress has recently expressed interest in improving the management of anti-terrorism programs that cut across multiple agencies. Some elected officials have even floated the idea of a "border czar" to address problems unique to the U.S./Mexico border area. This interest in crosscutting issues, combined with an increased emphasis on performance measurement, means that the ONDCP experience could prove very instructive as other administrators take on similar challenges.

What the future holds for the PME process is difficult to predict. Its fate will clearly be dependent upon a collection of factors both within, and outside, of the control of the ONDCP. Of course, given the number of obstacles that stood in the way initially, few would have been optimistic about it ever being constructed in the first place.

Endnotes

1. The U.S. General Accounting Office, the National Academy of Public Administration, and performance measurement experts have all recommended the use of stretch targets in performance measurement systems.

Bibliography

Barnow, B.S. (2000). "Exploring the Relationship Between Performance Management and Program Impact: A Case Study of the Job Training Partnership Act," *Journal of Policy Analysis and Management* 19: 118-141.

Carnevale, John and Patrick Murphy (1999). "Matching Rhetoric to Dollars: Twenty-five Years of Federal Drug Strategies and Drug Budgets," *Journal of Drug Issues*, 29, 2: 299-322.

Gore, Al (1993). *Report of the National Performance Review*. New York: Random House.

Hatry, Harry (1999). *Performance Measurement: Getting Results*. Washington, D.C.: The Urban Institute Press.

Keehley, Patricia, Steven Medlin, Sue MacBride, and Laura Longmire (1997). *Benchmarking for Best Practices in the Public Sector*. San Francisco: Jossey-Bass.

MacLaughlin, John A. and Gretchen B. Jordan (1999). "Logic Models: A Tool for Telling Your Program's Performance Story," *Evaluation and Program Planning*, 22: 65-72.

McCaffrey, Barry (1998). Letter to OMB Director Raines, dated January 12, 1998.

Millar, Annie, Ronald S. Simeone, and John T. Carnevale (2001). "Logic models: a systems tool for performance management." *Evaluation and Program Planning*, 24: 73-81

Mohr, Lawrence B. (1995). *Impact Analysis for Program Evaluation*. Sage.

National Academy of Public Administration, Center for Improving Government Performance (1998a), *Planning for Results*, Washington, D.C.

National Academy of Public Administration, Center for Improving Government Performance, (1998b) *Improving Performance Across Programs: Thinking About the Issue—Taking the First Steps*, Washington, D.C.

National Academy of Public Administration, Center for Improving Government Performance (1998c), *An Overview of Helpful Practices*, Washington, D.C.

National Academy of Public Administration, Center for Improving Government Performance (1998d), *Budget Alignments*, Washington, D.C.

Newcomer, Kathryn E. and Mary Ann Scheirer (2001). *Using Evaluation to Support Performance Management: A Guide for Federal Executives*. Arlington, VA: The Pricewaterhouse Coopers Endowment for The Business of Government.

Office of National Drug Control Policy (1998a). "The PME Process," internal draft working paper prepared by the Office of Programs, Budget, Research, and Evaluation.

Office of National Drug Control Policy (1998b). *Performance Measures of Effectiveness*. Washington, D.C.: ONDCP.

Office of National Drug Control Policy (1999). *Performance Measures of Effectiveness: Implementation and Findings*. Washington, D.C.: ONDCP.

Office of National Drug Control Policy (2000). *Performance Measures of Effectiveness: Progress Report*. Washington, D.C.: ONDCP.

O'Neill, Robert J., Jr. (2001). "Five Management Challenges Facing Your Administration." *Memos to the President: Management Advice from the Nation's Top Public Administrators*. Arlington, VA: The Pricewaterhouse Coopers Endowment for The Business of Government.

Osborne, David and Ted Gaebler (1992). *Reinventing Government: How the Entrepreneurial Spirit Is Transforming the Public Sector*. New York: Penguin Group.

Perrin, Edward B., Jane S. Durch, and Susan M. Skillman, Eds. (1999). *Health Performance Measurement in the Public Sector: Principles and Policies for Implementing an Information Network*. Washington, D.C.: National Academy Press.

Popovich, Mark G., editor (1998). *Creating High-Performance Government Organizations*. San Francisco: Jossey-Bass Publishers.

Public Law 103-62 (1993). Government Performance and Results Act of 1993, 107 Stat. 285.

Public Law 105-277 (1998). An Act Making Omnibus and Consolidated Appropriations for the Fiscal Year Ending September 30, 1999. P.L. 105-277, 112 Stat. 2681.

Radin, Beryl A. (2000). *The Challenge of Managing Across Boundaries: The Case of the Office of the Secretary in the U.S. Department of Health and Human Services*. Arlington, VA: The Pricewaterhouse-Coopers Endowment for The Business of Government.

Uhalde, Raymond J. (1991). Testimony before the Committee on Governmental Affairs, U.S. Senate, May 23.

U.S. General Accounting Office (1997). *Managing for Results: Analytic Challenges in Measuring Performance*. (GAO/HEHS/GGD-97-138) Washington, D.C.: USGAO.

U.S. General Accounting Office (1998a). *Managing for Results: An Agenda to Improve the Usefulness of Agencies' Annual Performance Plans*. (GAO/GGD/AIMD-98-228) Washington, D.C.: USGAO.

U.S. General Accounting Office (1998b). *Managing for Results: Measuring Program Results that Are Under Limited Federal Control*. (GAO/GGD-99-16) Washington, D.C.: USGAO.

U.S. General Accounting Office (1999a). *Performance Budgeting: Initial Experience Under the Results Act in Linking Plans with Budgets*. (GAO/GGD-99-67) Washington, D.C.: USGAO.

U.S. General Accounting Office (1999b). *Drug Control: ONDCP Efforts to Manage the National Drug Control Budget*. (GAO/GGD-99-80) Washington, D.C.: USGAO.

U.S. General Accounting Office (2000a). *Managing for Results: Continuing Challenges to Effective GPRA Implementation*. (GAO/T-GGD-00-178) Washington, D.C.: USGAO.

U.S. General Accounting Office (2000b). *Program Evaluation: Studies Helped Agencies Measure or Explain Performance*. (GAO/GGD-00-204) Washington, D.C.: USGAO.

Wholey, Joseph S. (1979). *Evaluation: Promise and Performance*. Washington, D.C.: The Urban Institute.

Wholey, Joseph S. (1999). "Performance-based Measurement: Responding to the Challenges," *Public Productivity and Management Review*, 2, 3: 288-307.

Walters, Jonathan (1998). *Measuring Up: Governing's Guide to Performance Measurement for Geniuses (and Other Public Managers)*. Washington, D.C.: Governing Books.

Appendix I: Departments, Bureaus, and Independent Agencies Involved in Federal Drug Control

(primary drug control functions in parentheses)

Department of Agriculture*
- Agricultural Research Service (research)
- U.S. Forest Service (law enforcement)
- Supplemental Nutrition for Women, Infants, and Children (prevention)

Corporation for National Service (prevention)

Court Services and Offender Supervision Agency (corrections)

Department of Defense* (law enforcement; interdiction)

Department of Education* (prevention)

Department of Health and Human Services*
- Administration for Children and Families (prevention and treatment)
- Centers for Disease Control and Prevention* (prevention)
- Food and Drug Administration (prevention)
- Health Care Financing Administration (treatment)
- Health Resources and Services Administration (treatment)
- Indian Health Service (prevention and treatment)
- National Institutes of Health* (prevention and treatment research)
- Substance Abuse and Mental Health Services Administration* (prevention and treatment)

Department of Housing and Urban Development* (prevention)

Department of the Interior
- Bureau of Indian Affairs (law enforcement)
- Bureau of Land Management (law enforcement)
- U.S. Fish and Wildlife Service (law enforcement)
- National Park Service (law enforcement)

**Denotes agencies with personnel who participated in the PME process.*

Federal Judiciary (prosecutions; corrections)

Department of Justice*

- Assets Forfeiture Fund (law enforcement)
- U.S. Attorneys (prosecutions)
- Bureau of Prisons (corrections)
- Community Oriented Policing Services* (state and local grants)
- Criminal Division* (prosecutions)
- Drug Enforcement Administration* (law enforcement)
- Federal Bureau of Investigation* (law enforcement)
- Federal Prisoner Detention (corrections)
- Immigration and Naturalization Service (law enforcement; interdiction)
- Interagency Crime and Drug Enforcement (law enforcement)
- INTERPOL (international law enforcement)
- U.S. Marshals Service (law enforcement; prosecutions)
- Office of Justice Programs* (law enforcement; state and local grants)
- Tax Division (prosecutions)

Department of Labor* (prevention)

Office of National Drug Control Policy*

Small Business Administration* (prevention)

Department of State*

- Public Diplomacy (international law enforcement)
- Bureau of International Narcotics and Law Enforcement Affairs (international law enforcement)
- Emergencies in the Diplomatic and Consular Service (international law enforcement)

Department of Transportation*

- U.S. Coast Guard* (law enforcement; interdiction)
- Federal Aviation Administration (law enforcement; interdiction; prevention)
- National Highway Traffic Safety Administration (prevention; state and local grants)

**Denotes agencies with personnel who participated in the PME process.*

Department of the Treasury*

- Bureau of Alcohol, Tobacco, and Firearms* (law enforcement)
- U.S. Customs Service* (law enforcement; interdiction)
- Federal Law Enforcement Training Center (law enforcement, training)
- Financial Crimes Enforcement Network* (law enforcement; money laundering)
- Interagency Crime and Drug Enforcement (law enforcement)
- Internal Revenue Service* (law enforcement)
- U.S. Secret Service (law enforcement)
- Treasury Forfeiture Fund (law enforcement)

Department of Veterans Affairs* (treatment)

**Denotes agencies with personnel who participated in the PME process.*

Appendix II:
Logic Models and Performance Management*

Logic models depict real-life events or relationships through the use of words or charts. They attempt to capture the underlying assumptions or bases upon which one act or event is expected to lead to the occurrence of another. Logic models, then, consist of causal chains that seek to explain the occurrence or non-occurrence of phenomena through a series of controllable activities. By trying to portray real life in pictures, they force the administrator to state explicitly the set of causal relationships surrounding the problem in question.

For the past 20 years, logic models have been used largely in program evaluations to chart out what should have happened and what did or did not occur as intended. These logic models start with the inputs of the program being evaluated and work their way through the processes to end with the desired end state, whether output or outcome. Evaluation specialists, with some input from policy/planning staff and program managers, usually undertook these modeling efforts (Mohr, 1995).

More recently, public managers have begun to employ logic models as part of the effort to introduce more accountability into government. These tools prove useful to any person trying to plan, manage, account for, audit, evaluate, or explain the connections between what a program's spending and its objectives. The logic models used by the ONDCP, then, were developed from the perspective of government managers seeking to implement policies to effect change. They reflected the logic behind a government programs. These models suggested that government intervention in one or more areas will set off a causal chain of responses or effects. At the end of that chain, ideally, would be a desired policy outcome.

Monitoring a program's outputs (e.g., services or products produced) is relatively easy for a manager. Determining a program's impact on society—its outcomes—is considerably harder. The relationship among variables is complex and the measurements elusive. Decreasing drug use by youth presents one such case. By developing a logic model, the manager can identify, at least conceptually, the issues that need to be addressed when seeking to change this behavior. Though some of these elements may be beyond the control of public administrators, they will have at least identified the components upon which successful performance is dependent.

Figure 3.3 provides an example of one piece of the larger PME system. It presents how the ONDCP conceptualizes the effect pursuit of a media

* *For a more complete discussion of logic models and performance measurement, see Millar, Simone, and Carnevale, 2001.*

campaign will have on drug use by youth. It also places that objective in the context of reducing the demand for drugs overall. Quantifiable measures are then identified for the outcomes. Once completed, the model can be used to identify how changes in policy will influence one element in the model and, in turn, ripple through the system, affecting other relationships. In this way, the model can be used to guide policy choices and, by monitoring changes in the target measures, measure performance.

Figure 3.3: Reducing Drug Use Among Youth

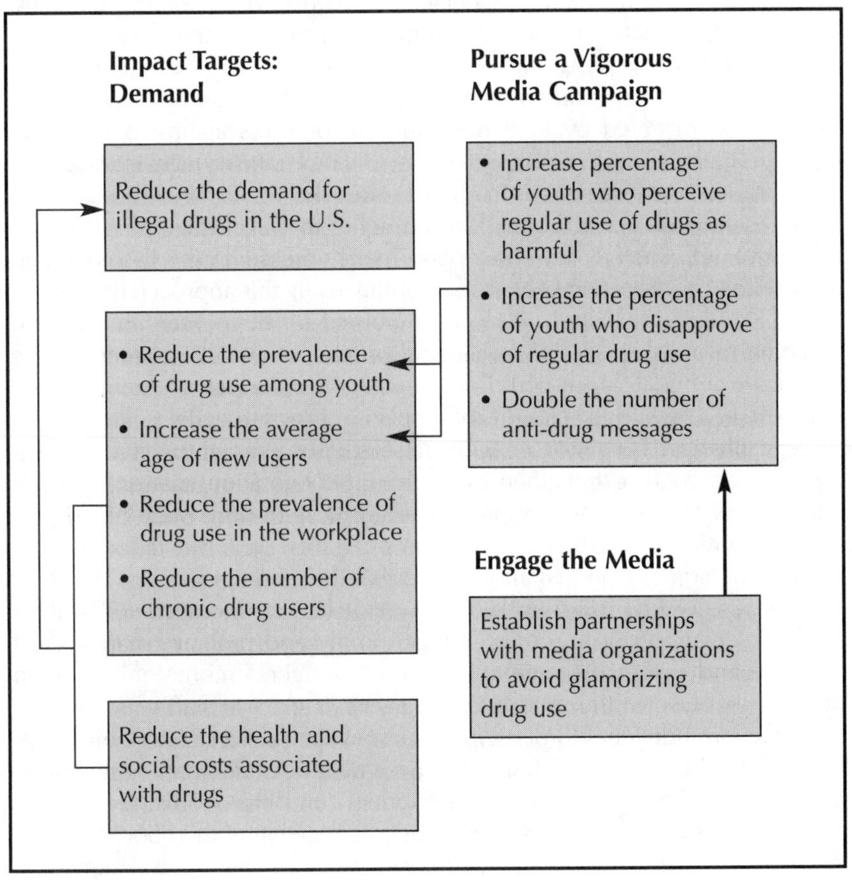

Appendix III: John Carnevale on Managing the PME Process

As the former director of programs, budget, research, and evaluation for the ONDCP, much of the substantive work on the PME system was the responsibility of my staff. Early on, I realized that successful development and formulation of the performance measurement system required buy-in from each of the departments and agencies involved in drug control activities. The challenge was to gain buy-in without compromising the integrity of the system. After all, the possibility of being held accountable for outcomes that could be affected by others was not too attractive to most agencies. At the same time, frustrated by a seeming lack of progress against overall and youth drug use, Congress demanded that ONDCP take its legal mandate for performance measurement much more seriously.

My approach was grounded in the belief that exclusive reliance on a bottom-up approach to develop a performance measurement system would not work. An earlier attempt at accountability using this approach had failed. ONDCP's Office of Supply Reduction worked for three years to establish outcome measures just for international programs—about 5 percent of the drug control budget—but could only manage to produce program activity targets (e.g., measuring seizures for a specific program activity) rather than strategically based targets (e.g., why are seizures important to the then existing strategic goal to strengthen international cooperation against narcotics trafficking?). The bottom-up approach asked those responsible for field program operations to explain how their programs contributed to national strategic outcomes. The real answer was that they did not know.

Because of that experience, I knew that leaving the agencies to their own devices was not an option. Those policy and program managers at ONDCP and within the federal drug control agency community had to become involved in the process. Each agency's chief of staff was asked to designate an individual to participate in the process. To ensure their cooperation, we did an unusual thing. The designated experts were "guaranteed anonymity" with regard to their contribution. In other words, we at least gave them the opportunity to "check their agency hat at the door" and free them up to share their expertise. Simply because they as an individual agreed on a particular issue would not be construed as clearance by their agency. That would come later.

Having a strong sense of purpose was critical. I wanted the performance measurement system to be cast in a logic model framework that would explain how the five goals and then 32 objectives contributed to an end state established 10 years into the future. Why 10 years? Led by the new drug czar, Barry R. McCaffrey, the discussion about the strategic plan focused on a long-term, 10-year plan to reduce drug use, availability, and consequences. So establishing 10-year targets and measures made sense.

Three specific elements proved critical to me as a manager throughout the process. First, I had the clear support of the ONDCP director. ONDCP's authorizers in the Congress had told Director McCaffrey to produce a performance measurement system, or else they would do it for him. Luckily, he understood the importance of accountability and wanted a performance measurement system even more than his congressional managers. His commitment to the project helped me to manage the interagency process from start to finish. Agency participants knew that one way or another, ONDCP's new czar was determined to develop a system—he had to—and understood they had more to gain by being involved.

The second critical element was my ability to tap outside expertise. Through a policy research contract, we could seek outside opinions on our work in progress. The baggage of bureaucratic politics or agency loyalties did not encumber these outsiders. As a result, they sometimes even played the role of referee. Finally, our effort greatly benefited from the presence of a noted national performance management expert on staff. Annie Millar brought to the project her considerable knowledge and experience as well as access to the best-known scholars in the performance measurement field.

It is worth highlighting one complex issue that threatened to derail the process: the imposition of stretch targets. The working groups identified 10-year targets that often simply extended current trend lines. For example, the working group that looked at outcomes for overall illicit drug use levels (measured by a national household survey) proposed a target of a 35 percent reduction in use relative to the 1996 baseline. Their rationale was that such a reduction reflected current use trends combined with pessimistic projections about future congressional funding. Such an approach, however, failed to recognize that the national strategy was supposed to take the nation beyond the point where the current trend might go. It also ignored the possibility of using the system to challenge the Congress to fund these programs.

The performance measurement literature maintains that sometimes targets have to be "stretched" if the reason is to motivate policy and program managers to do more than maintain current trends. It is a responsibility that falls squarely in the lap of the drug czar. So, we stretched. In the above case, the working group's recommendation was stretched to become a 50 percent reduction in drug use. Other similarly ambitious targets also were imposed.

The decision to stretch the performance targets was not a popular one and threatened the goodwill and cooperation we had cultivated to that point. The working group members claimed (in part, correctly) that the decision was politically motivated. More importantly, they feared their programs would be in peril if the targets were missed. They did not believe that the Congress would ever provide the funds necessary to achieve the ambitious goals we had laid out.

From where I sat, they were missing the point. It was the drug czar's job to organize a strategic effort to achieve the targets by getting the right programs and resources from Congress to achieve the 10-year targets. The drug czar would prepare a strategy and budget for the president to take to Congress. Ultimately, the burden would fall to Congress to approve the long-term strategic plan and to provide the necessary resources to implement it. We understood that the performance targets necessarily would be revised depending on Congress' cooperation. I think the agency participants understood my reasoning, but never completely accepted it. It is worth mentioning, though, that Congress itself caught the stretch target bug: It legislated its own version of policy targets for itself with respect to drug policy that far exceeded the administration's targets.

What would I do differently if I had to do it all over again? Not much would change. Having access to the many talented individuals who participated and their willingness to cooperate allowed the effort to succeed. The process was by no means perfect—sometimes it was like herding cats—but it was open. One area that I would strengthen is the involvement of other levels of government and outside groups in the process. The process I managed reflected the reality that underlies U.S. drug policy: While the strategy claims to be a national one, it is really federal in that it organizes the resources and activities of federal drug control agencies. It would have been interesting to see what state and local governments would add to the process. It would take a difficult task and make it even harder, but then we could claim a truly national strategic effort.

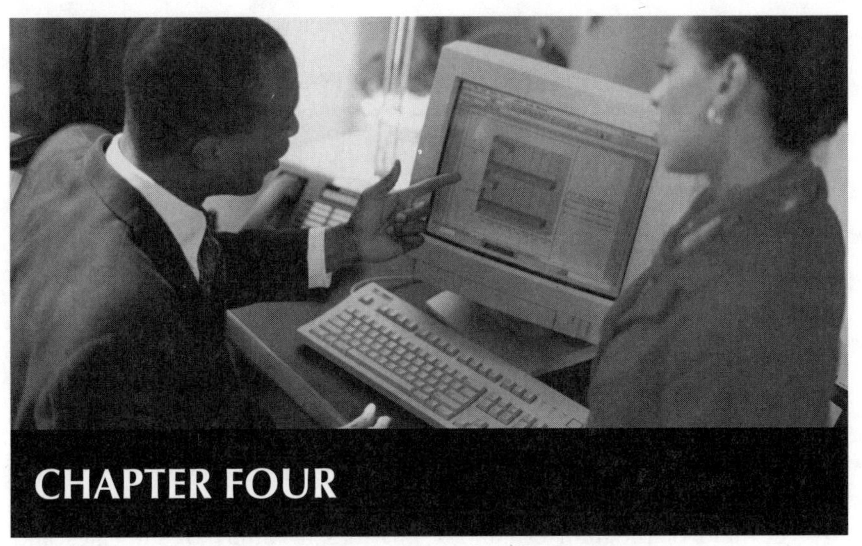

CHAPTER FOUR

Using Evaluation to Support Performance Management: A Guide for Federal Executives

Kathryn E. Newcomer
Professor and Chair
Department of Public Administration
George Washington University

Mary Ann Scheirer

Introduction

In the spring of 2000, federal managers completed the first cycle of planning, measuring, and reporting on programmatic performance required by the Government Performance and Results Act (GPRA) by submitting their first performance reports. The efforts undertaken to report on performance raise many issues that need continued involvement from agency executives and managers. GPRA requires agencies to routinely collect data on the level and type of program activities (processes), the direct products and services delivered by the program (outputs), and the results of those activities (outcomes) (GAO, 2000, p. 3). For their performance reports, agencies are expected to analyze performance data, draw apt comparisons, and probe the validity of the measures as they explain the operations and outcomes of their programs.

The field of program evaluation provides a variety of strategies and tools that support the ongoing performance measurement required by GPRA. While it does not specifically require agencies to undertake program evaluation studies, GPRA recognizes the complementary nature of program evaluation and performance measurement. The law requires agencies to describe program evaluations used to establish and revise goals, to include a schedule for evaluations in their strategic plans and to summarize the findings of relevant evaluations in their Annual Performance Reports (GAO, 2000, p. 4). In addition, GPRA requires agencies to provide explanations for why performance targets are not met, another clear opportunity for the application of program evaluation methods. This chapter suggests strategies and tools for agency executives to use in meeting these requirements.

This chapter draws upon a study of the current capacities for and uses of program evaluation to support performance management within 13 large federal departments and 10 agencies. The experiences of federal managers are summarized to offer advice to federal executives on:

- Program evaluation tools to support performance management;
- Leveraging evaluation capacity to contribute to performance management; and
- Organizational opportunities for integrating program evaluation and performance management.

Tips on using and leveraging evaluation to support performance management are offered. Then recommendations are suggested to identify ways that program evaluation capacity might be leveraged to effectively improve performance measurement and management. Findings and recommendations offered here could also be applicable to agencies in many other jurisdictions facing similar demands for sound performance information.

The Role of the Federal Executive in Performance Management

While GPRA is the major driver of performance measurement and management at the federal level of government, there are many other legislative requirements to report on performance, for agencies at the federal as well as state and local levels of government. Table 4.1 lists the many factors pressing federal agencies to focus on performance reporting (Newcomer, 2000). As indicated, the examples of other countries and jurisdictions, as well as a continuous series of executive and legislative actions, have initiated a culture of "performance-based management." Traditional political and interest group pressures on decision making are being supplemented, but not replaced, by demands for data about the operations and results of government programs.

Table 4.1: Drivers of Performance Management in the Federal Government

Pressures External to the Federal Government

- International success stories (e.g., New Zealand, UK)
- State and local government success stories
- The Governmental Accounting Standards Board call for "service efforts and accomplishments" reporting
- Total Quality Management (TQM) and other initiatives focusing attention on customers

Executive Initiatives

- The National Performance Review/National Partnership for Reinventing Government, 1993-2000
- Office of Management and Budget requirements for performance information to accompany budget requests (beginning May 5, 1992)
- Executive Order 12862—To survey customers

Legislative Initiatives

- Chief Financial Officers Act of 1990
- Government Performance and Results Act of 1993
- Government Management and Reform Act of 1994
- Chief Information Officers Act of 1996
- Federal Financial Management Improvement Act of 1996
- Many other laws requiring performance measurement in specific policy areas passed after 1995.

These demands for performance data require analytic capacity and resources often labeled as "program evaluation." However, support for program evaluation capacity across federal agencies has actually declined during the last two decades (Newcomer, 1994). The number of full-time staff dedicated to conducting program evaluation work within federal agencies declined fairly steadily from the late 1970s into the 1990s. Nine of the 13 federal departments contacted for this study downsized their central evaluation capacity since the 1980s or never had a central evaluation office. Recognizing the diminished ability of federal agencies to assess systematically how well programs are working, the authors of GPRA state they inserted language about the use of program evaluation in GPRA to stimulate interest and resources for evaluation work across agencies (NAPA, 2000).

Given the generally low capacity for program evaluation in most federal agencies, and the high demands for valid and reliable evidence of the results of federal efforts required by GPRA, how might federal executives rise to the analytical challenges thrust upon them? We conducted this study to identify ways that federal managers are using program evaluation to contribute to these analytical challenges. The objectives of this work were the following:

- To document ways that program evaluation strategies and tools are being employed to support implementation of GPRA, and
- To offer recommendations for improving the linkages between program evaluation and performance management in the federal government.

The current environment in the federal government requires federal executives to measure and report on programmatic performance. Performance-oriented political appointees, staff of the Office of Management and Budget (OMB), congressional committees, and interest groups are asking good, hard questions about performance. Federal executives need to know how to marshal resources to ensure that their agencies provide good data. Federal executives should know:

- What program evaluation is, particularly the wide range of its potential uses;
- The array of possible tools that program evaluation and analytical staff can use to support performance measurement and management;
- The level and availability of evaluation capacity in their agencies;
- The evaluation knowledge and skills needed by line managers in their agencies as well as by analytical staff;
- Effective strategies for leveraging evaluation capacity through cross-fertilization of staff and their skills; and
- Opportunities available for marshaling evaluation to support performance management.

Program evaluation is defined fairly broadly in this study as the application of systematic analytic methods to address questions about program operations and results. In fact, the federal officials interviewed were encouraged to explain how they view program evaluation. This approach uncovered more uses and planned uses than have been reported in published documents such as the FY 1999 performance reports. Our interviews suggest that official reporting under GPRA may reveal only the "tip of the iceberg" regarding the tremendous amount of analytical work underway in federal agencies as programmatic performance is monitored and probed.

Methodology

This chapter draws upon exploratory research in 13 major departments of the federal government, plus 10 of their component agencies. Federal agency evaluators, and staff members in offices of Inspector General (OIG), policy and planning offices, and budget offices involved with implementing GPRA were interviewed between February and June of 2000. Letters were sent to each interviewee in advance explaining the project, assuring confidentiality, and requesting participation. The interview protocol was often faxed to each interviewee after appointments for in-person or telephone interviews were confirmed. The interview protocol contained mostly open-ended questions developed from the primary research questions for the study. Pre-test interviews to improve the instrument were undertaken with highly experienced evaluation managers within three agencies.

Agencies and respondents were selected using a snowball sampling technique. Initial contacts were made with agencies with track records of experience in evaluation. Other federal agencies were included to broaden the range of federal programs covered. There should be no inference drawn from this study that agencies excluded are not using evaluation to support implementation of GPRA. The agencies included in the study are listed in Table 4.2. For many agencies, staff in one or more operating units within the agency—e.g, the National Highway Traffic Safety Administration and the Centers for Disease Control—were also interviewed. The operating units were selected based upon the recommendations of central departmental staff, and were typically recommended because of the noteworthy evaluation work they have undertaken.

Thirty-seven interviews were conducted in 23 federal departments and agencies; the interviews involved a total of 61 federal officials, as some included more than one person. The researchers sought out those who had been actually involved in preparing strategic plans, performance plans, and performance reports required under GPRA.

Table 4.2: Federal Agencies in the Study (with abbreviations)

Department of Agriculture (USDA)
Food and Nutrition Service (FNS)
Department of Education (ED)
Office of Student Financial Assistance Programs (SFA)
Environmental Protection Agency (EPA)
Department of Health and Human Services (HHS)
Health Resources and Services Administration (HRSA)
Centers for Disease Control and Prevention (CDC)
Department of Housing and Urban Development (HUD)
Department of Interior (DOI)
Department of Justice (DOJ)
Bureau of Prisons (BOP)
National Institute of Justice (NIJ)
Department of Labor (DOL)
Employment and Training Administration (ETA)
National Aeronautics and Space Administration (NASA)
Social Security Administration (SSA)
Department of Transportation (DOT)
National Highway Traffic Safety Administration (NHTSA)
Maritime Administration (MARAD)
Research and Special Programs Administration (RSPA)
United States Agency for International Development (USAID)
Department of Veterans Affairs (VA)

Program Evaluation Tools to Support Performance Management

Prior discussions of performance measurement and program evaluation often contrast these functions as being *different strategies* for collecting and using information about program performance. For example, the General Accounting Office (GAO) has been active in stimulating and monitoring performance management and its relationships with program evaluation. GAO defines performance measurement as "the ongoing monitoring and reporting of program accomplishments, particularly progress towards preestablished goals." It states that "program evaluations are individual systematic studies conducted periodically or on an ad hoc basis to assess how well a program is working" (USGAO, 1998).

However, our research revealed that many program managers view their performance measures as a major means of programmatic evaluation, and do not make the conceptual distinctions implicit in the GAO definitions. Instead, evaluative functions are pervasive in the developmental work supporting performance measurement, including tasks such as defining the program outcomes to be measured, designing or discovering measuring tools for these outcomes, collecting valid data, analyzing these data, and presenting results in formats useful to a variety of audiences. But some agencies are not viewing these tasks as part of program evaluation, and often do not assign them to staff members with skills in these functions. By adopting a broader definition of program evaluation, one which includes performance measurement as a relevant application of evaluators' skills, agencies might integrate more fully their analytic capacities into their work in implementing GPRA.

Requirements for Performance Management

Performance management involves more than simply recording measures of program performance and reporting them upwards to oversight bodies and public stakeholders. Several steps are needed to develop and collect performance measures that can be useful to management in decision making:

- Programmatic stakeholders must come together to reach agreement on strategic and performance objectives and the strategies for achieving them;
- Indicators must be defined for program components that capture program outputs (e.g.,the extent of services provided) and/or outcomes (e.g., behaviors of beneficiaries influenced by the services);
- Data sources must be developed or discovered for those indicators;
- Data must be collected with systematic methods, often in multiple jurisdictions (e.g., states, grant-funded projects, etc.);
- Data must be aggregated and reported in user-friendly formats;
- The data must be used by program managers and decision makers to assess and improve results; and
- Data quality must be addressed at every step of its journey from original collection to final reporting.

All of these steps are taken in relation to an agency's program strategies and activities to address the problem or content domain targeted in the agency's mission.

A central theme of performance measurement is to collect useful evidence, usually quantitative data, about the delivery and results of agency actions. This process is often called evidence-based management in the health services context. The tools of program evaluation and the skills of program evaluators can contribute substantially to the multiple steps needed for institutionalizing useful performance measurement systems. This section discusses the many ways that evaluation strategies, tools, and studies can support performance management, going far beyond a narrow view of evaluation that focuses primarily on impact research.

Federal agency officials suggested that evaluation is not only a set of specific, discrete studies of programs, but is an ongoing function served by both performance measurement and more targeted studies. Interviewees acknowledged that focused evaluation studies are needed to provide more in-depth understanding of program implementation, to supply evidence of the causal links assumed to connect outputs with intended outcomes, as well as to examine the contextual background for ongoing performance data. Performance measurement provides the central core of routinely collected evaluative data about program operations and outcomes. Additional evaluation studies provide complementary evidence and logical frameworks for increasing the depth of knowledge for interpretation of the performance data.

Types and Methods of Program Evaluation

Over the past 30 years, evaluators have developed an extensive array of approaches and methods to address a variety of client needs and situations. Methods for process evaluation, theory-based evaluation, impact assessment, and participative evaluation, among others, all provide alternative approaches to data collection and analysis. While this array of evaluative approaches is sometimes bewildering to program managers, it does provide a diversity of tools that can be applied to various tasks needed for developing and using performance measurement systems for evidence-based management.

To illustrate the varied ways that program evaluation can contribute to the many processes involved in performance management, we developed the conceptual framework shown in Table 4.3. The columns describe major stages in the development and use of systematic information for performance management, including:

- **Support for strategic and program planning**—for GPRA, developing Strategic Plans and Annual Performance Plans;
- **Support for improving program delivery**—the heart of program management, by using the planned strategies and data feedback to inform decision making on delivering services, designing and implementing regulations, and providing grants for research or service delivery;

Table 4.3: Framework Showing Potential Uses of Program Evaluation in Support of Performance Management

	Stages in the Use of Performance Information for Performance Management			
Types and Methods of Program Evaluation	*Support for Strategic and Program Planning*	*Support for Improving Program Delivery*	*Support for Accountability*	*Support for Attributing Results to Agency's Programs*
Conceptual Development	**a.** To show expected links via logic models **b.** For policy analysis of options available	**a.** Use of logic models to show intended delivery **b.** Use of prior literature about program strategies	**a.** To show links among inputs, outputs, and outcomes with logic models	**a.** Use of theory-based evaluation **b.** Use of logic models
Development of Evaluation Methods and Quality Control	**c.** To develop meta-analysis methods for summarizing findings from previous evaluation and research	**c.** To develop data systems for monitoring program delivery and management	**b.** To develop performance measures and data sources **c.** To verify and validate data	**c.** To develop evaluation research designs and measurement tools
Use of Data Systems	**d.** For needs assessment, via population-based data and periodic surveys **e.** Setting targets for performance measures	**d.** Use of MIS data to monitor diverse program sites or states **e.** Geographic-based analysis	**d.** Use of MIS to produce output and outcome data	**d.** By causal modeling (e.g., time-series and regression models) using MIS data
Process and Impact Evaluation Studies	**f.** To summarize findings from prior evaluations and research: "What works?"	**f.** For process and implementation evaluation (one-time or periodic)	**e.** For descriptive outcome data (e.g., using surveys)	**e.** For impact evaluation, with experimental or quasi-experimental design **f.** To analyze plausible associations; pattern matching

- **Support for accountability**—reporting the performance data in GPRA Annual Performance Reports and other reports to oversight bodies, such as Congress and the public; and
- **Support for attributing results to agency's programs**—providing research and evaluation to analyze the causal effectiveness of the programs and strategies whose "results" are reported in other documents.

The stages of performance management occur in cycles in most agencies, and may overlap (particularly the work involved in attributing results to agency programs, which may be ongoing). For example, the officials we interviewed had just completed their first Annual Performance Reports and were starting to revise their Strategic Plans. They were explicitly building on their prior work and trying to improve it, using feedback from both internal and external sources. The rows of Table 4.3 summarize major types of program evaluation that can contribute to each stage in performance management (see accompanying box for definitions). The cells of Table 4.3 then illustrate the many and varied potential uses for evaluative information in support of performance management. These diverse uses illustrate our broad definition of evaluation as "the application of systematic analytic methods to address questions about program operations and results."

The following section details the multiple ways that evaluation approaches are being used to support performance management efforts, to amplify the suggestions in Table 4.3. A "menu of approaches" is offered that agency executives, program managers, and their partner agencies might consider when planning data collection strategies that would provide useful information to support performance management. As will be evident

Definitions of Types and Methods for Program Evaluation

Conceptual Development—Methods for detailing the pathways by which programs are intended to work.

Development of Evaluation Methods and Quality Control—Detailing the procedures and specifications to be used for collecting data, for evaluation study designs, and for verification and validation of data quality.

Use of Data Systems—Using data from available statistical indicators (e.g., state-collected "vital statistics" or regularly collected surveys), from program-specific Management Information Systems, and/or from Geographic Information Systems.

Process and Impact Evaluation Studies—Systematically conducted assessments, usually on a one-time basis, of the activities or interventions undertaken by a program, and/or of the results attributable to that program.

from the variety of examples described below, these uses of evaluation tools are far more diverse than the traditional distinction between evaluation and performance measurement would suggest.

Conceptual Development—Using Logic Models and Program Theory

Evaluation tools can support the conceptual work needed to describe the agency's intended programs and their strategies. Program evaluators (e.g., Wholey, 1979, 1987; McLaughlin and Jordan, 1999) have long advocated the use of logic models to show the flow of program operations, including:

- resources (inputs) and/or initial assumptions;
- implemented program activities;
- program outputs (products); and
- short-term, intermediate, and long-term outcomes.

GPRA legislation and guidance from the General Accounting Office support this focus by suggesting that agency strategic plans and performance measures should include inputs, outputs, and outcomes to show a logical sequence of strategies and results, as well as their measures (U.S. GAO, 1997).

Further, the use of logic models encourages connections to theory-based evaluation (Bickman, 1987; Chen, 1990; Weiss, 1998) by detailing the logic and assumptions connecting the activities delivered by a program and its expected results. Program staff can work with stakeholders to develop logic models and hypothesized program theories to assess the plausibility of expectations for program goals and results. Such conceptual assessment also encompasses the likelihood that intended delivery will be implemented, and that the resources and other requirements will be available to enable those program activities to take place.

Focusing on the conceptual background underlying a program, such as by developing a logic model, can be a valuable tool for agency use in gain-

Using a Program Flow Model at the Department of Education

A senior administrator in the Student Financial Aid program at ED developed a 13-step logical flow model of students' decision processes in obtaining higher education and financial aid, including the occurrence of loan repayment problems. ED programs that affect each step were listed. The model occupied a whole wall of the administrator's office, and had been iteratively developed using Post-it notes to add or delete specific elements suggested by program managers or other stakeholders. This administrator referred to the model when discussing program strategies and alternative interventions with program managers, particularly to identify likely intervention points that could make a difference in the outcomes of student financial aid programs.

ing agreement among stakeholders on the intended program, and in clearly communicating program results as a logical sequence among program measures and targeted outcomes. For some measures, particularly agency outputs, agencies ought to be able to specify targeted performance rather precisely. For longer-term outcomes or "results," targets are likely to be less precise, because many other partners and environmental factors affect those outcomes, and agencies have less immediate control over them. A logic model helps to show the "chain of results" between an agency's concrete activities and its long-term goals or purposes.

Rather surprisingly, we found only a few explicit examples of the use of logic models in GPRA plans and performance measures. Much of the initial guidance to agency staff on developing performance measures focused heavily on moving beyond outputs to specify and develop measures of outcomes. Perhaps agency staff who developed these documents did not feel it was necessary to show the linkages among their measures or the "theory" underlying their strategies. However, some analytic staff members indicated the need for their agencies to focus on these links in the future, particularly in programs that involve state and local partners.

In areas where there has been a long history of measurement, such as in the National Highway Traffic Safety Administration (NHTSA), there is a higher level of comfort with complex logic models. Counting highway traffic casualties has been part of work as usual at NHTSA since it was founded, and staff can use complex models with facility. In other instances, the need to re-engineer program processes to focus agency efforts on feasible intervention points has pushed staff to such an analytical approach, as illustrated by the program flow model for the Department of Education's student aid program.

Development of Evaluation Methods and Quality Control

A second contribution that evaluation tools can make to performance measurement is in the development of valid indicators and their associated data collection methods, as well as data quality control methods in ongoing data collection. Development of measures is certainly a traditional role for evaluators, a function recognized by most of those interviewed. Evaluators who specialize in specific content areas can often serve as the "bridge" to outside content area experts to help agency officials select the most up-to-date and valid measures to operationalize an intended performance construct. For example, a Healthy Eating Index used by the Department of Agriculture's Food and Nutrition Service (FNS) was developed over a three-year period, with primary data collection from a nationally representative survey of food intake, along with the involvement of diverse stakeholders such as academics and advocates.

Further, evaluators' technical expertise can often help in specifying the details of data collection methods needed for reliable data. Evaluators and other social researchers have developed professionally approved methods for a wide range of data, such as:

- Collecting data in sample surveys;
- Systematically recording field observations;
- Conducting key informant interviews;
- Entering and maintaining data via handheld computers or local agency management information systems; and
- Collecting qualitative data systematically, with methods such as focus groups, expert panel judgments, and case studies.

In addition, evaluators frequently are experienced in delivering the training needed by agency staff and administrators to ensure the integrity of data collection. These data development and collection methods can be usefully applied to performance measurement when evaluators and agency officials work closely together to integrate needed measures with technically appropriate methodologies.

Prior evaluation and research results can also help agencies to set realistic targets, for example, in GPRA Annual Performance Plans. Prior evidence might be available about the extent of change achieved by use of a specific agency strategy, the time spans needed to achieve those changes, and the extent of variability to expect among delivery sites. Such data can help an agency to be realistic in setting specific targets for its performance measures in each annual plan by linking its strategies and outputs to the prior evidence on the extent of change ("results") likely to be achieved. Use of evidence can also help in communicating to key stakeholders a realistic view of what is achievable within a short time period in moving toward the long-term desired results. For example, the U.S. Coast Guard has been a leader in analyzing data on marine safety to ensure the managers understand how to interpret trends as they set performance targets, and data-driven management has caught on across the agency.

A further use of program evaluation skills is to assess the quality and integrity of data used for performance measures. For performance data to be credible to users, and to withstand potential criticism, the data must be documentably unbiased and relevant for assessing the agency's performance. While many agencies have collected substantial archives of data over time, several administrators acknowledged that data quality characteristics were often questionable or unknown. Problems with data collected by diverse partners at multiple levels can take many forms, such as the following:

- Definitions of data elements may be unclear, so that local data collectors interpret them differently and thus enter data differently;
- Training and/or supervision of local data collection may be lax, resulting in unreliable initial data recording or entry;
- Different jurisdictions may have used different time frames when supplying data to a federal office, such as their varying "fiscal years," which

makes it difficult to aggregate the data into national performance indicators; and

- Data processing systems may have used different standards, or be differentially accurate, in the processing and transmission of data sets across jurisdictions or data systems.

Evaluators with appropriate technical expertise can assist in both identifying the nature and implications of such problems and in suggesting the "fixes" or training needed to avoid similar future data problems. For example, the Department of Education is using both evaluation and program staff input, as well as major stakeholder input from states, to redesign the data to be submitted by states concerning their elementary and secondary educational activities in an "Integrated Performance and Benchmarking System."

Use of Data Systems

Performance management can be supported in many ways by regularly collected data systems, including publicly available statistics, management information systems (MIS), and Geographic Information Systems (GIS). Even for the initial stages of strategic planning and developing program strategies, existing statistical data sources such as census data or vital statistics can be extremely useful. They can provide data for needs assessment, for estimating the scope of a target population, and for showing the underlying recent trends for potential key outcome indicators. Analytic skills are likely to be needed to identify appropriate existing data sources and to pull out the needed specific information from the broader data archives.

Management information systems are often used to provide periodic data about programmatic activities and outcomes. These systems house evaluative data that are rightly viewed as integral elements of program evaluation, as well as supplying the externally reported performance measures. Monitoring program delivery to describe what is provided to whom has tra-

A Multi-Purpose Management Information System (MIS) at the Department of Labor's Employment and Training Administration (ETA)

ETA is creating an information system for its new Workforce Incentives Act programs which will also integrate data on participants from its multiple employment assistance programs, including the US Employment Service, Job Corps services and others. This MIS will be used for GPRA and other reporting requirements, will be accessible to its state contributors, and will allow ETA to assess the relationships among program participation, participant characteristics, and outcomes.

ditionally been a key component of process evaluation (Scheirer, 1994). This approach has recently been extended to evaluation in numerous local service agencies via the United Way's influential *Measuring Program Outcomes* guide and associated technical assistance (United Way of America, 1996). Those advocating outcomes monitoring are extending performance measurement to capture results of program delivery rather than simply counting program actions or such things as persons served (Hatry, 1999).

In some cases, data originally developed for evaluative and monitoring purposes are used by agencies as performance indicators for key outcomes. For example, the Department of Housing and Urban Development (HUD) is using data from the American Housing Survey (AHS), conducted biannually for HUD by the Bureau of the Census, for several GPRA indicators. These include the number of households with "worst case" housing needs and a new index of the number of housing units in "substandard condition." Its analysts drew on several years of analytic work with the AHS to develop a composite measure of "substandard condition."

Other agencies are developing integrated management information systems for performance management that pull together data about program operations, outcomes, and results, often from diverse data sources. Analysts intend to use these MIS resources not only for descriptive data reporting for GPRA, but also for more in-depth data analyses usually considered "social research" or "program evaluation." These data can be used for multivariate modeling to examine the linkage between variations in program strategies and the outcomes achieved in diverse locations, with controls for other differences in the environment or client characteristics of those locations. When enough data points are available in such systems, data collected over time to show descriptive trends can also be used for more detailed program modeling, such as assessing the impact of a legislative or policy change using an interrupted time-series design.

Another innovative tool is the use of Geographic Information Systems to examine the co-occurrence of programmatic and other indicators (e.g., demographic characteristics, SES statuses, housing characteristics, etc.) by location, such as states, counties, or ZIP codes within a city. For example, the Department of Justice is using geographic information to relate the deployment of federal law enforcement resources among federal judicial districts to caseloads of its component agencies in the same districts, in order to help optimize resource allocation.

Process and Impact Evaluation Studies

Processes of strategic planning, indicator development, and setting targets all require grounding in the evidence produced by prior program evaluations and applied research in the relevant content areas. For agency strategic plans to be realistic, they need to be based on the cumulative evidence concerning "what works" for achieving the intended outcomes. For example, the Food and Nutrition Service (FNS) conducted an observational study of the nutrition actually supplied in the facilities funded in its Child and Adult Care program, to establish feasible performance measures for this program and to determine whether revised guidelines were needed. The study showed that many care givers provided good nutrition to their children or adult beneficiaries, and FNS made a policy decision that further regulations were not needed.

Evaluation tools for the synthesis of prior studies may be needed for this task, particularly meta-analysis and other methods for reviewing and assessing prior literature. If the literature review is combined with a program logic model, the evaluator can indicate the nature and strength of available evidence underlying causal arrows in the model. For example, the U.S. Agency for International Development (USAID) used basic research methods to establish the link between the presence of medically trained birth attendants and lower maternal mortality in developing countries. This evidence then justifies AID's use of the indicator "percentage of births attended by medically trained personnel" as a measure of improved maternal health systems, rather than using less reliable data about long-term maternal mortality from diverse countries' government information systems.

Another tool from program evaluation is the use of process evaluation methods to amplify the descriptive information in performance measures, which usually simply describe *what* is occurring within a program, but not *how* or *why*. Evaluation methods for assessing the processes involved in implementing the program in diverse delivery sites, as well as the extent and accuracy of delivery, can help to illuminate how the program operates and, therefore, why performance targets are or are not achieved. This more in-depth information can be used to help improve program results by suggesting needed changes in delivery strategies to increase fidelity to the intended program components. This type of evidence might already be available from prior evaluation studies that provide detailed descriptions of implementation variations. Or, as performance measurement data are obtained, they may raise questions concerning variations among delivery sites that could call for conducting a new process evaluation. For example, international data from USAID's ongoing demographic and health surveys began to show lower rates of childhood immunization in several countries. This reduced implementation prompted the agency to boost its programming in the affected countries to increase immunization rates, a key indicator for its GPRA reporting on children's health status.

Implementation evaluations can use a variety of data collection strategies, including:

- Conducting site visits and case studies of diverse sites;
- Analyzing more detailed data about variations in intervention delivery (perhaps from an ongoing MIS or GIS);

- Holding focus groups to obtain in-depth understanding about program operation, such as from the perspectives of program clients; and
- Interviewing key informants such as local delivery staff or knowledgeable local observers about factors facilitating or impeding local implementation.

The Department of Veterans Affairs (VA) has been a leader in applying these evaluation strategies to clarify understanding of how their educational benefits program is working. They are currently undertaking similar evaluation work in their cardiac care and survivors' benefits programs.

Many interviewees raised concerns about attributing their reported "results" to their often limited program interventions when multiple factors influence these broad societal goals. As Michael Hendricks has aptly noted, attribution is the "Achilles' heel" of performance measurement (Hendricks, 2000). That is, routinely collected data about results allegedly affected by governmental efforts, such as improved student achievement scores, reduced traffic fatalities, and reduced air-traffic "near collisions," are usually not sufficient to "prove" that the governmental actions caused improvements in the conditions monitored. Impact evaluations can be used to address this problem by providing evidence concerning the hypothesized links between agency outputs and program impacts, for example, by using an experimental or quasi-experimental design. Several agencies reported their intentions to expand their use of causal impact studies to support their reporting of results. But such studies are often time-consuming and expensive. Further, the complexity of the statistical methods required for these evaluations often makes it difficult for program managers to assess and use these tools.

Program evaluation professionals have also suggested less rigorous strategies to address the attribution dilemma (Reynolds, 1998). Larry Cooley's ideas about "plausible association" between program efforts and performance help by focusing attention on the choices that must be made about an appropriate standard of evidence in drawing inferences about attribution (Cooley, 1994). John Mayne has suggested some helpful ways to appropriately interpret performance data; for example, he places responsibility on the managers closest to the data to reduce the uncertainty, provide considerable evidence, offer a credible picture of attribution, and acknowledge external (rival) factors in providing a credible performance story (Mayne, 1999). The Department of Transportation (DOT) drew accolades from the Congress and the General Accounting Office for its FY 2000 Performance Report, in part because external factors also affecting monitored behaviors were acknowledged in credible performance stories that the report conveyed in many areas of transportation safety.

Addressing the challenge of causal inference in reporting outcomes of public programs is definitely an area where program evaluation offers many conceptual strategies and tools. To ensure that performance measurement is implemented and reported to support a plausible association between programs and the outcomes measured, targeted evaluation work can be invaluable. For example, evaluations of variability in implementation across sites and longitudinal trends in program participants' behaviors can be used to help make the case for attribution of observed improvements to program actions by tracing the patterns of outcomes in relation to a hypothesized causal sequence (Marquart, 1990). If several waves of performance measures are available, and systematic interventions are undertaken between waves of data, then examining differences among sites before and after the intervention may contribute evidence of the program's contribution to the results achieved (Scheirer, in press, 2000). Evaluations targeted at the linkages identified in program logic modeling efforts can increase confidence that the programs are working.

On the other hand, impact evaluations that systematically trace the implementation and/or the effects of program activities are extremely helpful when performance data indicate that programs are not working. In fact, the Government Performance and Results Act requires agencies to employ program evaluation studies to explain instances where performance fails to achieve targets. While the legislative mandate focuses attention on learning why programs fail, targeted evaluation work can also advance knowledge of when and why programs work.

Evaluation Uses in the 23 Federal Departments and Component Agencies

As indicated above, we found many examples of a diversity of types of evaluation used to support performance management among the agencies in this study. To provide an indication of the scope of evaluation use, we tabulated the agencies by their types of use. The department or agency was included as "used" or "planned to use" for each type of evaluation if any of those interviewed at that agency mentioned an example of that type of use. The example of use could either be one or more studies cited in one of their GPRA documents or an example that supported their GPRA work but was not explicitly cited in their reports.

Nearly half of the agencies (9 to 11 of the 23) had used evaluation to support the central processes for performance measurement, and 4 to 7 additional agencies planned to use evaluation for these purposes:

- Defining expected performance and targets;
- Developing indicators and data collection methods;
- Measuring outcomes; and
- Assessing program implementation and delivery.

Fewer agencies reported using or planning to use logic models (7 agencies), using or planning to use evaluation to assess the quality of their performance data (10 agencies), or conducting/planning impact evaluations to attribute their results to program interventions (12 agencies). Thus, many agencies were familiar with a variety of types of evaluation use, but these were often just one or two examples in an agency with multiple programs and indicators (sometimes hundreds of them).

The infrequent use of logic models was somewhat surprising to us, as this tool has been widely discussed in connection with GPRA processes. Several respondents who were familiar with logic models but had not used them in their GPRA documents mentioned that logic modeling seems more appropriate for a specific program with a defined set of activities. In contrast, their GPRA plans and indicators are often for broad outcomes that cross-cut more than one of their funded programs. Further, sometimes their managers were reluctant to show outcomes in a logic model that their programs could not directly control, the "attribution for results" problem discussed earlier. (For a further discussion of logic models, see pages 65 and 98.)

These study findings indicate that many agencies can and do use evaluation when it is available. Nearly all interviewees believed in the value of systematic evidence to support their agency's work and wanted to apply more evaluation expertise than their agency is currently supporting. Many cited concrete examples of work on specific evaluations or management information systems that would provide expanded information in the future. While nearly all are constrained by their agencies' limited capacities for evaluation activities, many described a number of management strategies being used to foster the use of program evaluation.

Leveraging Evaluation Capacity to Contribute to Performance Management

Evaluation capacity was viewed fairly broadly in this study. The components of "capacity" can include the numbers and skills of available evaluation staff, the extent of funding for contracting evaluation studies, and the organizational support for workforce training and professional development to enhance evaluation knowhow. Table 4.4 provides a broadbrush picture of how respondents in this study assess the current status of evaluation capacity in their agencies. As noted in the table, respondents from central departmental staff offices were asked about staffing at their level, while staff in operating units were asked about analytical staff only in their own units. Respondents were asked about analytical staff available to assist with pro-

Table 4.4: Current Status of Program Evaluation Capacity in the Agencies Profiled

	In Need of Improvement	Mixed	Comfortable
Resources			
Adequacy of # of FTEs in Centralized Policy/ Evaluation Offices[a]	6	5	2
Adequacy of # of FTEs in Decentralized Policy/ Evaluation Offices Contacted[b]	3	3	5
Budget for Contracting-Out Evaluation Work[a]	5	5	3
Workforce and Professional Development			
Resources to Support Staff Training in Evaluation[a]	9	2	2

a The N = 13, including: Agriculture, Education, EPA, HHS, HUD, Interior, Justice, Labor, NASA, SSA, Transportation, USAID and VA.

b The N = 11, including: Labor: Employment and Training Administration; Justice: Bureau of Prison; and National Institute of Justice; Agriculture: Food and Nutrition Service; USAID; Education: Office of Student Financial Assistance; HHS: Health Resources and Service Administration and Center for Disease Control and Prevention; and Transportation: NHTSA, Maritime Administration and RSPA.

gram evaluation and not to confine their assessment to "evaluation" offices. Only three of the 13 federal departments contacted had centrally located evaluation offices, with three others in the process of developing this capacity. As indicated in Table 4.4, few agencies were viewed as "comfortable" in any of the dimensions of capacity, and resources to support training were particularly lacking.

The relatively higher level of satisfaction with current evaluation staffing levels expressed by staff in operating units than by their counterparts in central departmental offices reflects, in large part, the purposive agency selection technique used. That is, the operating units were typically selected due to their more extensive experience with evaluation. For example, the National Highway Traffic Safety Administration was established in 1966 to measure and report data on highway safety, and its staff is comprised largely of statisticians and other professionals quite comfortable with evaluation methodology.

On the other hand, respondents in centralized departmental offices typically reported that the level of both resources and evaluation skills and/or appreciation varied substantially across their departments. In most large federal departments, some operating units may possess both evaluation staff and commitment for evaluation, but typically that is not the case across the entire department. As GPRA reporting documents are usually prepared by a central office, the evaluation work performed by operating units may or may not be reflected in the department-level documents.

Agency staff who are familiar with GPRA requirements for agencies to document their use of program evaluation have typically become aware of their organization's evaluation capacity. Three themes in leveraging evaluation capacity emerged in interviews. Our respondents were very forthright in noting that:

- Evaluation capacity is difficult to identify;
- Building evaluation skills and knowledge is necessary; and
- Line managers' knowledge needs to be enhanced about the right kinds of evaluative questions to raise about programmatic performance.

These themes are amplified below.

Finding Evaluation Capacity

Respondents in this study presumably are as familiar as any staff with the level of evaluation capacity in their agencies, yet most were hesitant to offer global judgments. When asked to count the number of evaluators in central policy and planning offices or in counterpart offices in operating units, many were careful to couch their responses. Some operating units contacted are extremely research-oriented, such as HHS' Centers for Disease Control and DOT's Research and Special Program Administration, and respondents found it difficult to differentiate evaluators from other analytical staff. In some operating units, respondents were unsure whom to count as evaluators because "it may not be in their job description." In several central budget and planning offices, the respondents identified specific staff as evaluators, but then noted that "they do not really evaluate programs." In general, agencies did not have a defined set of criteria or a qualifications statement for what skills are needed to be an "evaluator."

Clarity on what constitutes evaluation capacity varied greatly across respondents. In some cases, respondents readily volunteered that program evaluation has recently been revitalized in their agency, acknowledging that this has been due in large part to GPRA. For example, the Central Planning Office in the Department of Veterans Affairs reopened an evaluation unit two years ago, after closing it eight years before. The Office of Inspector General at the Environmental Protection Agency (EPA) obtained approval to open a

Program Evaluation unit in February of 2000 with 15 new full-time equivalent (FTE) evaluators. New hires in evaluation shops were not apparent across all the agencies surveyed, but there was certainly evidence that there have been some new hires dedicated to evaluation work—even if what these staff will actually do on the job may not be clear. Several respondents mentioned obstacles in federal hiring procedures that make it difficult to hire staff with needed skills.

Building Evaluation Skills and Knowledge

Funding to provide training on evaluation for staff in policy and evaluation offices and for line managers is critical, yet it was viewed as inadequate across virtually all of the agencies contacted. Most respondents volunteered that personnel in both staff and line offices need more evaluation knowledge and skills, but that training in this area is typically not viewed as a high priority. There has been a flurry of workshops on GPRA implementation and basic performance measurement concepts offered to agency staff directly involved in implementing GPRA, but this training has been tightly focused on immediate responsiveness to GPRA and has typically not been offered to line managers across the agencies.

Some respondents volunteered that a carrot and stick approach to enhancing evaluation knowledge among staff will be necessary. They suggest that more funding for training is necessary. However, they believe that until staff sees evidence that using evaluation to support performance measurement and management brings positive consequences, initiatives to strengthen evaluation skills and knowledge will not be a priority. The incentives must come from top leadership in the agencies, along with the resources.

Asking the Right Evaluative Questions about Performance

Building evaluation capacity to effectively support performance management in agencies extends to expanding the knowledge and skills held by line managers as well as the priority given to evaluation in the organizational culture. Virtually all respondents recognized the challenges placed upon line managers to ask good, targeted questions about the performance data they are now collecting and/or reviewing. While many respondents were hesitant to identify specific aspects of program evaluation knowledge needed by line managers, they acknowledged a need to prepare managers to apply standards to these new tasks.

Program managers often serve as developers and monitors of their agency's contracts for evaluation studies, but lack the technical background

Department of Health and Human Services (HHS) Capacity Initiatives

The Office of the Assistant Secretary for Planning and Evaluation (ASPE) at HHS is devoting resources to two new initiatives intended to improve evaluation capacity across the operating units:

1. A pool of individual and small business consultants with evaluation expertise has been established via a task-order contracting mechanism to be on call to assist program staff across HHS with developing performance measures, designing evaluation studies that may be contracted out, or any other in-house evaluative work.
2. ASPE contracted for a training needs assessment to be undertaken across the department to identify the specific evaluation skills needed by contract managers in the operating agencies.

needed for this role. As one respondent aptly volunteered: "The key is to make the program managers more skilled at asking good, hard questions, plus being really good, critical consumers of evaluation work. Managers need to think more like evaluators and view program evaluation as a useful tool."

GPRA has required agencies to measure performance, but the law cannot make managers use the performance data to improve their programs.

The requirements to measure and report on program achievements have pushed managers across most agencies to think about the link between what they do and their performance measures, as well as the quality of the data they receive. While "thinking like an evaluator" about the validity and reliability of data is not new to managers in research-oriented agencies, it is a new task for many managers in other locations.

Pressures from GPRA requirements and agency executives to measure program results or outcomes as well as workloads have also increased pressures for program managers to think critically about the logic underlying their programs. Systematically modeling programs to identify what to measure requires evaluation knowhow, particularly the use of tools for conceptual development.

Sensitizing program managers to the usefulness of evaluation thinking and tools may require additional training. It definitely requires an organizational culture that supports managers who take the time and effort to systematically and empirically assess their programs.

Successful evaluation projects that inform managers' efforts to measure performance build a more supportive culture for evaluation. Respondents across the Department of Transportation mentioned the value of a recently completed evaluation study on the transportation of hazardous materials (Hazmat) that brought together staff from all its agencies concerned with various transportation modes. The Hazmat evaluation was well received by managers across DOT for a variety of reasons: it demonstrated cooperation across otherwise quite separate operating units; it was designed and overseen by a team of representatives from all the modal agencies working alongside a very supportive Inspector General; it provided useful information to assist managers in improving performance measures and targets; and it provided timely, clear, useful recommendations. Respondents at DOT highlight the impact that the Hazmat evaluation had upon improving the general posture toward evaluation thinking among managers across DOT.

The benefits of such positive evaluation experiences for improving the organizational culture regarding evaluation are invaluable. Positive experiences where the insight offered to managers clearly outweighs the costs imposed upon them are especially effective in building support for evaluation and for enhancing evaluation capacity.

Organizational Opportunities for Integrating Program Evaluation and Performance Management

Agencies now face both challenges and opportunities that should be addressed by federal executives. Our respondents emphasized seven major organizational strategies that can be used to support the integration of program evaluation into performance management:

- Secure support from top administrators;
- Institutionalize continuous performance improvement strategies;
- Use a variety of coordinating processes to bring skilled staff together;
- Clarify the roles of key players;
- Work proactively with Congress;
- Build upon information technology to support performance management; and
- Take advantage of initial groundwork institutionalizing performance measurement.

This section briefly describes each of these strategies, with illustrations from the agencies. With the complexity and diversity of operations among the agencies included in this study, we did not find any single key to more effective use of program evaluation. Just as there are many ways in which the diversity of program evaluation methods can be used to support improved program management, so are there many organizational approaches that support these steps toward performance-based management.

Secure Support from Top Administrators

Agency respondents were nearly universal in their emphasis on the key roles of top executives. Often a department's deputy secretary has played a major role in obtaining the buy-in of agency administrators by becoming a "champion" for the use of data.

As one federal manager explained: "Starting with the FY 2000 Plan, the deputy secretary took charge. He provides leadership to resolve issues and meet deadlines. He adjudicates major disputes. When managers explain that 'We can't possibly control that situation!' [affecting an indicator], he urges them to use the outcomes more: 'You should try to meet that indicator.' In this agency, the Office of the Deputy Secretary is centralized over all the bureaus and provides a centralizing logic for program development."

Federal departments differ in their extent of centralized versus decentralized evaluation offices and staff. Some respondents described their agency as having program "stovepipes," with each of its component parts nearly independent, and the departmental Secretary's office as a "holding company" rather than an active manager of its agency operations. For example, agencies such as the Federal Bureau of Investigation and the Immigration and Naturalization Service have high autonomy within the Department

Capturing the Interest of Top Administrators

Respondents mentioned several strategies to increase the interest of top administrators in the use of evaluative data and thus increase their support for it:

- Present data in a way that gets their interest; good graphics are especially useful.
- Summarize information on their pressing policy questions into "quick and easy answers."
- Provide visibility by asking them to address workshops or other training sessions.
- Build performance reporting into policy initiatives they support.
- Use program "failures" or crises as opportunities for program evaluation to diagnose the source of the problems and show its usefulness.

of Justice, as do the operating agencies within the Department of Health and Human Services, such as the Centers for Disease Control and the National Institutes of Health. These "stovepipe" organizations tend not to have a large central evaluation office, and their extent of evaluation use is very mixed, depending on their component agencies' administrative support for it. The absence of a directive for centralized management means that executive support for evaluation must be present in each component agency in order to strengthen the links to departmental performance management.

In other departments, a centralized evaluation office provides information and guidance on evaluative functions across the agency, such as the Planning and Evaluation Service for the Department of Education. Such central offices were present in only three of the 13 departments contacted, with three others developing this type of office or having some central capacity. These central offices often provide skilled analytic staff for the production of GPRA plans and reports. Respondents in these departments could cite more examples of how they are using program evaluation and other systematic data for GPRA documents and the improvement of program management than did respondents in decentralized departments. *If their central administrators took actions to support data-based management,* then the central evaluation offices seemed to be more involved in using evaluation to support the products and processes for GPRA. In several cases, a new administrator provided the impetus for increased attention to the data available about program performance, which then cascaded through the agency.

Institutionalize Continuous Performance Improvement Strategies

Many agencies are evolving toward processes that promote continuous improvement in both the use of various types of data to improve program outcomes and in the content of their performance measures. Several respondents characterized these changes as moving toward a "learning organization." In the first several years of the GPRA requirements, many agencies produced their documents primarily because they were required. Gradually, their managers have begun to see the usefulness of the data. As one observed, "We are now going toward a problem solving mode in trying to solve the problems identified by the performance measures."

These agencies usually have regular management reviews of their performance data at least once per quarter, not just annually for the GPRA report. They often have many more indicators and data sources for each program than they can report in the Annual Performance Plan or Report, in order to track important program delivery processes and their outcomes. Several mentioned the need to obtain data from program evaluations more quickly than is traditionally possible with contracting mechanisms, such as telephone surveys of consumers or a rapid field appraisal. They emphasize that the involvement and support of top administrators is essential for continuous improvement strategies to be implemented.

Continuous Improvement at the Department of Justice's Bureau of Prisons

The Bureau of Prisons uses 20 indicators in its Key Executive Indicators System, which its executive staff examine quarterly. These include intakes and outgoes, population diversity, assault rates, disciplinary actions, educational program enrollment, etc. They look at comparisons among prisons and over time, and if changes occur in one prison but not others, they ask why. The data may be used to trigger a more intensive evaluation, using inside staff experienced with the prison system.

The time frames for developing and using valid indicators can be extensive. Many agencies reported they are now changing the indicators that they proposed in their early GPRA Plans, as they put more emphasis on outcomes as well as outputs, obtain feedback on the deficiencies in initial indicators, and develop or obtain access to improved data sources. These continuous improvement processes also depend on team building among the staff involved to make sure that all understand the purposes behind the requirements and to develop the "buy-in" needed among all team members.

In some agencies, the collection and use of information to support program management has long precedents, which has facilitated the availability of measurement data for GPRA and for continuous improvement. For example, an analyst at the U.S. Agency for International Development noted that country-level mission staff for demography and health are quite adept in using indicators that have been available for some time: "The level of sophistication in using indicators depends on how long we have had program initiatives in that content area. We started earliest with indicators for population and reproductive health, in the 1960s and '70s, then child health in the '80s, and HIV/AIDS and maternal health in the '90s. We started working on infectious disease in 1997, and still don't have good indicators for this area."

Use a Variety of Coordinating Processes

Formal and informal task forces or committees can be used to bring evaluators together with other types of staff to help integrate evaluation and performance management. Most agencies use some type of formal task force or work group charged with putting together performance documents, usually with representatives from each of their operational divisions. Sometimes these representatives are evaluators, but this is not a common requirement. In addition to program staff and evaluators, the work groups often include staff from the budget office, the office of the chief financial officer, the inspector general's office, and scientific support offices, as well as policy development offices. Several agencies have a cascading series of groups, such as a Strategic and Performance Planning Work Group reporting to the top-level Management Review Council in the Department of Labor. These dual arrangements help emphasize high-level interest in the process, while using a task group of mid-level staff to coordinate the more detailed production work among component agencies.

These groups were often begun as temporary structures to meet GPRA requirements, but in several agencies they are now evolving into more permanent coordinating bodies to address issues of strategic planning and evaluation that cut across the department's agencies. For example, both EPA and the Department of Transportation have started a Program Evaluation Council or Network to coordinate evaluation and its relationships to performance measures. In some cases, training or technical assistance is provided to members of the work groups, with the intention to achieve more stability and experience in these processes. Some of these working groups are focused on a specific topic or issue that needs cross-agency coordination, such as "litigation" within the Department of Justice or transportation of hazardous materials for the Department of Transportation.

Informal relationships are viewed as just as important as the formal processes in many agencies. Respondents stressed the importance of frequent telephone calls, visiting each others' offices, "hand-holding with the program managers," and informal conversations in identifying relevant measurement tools and prior evaluations that could enhance a performance report. One of the unanticipated consequences of GPRA may be the stimulus it provides for staff from different parts of an agency, and in different functions, to learn about each others' roles and about the program strategies of related agencies. For example, in planning for a new cardiac care evaluation, the VA brought together a work group from relevant offices across the agency, including evaluators and program staff, to develop eight focused research questions for the study.

Clarify the Roles of Key Players

As in all efforts to change organizational processes and cultures, the roles and skills of individuals are central to success. Bringing together the diversity of potential evaluative data with the new requirements for GPRA has mandated that people from diverse offices work together more closely and in new ways. Performance management involves a wide variety of people who may not have worked together before, including budget officers, policy developers, program managers, and agency executives, as well as program evaluators and analysts, who often supply the performance data. The intended roles of each type of staff need to be clearly articulated to utilize the skills of all and avoid conflict or duplication of effort.

Performance management may demand more change from program managers than from other types of staff. Often for the first time, they are being asked to think in terms of outcomes for their programs, and to explain program performance measures to agency executives or Congress. Many respondents noted that managers are the ones on the front line if results do not meet targets. A sampling of their comments: "It is sometimes scary for them." "Managers may avoid the risk of negative information from evaluation." "How can they put into place an action plan to improve results for an indicator not under federal control?" "Fear of the unknown is high among program managers when they don't know how the data will be used." Positive incentives are needed for managers who obtain and review data about their programs, rather than punishment for not meeting "targets." Agency executives may need to work with line managers to help them align feasible program strategies with realistic performance measures.

One impetus for managerial change is having the opportunity to examine real data about their programs, a stimulus noted by several interviewees. As one of them put it:

> Having the data is a driving factor. Now program managers are finally getting it when they see their data. They are asking good questions about "success" and meeting the targets. What are the comparisons between their "predicted" targets and what the data results showed? They are also thinking more about the measures and their meaning. Some programs within the agency have been embarrassed when other programs have data for performance measures and they don't. They are asked, if (other programs) can do it, why can't your program do performance measures?

Similarly, when agencies produce evaluations that a manager finds useful and helpful, the administrators of other programs may ask, "Why aren't you evaluating my program?"

Attribution for "results" is a key issue for many managers, who recognize that their programs are small pieces in much larger puzzles of federal, state, and local processes. The term "results" implies that the outcome measures are within the control of the federal agency proposing that indicator, but many federal program managers believe they do not control these results for their own programs. As one administrator explained: "It takes research to find out what strategies are needed and to link program performance and outcomes. Now program managers must make strategy decisions on how to manage their programs and often don't have data to guide them. Congress and external audiences act as if these relationships are well understood, but they are not."

Attributing results to program interventions and assessing the linkages between program outputs and outcomes are challenges that can be addressed by program evaluation methods. But the application of these methods requires time, evaluation expertise, and resources to do studies. As indicated by our prior discussion of capacity issues, many agencies do not have or have not budgeted for the resources to do these evaluation studies.

Further, many agencies work in partnership with states, local governments, or other entities, and obtaining performance data from them involves detailed negotiations to obtain good quality, comparable data. Under block grants, there has been limited accountability, and were that to change, local officials may protest, "Just give us the money, and leave us alone!" The new era of accountability also requires a change in the culture of state and local relationships with federal officials. In order to manage the programs to achieve intended results and for GPRA reporting, federal staff need good quality data from their partners and grantees. Yet it takes substantial time, often several years, to work through the problems of indicator definitions and data collection strategies when multiple partners are involved.

Work Proactively with Congress

Timing is especially relevant for federal executives currently attempting to integrate program evaluation and performance measurement given changes in Congress and the presidential administration. Anticipated changes in the composition of congressional appropriations and authorization committees and in agency leadership may induce anxiety for some. But, somewhat surprisingly, the majority of respondents did not fear that momentum in their analytical accomplishments would be lost due to changes in political leadership, because good performance data will be needed by any new administration.

Officials interviewed were asked whether they have found the relative emphasis in implementing GPRA to be on accountability, specifically reporting to Congress, or on program improvement. The majority responded that so far the emphasis within the agencies has been on accountability, but with a growing focus on using data for program improvement.

The first full cycle of GPRA planning and reporting has been a learning process for all parties. Most agencies started with far too many performance measures, then observed that their appropriations committees were not highly interested anyway. Many agencies are now using a dual strategy of reporting a few broad measures in GPRA accountability documents, but collecting many more indicators for program-specific management and improvement.

Working with Congress to move agencies forward in performance management continues to present a challenge. The role of Congress in encouraging the implementation of GPRA has been sporadic and somewhat confusing for agency staff. Many agency respondents were concerned that if Congress uses GPRA reporting documents in a "heavy-handed way," it will undermine their efforts to improve data and to use it for performance management. "Fear of the unknown is high among managers when they don't know how the data will be used," said one.

Some congressional members have shown an interest in seeing performance information, but most appropriations committees reportedly have worked through the budget as if there were no GPRA. A few appropriations committees have been micro-managing agencies in reviewing their performance plans, but they are the exception, rather than the rule. There have not been consistent signals coming from the appropriations committees on how performance reports will be used in the budget process. And as one respondent noted, generally speaking "it is only the good government types on the Hill who care about GPRA, not appropriations committees."

Perhaps the best way to summarize the views about Congress' role in using program evaluation to support GPRA implementation is uncertainty about the extent of congressional support and extreme variability across the committees. HHS has a legislated one percent set-aside for evaluations of public health service programs. The respondents believed that such legislative budget support is absolutely essential. They pointed out that if Congress asks for systematic evaluation of a program, it gets done, but without such direct requests, it is difficult to include such expenditures in their budgets. If GPRA serves to accustom appropriations committees to receiving useful performance data, it is likely that the learning process will help raise evaluation-type questions. Then, congressional requests will likely increase rather than decrease. In any case, proactive action on the part of executives to focus committees on agency performance is preferable than waiting for Congress to lead.

Build Upon Information Technology to Support Performance Management

Many respondents volunteered that the use of information technology in management information systems supports both performance measurement and further evaluation. It opens opportunities for ongoing evaluation for program improvement when the technology facilitates more frequent submission of data. MIS systems for multi-state programs open opportunities for data mining, such as disaggregation to address significant questions about targeting services and the variability in outcomes among sites. With the accumulation of data over time from multiple participants and partners, rigorous analysis of the impacts of program changes or variations is often possible, using causal modeling.

Further, use of graphics capabilities in modern analytic software helps to communicate evaluation and performance results in "user-friendly" formats. Sophisticated use of Geographic Information Systems at the Department of Justice, and multi-purpose management information systems at the Department of Labor's Employment and Training Administration, illustrate ways that information technology opens opportunities for managers to present their data clearly and to ask more sophisticated analytical questions about programs and their performance. After their successful maneuvers to combat the "Y2K bug," information technology staff may also be available to redirect their MIS systems toward greater support of performance measurement and evaluation.

Take Advantage of Initial Groundwork for Institutionalizing Performance Measurement

Federal executives should build on the momentum already achieved in institutionalizing performance management. While the responses to GPRA among agencies are somewhat uneven, it is still early and much learning has already taken place. The general tone of respondents was very optimistic about the potential for evidence-based performance management in their agencies. Changes are occurring in the ways that managers operate when they have performance data available. For example, managers across agencies are talking about "verification and validation" of data because they know that quality performance measurement and reporting is now business as usual. The respondents noted that now, finally, managers throughout their agencies recognize that GPRA is not simply a paperwork exercise that will go away soon, as have many other government reforms attempted in the past.

Thus far, implementation of GPRA has initiated the mechanisms to support performance management. Performance is being measured and reported, and program strategies are being re-assessed as performance results are reviewed. Initial efforts at measurement have pushed managers to ask good questions about how relevant the measures are to what they do and how good the data actually are. This is progress. In fact, the tools are now in place to permit the Bush administration to move ahead with performance-based management—if they so choose.

The arrival of a new administration presents an important opportunity for evaluation capacity to be expanded and utilized more effectively to support performance management. In many agencies, much painful deliberation and "heavy lifting" have already taken place regarding GPRA. In some, resources are being allocated to build performance information systems and to support some of the needed analytical work. Drafters of future Annual Performance Reports have a distinct advantage as they learn from the early performance reporting experiences. False starts and misplaced optimism about what is achievable have occurred, but agency staff have made great progress along the learning curve. The new administration will find an "older and wiser" GPRA staff awaiting them with better and more informed expertise about how best to use performance measurement systems to move their agencies forward. The most fortunate new executives are those coming to take the helm from top management teams that fared especially well in the first round of GPRA. Much trial and error learning has taken place across the federal government. This experience lays a strong foundation for the new agency executives who take over while the momentum is moving forward, as they build upon the performance systems initiated in the early GPRA work.

Conclusions and Recommendations

Federal agencies are rising to the analytical challenges thrust upon them by GPRA through effective use of talented staff who have tried to cope with inadequate evaluation capacity through resourceful maneuvers. This chapter identifies numerous ways in which federal agencies are using program evaluation strategies and tools to support the implementation of GPRA.

A key study finding is that GPRA has raised expectations and demands for the application of evaluation expertise to support systematic analysis of program performance in the federal government. The officials interviewed believed that opportunities for using program evaluation strategies and tools can help performance measurement efforts to improve management and the results of programs. However, in general, evaluation capacity within these agencies is not adequate to contribute effectively to performance measurement and management. Most agencies do not allocate funding to support an adequate number of evaluation staff, nor provide the training needed for either the analytical staff already there or the line managers who are being asked to cope with new analytical challenges.

Most respondents recognized the need for program evaluation strategies and tools to support ongoing performance management. Many examples were described that demonstrate the diversity of ways that evaluation tools are being used or could be used to support this work. Yet most agencies were using evaluation only tangentially, and their staff acknowledged that evaluation and performance measurement are not yet integrated for many of their programs.

This study developed a conceptual framework to help categorize potential uses of evaluation and to encourage fuller use of this potential as agencies plan for future evaluation. The framework suggests that evaluation can be marshaled to support four stages in agencies' growth toward performance management: strategic and program planning; improving program delivery; accountability to external bodies, such as Congress; and attributing results to the agency's programs. These stages are of course cyclical, and evaluation for each stage can contribute feedback to earlier processes. Four major types of evaluation methods form the rows of the framework: conceptual development tools, such as logic modeling; data collection and quality control; the use of statistical and management information systems; and the use of process and impact evaluation studies. The cells of the framework in Table 4.3 illustrate the great variety of ways that evaluative data could enhance performance management. With broader thinking and planning for the full potential range of evaluation uses, executives can stimulate their agencies to achieve much greater benefit from their existing evaluation resources for improved performance management.

Federal officials involved in GPRA implementation who were surveyed for this study identified a variety of very useful processes they employ to integrate program evaluation and performance measurement. They highlighted the need to receive demonstrated support for this effort from top administrators to create central evaluation capacity and to "champion" their efforts. Several are using "continuous improvement strategies" with at least quarterly reviews of performance data by several levels of management. These include both programmatic and executive level review of detailed performance data and the iterative development of improved measures over time. Good coordinating structures were seen as vital to this work, with task forces evolving into permanent intra-agency committees to achieve stability and continuity, but with continued emphasis on informal relationships among key staff in diverse locations.

The roles of many types of staff contribute to these evolving processes, and clarity of their "division of labor" among offices is needed. Operating-level program managers are likely to be most affected by GPRA reporting requirements, and most anxious about how GPRA will affect them. Evaluators and other analytic staff can relieve these fears by helping them to interpret and use performance data for improving their results, and by applying evaluation techniques to the key concerns about attributing "results" to their programs.

The respondents also identified a number of remaining challenges and opportunities they face as they move into further cycles of performance planning and reporting under GPRA. They are concerned about the uncertain support and mixed signals they receive about performance measurement from Congress, and insufficient resources for strengthening evaluation capacity within their agencies. They recognize that line managers need some retooling in this era of performance-oriented management to help them think more like evaluators as they collect, review, and use performance data, but that this will require resources and positive incentives. On the other hand, they voiced optimism about the opportunities presented by fuller use of information technology and the forward momentum for institutionalizing performance measurement and management in their agencies. They believe the groundwork has been laid and that managers are moving forward on the learning curve to present inviting opportunities for the new leadership arriving in January of 2001.

A variety of recommendations are offered here to improve the synergistic relationship between program evaluation and performance measurement to foster evidence-based management efforts in the federal government. Improving evaluation and analytical capacity is a key concern of the respondents here. They described many examples showing how ingenious staff leverage the resources available to use evaluative strategies and tools in creative ways. In response, these examples can inform and persuade managers of the potential for more effective use of evaluative information to support performance management. The bottom line is that strengthening evaluation capacity and use will enhance the likelihood that the performance measurement and management framework being institutionalized across the federal government will result in both improved program management and desired results.

Recommendations

Clearly, many opportunities are available for enlightened agency executives to utilize existing and evolving evaluation strategies and tools to support their agency's performance measurement efforts. The recommendations that follow identify several actions for executives, evaluators, and agency managers to bridge the gaps between many agencies' current practices in collecting and using performance data, and potential contributions from the broad field of evaluation.

Make Fuller Use of Program Evaluation Tools and Skills

1. Recognize the diversity of ways that evaluation tools can support performance management, and plan for a broad array of evaluative functions.

By recognizing evaluation as an ongoing function encompassing many opportunities, agencies can support each stage of their work toward full performance management. This study identifies a wide array of ways in which performance improvement and accountability can be enhanced both by fuller use of regularly collected performance data and by complementary discrete evaluative studies.

2. Conduct an inventory of the evaluation skills of the agency staff directly involved in planning performance measures and reporting them.

A good match between the evaluation skills needed and the available skills of those contributing to performance reports is likely to improve report quality. We observed that several agencies which integrated staff with evaluation skills into their GPRA production teams tended to receive high ratings for their GPRA efforts, such as the Departments of Education and Transportation. Improving this match may involve several options: 1) transferring staff skilled in evaluation into the offices most closely involved in performance measurement efforts; 2) more training on evaluation for existing staff who contribute to performance planning and reporting; and 3) more structured coordination of work conducted jointly by evaluators and the performance office staff. In agencies where the numbers of evaluators have been substantially reduced by personnel cuts, hiring more staff with evaluation skills may be needed.

3. Seek out staff with evaluation skills when implementing many of the steps in performance management.

Including evaluators and others with analytic skills as key members of GPRA work groups is likely to integrate these perspectives with those from other backgrounds. The field of evaluation is now much broader than its earlier focus on methods for rigorous impact evaluation, but many agency administrators do not have a full view of the potential roles for evaluators. Evaluators may need to "sell" the usefulness of their areas of expertise to managers who are skeptical of its applicability to performance measures. At the same time, evaluators need to be supportive of agencies' initial efforts in performance measurement, which may not meet ideal standards for data quality.

4. Provide more explicit guidance for program officers who oversee contractors conducting program evaluations.

Many of those interviewed suggested that more, not less, program evaluation work will be conducted in this period of performance-based government, and that large evaluation studies will continue to be contracted out. To ensure that contracted evaluations meet expectations for relevance and quality, those in charge of overseeing these contracts need sufficient knowledge to construct appropriate statements of work, to ask the right technical questions of the contractors before and while the contracted work is undertaken, and to review the quality of contractors' draft products (Behn and Kant, 1999).

Leverage Capacity for Implementing Performance-Based Management

5. Persuade new political appointees to allocate resources for building greater evaluation capacity.

The unambiguous message from respondents is that training and new hires are required to bring evaluation capacity in line with the analytical demands placed upon the agencies now and in the immediate future. Agencies that have developed central evaluation units and/or that have legislated set-aside budgets for evaluation have better track records for meeting GPRA requirements.

6. Assess and enhance, if necessary, the evaluation skills of the Office of Inspector General (OIG) staff involved in performance data development and auditing.

Those auditing data quality need to be cognizant of the relevant quality standards and methods for the content area of the performance data. Again, a good match between the measurement-related tasks and the appropriate skills for OIG staff might be improved through one of the methods noted above. The roles of OIG staff in auditing data quality may need ongoing coordination with the work of evaluators in data design for performance measures, via the use of a performance measures work group or another joint planning strategy.

7. Search out agency resources that might be re-allocated to support using data for performance management.

Relevant analytic skills may be located in units other than those labeled as "evaluation," such as in statistical sections, research units, or information technology groups. Again, a broader view of evaluative functions and skills can bring to bear agency data and other resources that might make greater contributions to performance measurement.

Integrate Program Evaluation and Performance Management

8. Institute and support ongoing teams that bring together evaluators from technical offices, program management, OIG staff, and performance planning and reporting staff.

These groups should be used to transfer knowledge throughout the agency about feasible uses of evaluation methods, as well as performance "success stories." For example, a Program Evaluation Council has been instituted at the Department of Transportation that provides many opportunities for improved communication among the multiple agencies that make up DOT.

9. Foster basic performance measurement and evaluation skills as important managerial competencies for all line managers.

At a minimum, program managers should be versed in the basics of program logic modeling, measurement development, descriptive data presentations, and data validity and reliability. The Department of Education is requiring program managers to attest to the quality of the performance data they submit about their programs, using quality criteria developed via a participative process, or to submit plans for data improvement if currently available data are known to be deficient. The department is also providing training and consultation for the managers to help them meet the quality standards.

10. Plan for continuous improvement in evaluation and performance measurement, building on the groundwork laid in the initial rounds of GPRA work.

Processes for building good data systems and evaluation findings often require a considerable period of time, even five to 10 years. But substantial progress has been made in many agencies in their initial steps toward meeting GPRA requirements. Agencies should assume that this work toward performance-based management will need to be continuous in order to achieve meaningful improvement in program results, rather than a temporary addition to "business as usual."

11. Publicly reward managers who obtain and use performance data in decision making, for existing as well as new programs.

The intended outcomes from many programs require longer time periods than the annual time frames in GPRA reporting, so focusing on annual targets may be tangential to their management. Rather than applauding managers who achieve often artificially set "targets," executives are more likely to help improve their agency's programs by supporting managers who allocate resources to obtain a meaningful set of output, outcome, and results measures, and then manage their programs to improve the full "chain of events" affecting their results.

12. Use evaluation findings in appropriate ways to amplify data about results when reporting to Congress on GPRA requirements.

Often a program's "performance story" is more complex than the broad measures selected to communicate an agency's high-level goals. By selectively including more detailed information from evaluation studies that illuminate how these results are achieved, agencies can provide a more convincing picture of how and why their programs help to achieve those results.

Bibliography

Behn, Robert D. and Peter A. Kant. (1999). "Strategies for Avoiding the Pitfalls of Performance Contracting," *Public Productivity and Management Review*, 22, 4: 470-489.

Bickman, Leonard (1987). "Using Program Theory in Evaluation," *New Directions for Program Evaluation*, 33, Spring.

Chen, Huey-Tsyh (1990). *Theory-Driven Evaluations*. (Newbury Park, CA: Sage Publications).

Cooley, Larry (1994). "Challenges and Opportunities for Performance Measurement at USAID," *USAID Evaluation News*, 1.

Hatry, Harry (1999). *Performance Measurement: Getting Results*. (Washington, D.C.: The Urban Institute Press).

Hendricks, Michael (2000). "Attribution: Can We Soothe the Achilles' Heel of Performance Measurement?" presentation at the CAP/GAO/ GWU Brown Bag Lunch Services, April 19.

Hendricks, Michael (1996). "Performance Monitoring," AEA Presentation, 1995; and "Performance Monitoring: How to Measure Effectively the Results of Our Efforts," AEA presentation workshop.

MacLaughlin, John A. and Gretchan B. Jordan (1999). "Logic Models: A Tool for Telling Your Program's Performance Story," *Evaluation and Program Planning*, 22: 65-72.

Marquart, Jules M. (1990). "A Pattern-Matching Approach to Link Program Theory and Evaluation Data," in *Advances in Program Theory*, L. Bickman, ed. (New Directions for Program Evaluation, #47) San Francisco: Jossey-Bass.

Mayne, John (1999). "Addressing Attribution Through Contribution Analysis: Using Performance Measures Sensibly." Paper Published by the Canadian Office of the Auditor General of Canada, June.

National Academy of Public Administration. (2000) Transition Session on the Results of GPRA, Washington, D.C., October.

Newcomer, Kathryn E. (2000). "Measuring Government Performance," in *Handbook of Public Management Practice and Reform*, K. Tom Liou, ed. (New York: Marcel Dekker, Inc).

Newcomer, Kathryn E. (1994). "Opportunities and Incentives for Improving Program Quality: Auditing and Evaluating," *Public Administration Review*, 54.

Perrin, Edward B., Jane S. Durch, and Susan M. Skillman, Eds. (1999). *Health Performance Measurement in the Public Sector: Principles and Policies for Implementing an Information Network*. (Washington, D.C.: National Academy Press).

Reynolds, Arthur F. (1998). "Confirmatory Program Evaluation: A Method for Strengthening Causal Inference," *American Journal of Evaluation*, 19, 2: 203-221.

Scheirer, Mary Ann (1994). "Designing and Using Process Evaluation," in *Handbook of Practical Program Evaluation*, J.S. Wholey, H.P. Hatry, and K.E. Newcomer, eds., (San Francisco: Jossey-Bass).

Scheirer, Mary Ann (2000). "Getting More 'Bang' for Your Performance Measures 'Bucks,'" *American Journal of Evaluation*, 21, 2: 139-149.

United Way of America (1996). *Measuring Program Outcomes: A Practical Approach*.

U.S. General Accounting Office (1998). *Managing for Results: An Agenda to Improve the Usefulness of Agencies' Annual Performance Plans*. (GAO/GGD/AIMD-98-228) Washington, D.C.: USGAO.

U.S. General Accounting Office (1997). *Managing for Results: Analytic Challenges in Measuring Performance*. (GAO/HEHS/GGD-97-138) Washington, D.C.: USGAO.

U.S. General Accounting Office (2000). *Managing for Results: Continuing Challenges to Effective GPRA Implementation*. (GAO/T-GGD-00-178) Washington, D.C.: USGAO.

U.S. General Accounting Office (1998). *Managing for Results: Measuring Program Results That Are Under Limited Federal Control*. (GAO/GGD-99-16) Washington, D.C.: USGAO.

U.S. General Accounting Office (1999). *Managing for Results: Opportunities for Continued Improvements in Agencies' Performance Plans*. (GAO/GGD/AIMD-99-215) Washington, D.C.: USGAO.

U.S. General Accounting Office (1998). *Performance Measurement and Evaluation: Definitions and Relationships*. (GAO/GGD-98-26) Washington, D.C.: USGAO.

U.S. General Accounting Office (1998). *Program Evaluation: Agencies Challenged by New Demand for Information on Program Results*. (GAO/GGD-98-53) Washington, D.C.: USGAO.

U.S. General Accounting Office (2000). *Program Evaluation: Studies Helped Agencies Measure or Explain Performance*. (GAO/GGD-00-204) Washington, D.C.: USGAO.

Weiss, Carol H. (1998). *Evaluation (Second Ed.)*. (Upper Saddle River, NJ: Prentice Hall).

Wholey, Joseph S. (1979). *Evaluation: Promise and Performance*. (Washington, D.C.: The Urban Institute).

Wholey, Joseph S. (1987). "Evaluability Assessment: Developing Program Theory," in *Using Program Theory in Evaluation*, L. Bickman, ed., (New Directions for Evaluation, #33) San Francisco: Jossey-Bass.

Wholey, Joseph S. (1999). "Performance-based Measurement: Responding to the Challenges," *Public Productivity and Management Review*, 2, 3: 288-307.

PART III

Using Information to Manage for Results

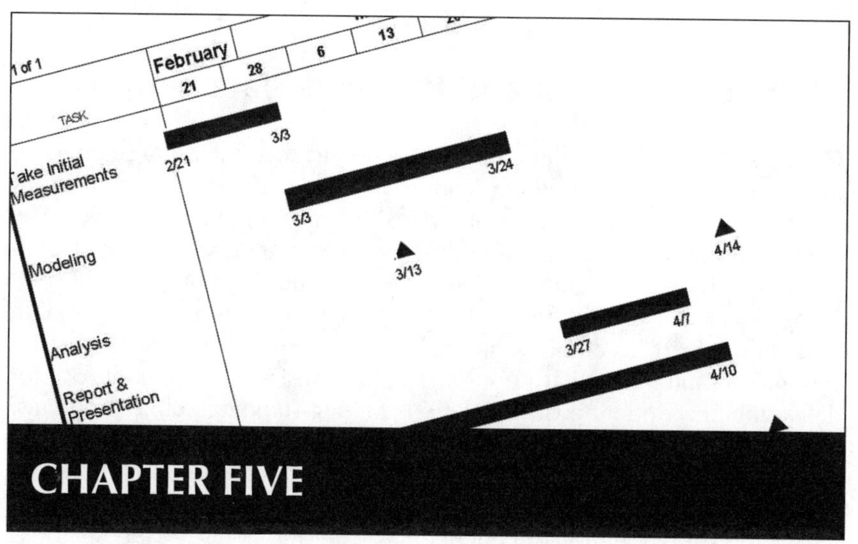

CHAPTER FIVE

Managing for Outcomes: Milestone Contracting in Oklahoma

Peter Frumkin
Assistant Professor of Public Policy
Kennedy School of Government
Harvard University

Background and Problem Statement

On the surface, nonprofit autonomy and public accountability seem to be in tension with one another. Nonprofit organizations want and need autonomy to design innovative programs that meet community needs. The independence that nonprofit organizations enjoy separates them from government and business organizations. Free from both the pressures of public opinion and the demands of shareholders, nonprofits are positioned, in principle at least, to act as vehicles for social experimentation and innovation. The autonomy that nonprofits enjoy can be an important tool for delivering new and innovative solutions to long-standing public problems. Many times, nonprofits working in fields as diverse as early childhood education and welfare-to-work transitions have made important breakthroughs that have influenced entire fields. Innovation is not the only justification for nonprofit independence. The autonomy of the sector is protected in order to create a realm where private visions of the common good can be pursued and where the values and commitments of individuals can find expression. The freedom that is granted to nonprofits by exempting them from taxation is thus designed to recognize their sovereignty and independence, while also giving them a subsidy to carry out their important work (Brody, 1998).

The very independence that lies at the heart of the nonprofit sector's privileged tax position can, however, be a major stumbling block when nonprofit organizations depend on direct financial support from government. In almost every case in which public funds pass from federal, state, or local authorities to nonprofit organizations, the public sector establishes and communicates expectations about both program design and performance. These expectations arise out of government's need for accountability and transparency. Public funds carry with them a special burden that neither private gifts nor fees for service need shoulder. Often anchored in a core commitment to equity and access, government grants must affirm and be applied to purposes that are in keeping with the public sector's broad public agenda, one that is far wider than that of most private contributors or paying clients. Accountability is a critical value in public sector organizations because it constitutes the foundation for both the legitimacy and support that government needs to carry out its work.

At one level, therefore, the values of autonomy and accountability seem at odds with one another. While nonprofit organizations might want to maximize the freedom they enjoy to experiment with new programs and service models, this impulse can and does come into conflict at some point with the public sector's need for a certain level of uniformity and consistency in the programs it funds (DeHoog, 1984; Smith and Lipsky, 1993). At the same time, while government might want to achieve very high levels of accountability in all the projects it funds, this impulse often comes into conflict with the desires of nonprofits to pursue their missions as they see fit (Gooden, 1998; Kearns, 1996). This tension between sectors can be depicted along a tradeoff line stretching from a combination of a high level of nonprofit autonomy and a low level of government accountability to a combination of a high level of government accountability and a low level of nonprofit autonomy. Government has traditionally staked out a position somewhere near point A on the tradeoff line, while nonprofits have gravitated more in the direction of point B (see Figure 5.1).

In most circumstances, this classic contracting tension is resolved in one of three ways: (1) The government adheres to a given decision making process and refuses compromise, fearing a loss of accountability, uniformity, and fairness; (2) The nonprofit organization refuses to give in to the demands of the government and either forgoes public funding or takes the funding but does not comply with mandates; or (3) Government and nonprofits reach an accommodation of sorts that produces less accountability and less autonomy.

This third solution results in both sides moving to point C in Figure 5.1. Often, this third option represents a sub-optimal, political compromise

Figure 5.1: Accountability and Autonomy in Public-Nonprofit Contracting

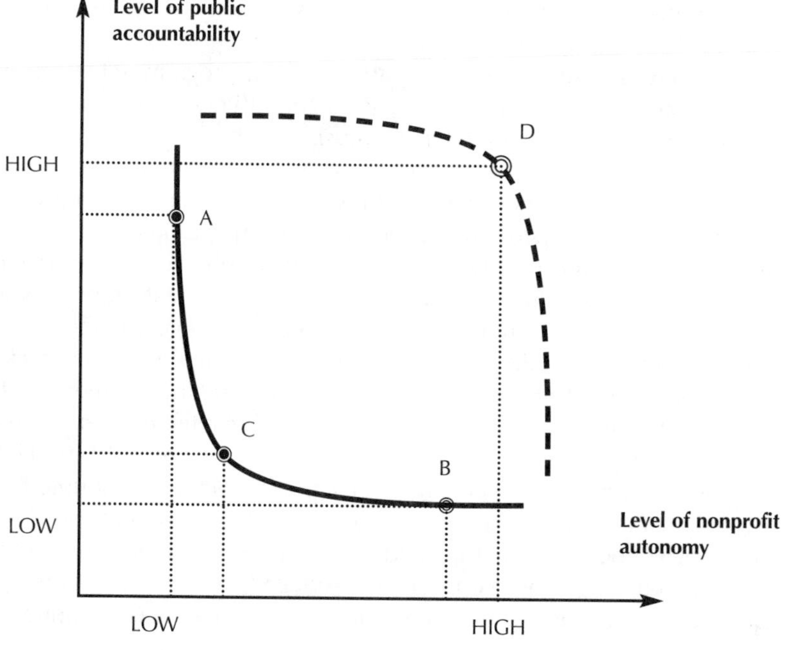

that satisfies neither side. A central challenge for both public and nonprofit management comes down to finding a fourth alternative to this classic dilemma, an alternative that allows government and nonprofits to simultaneously maximize both the accountability and autonomy dimensions (point D in Figure 5.1). Such a solution involves moving the production possibility frontier outward to reflect a new range of tradeoffs, a frontier on which a point can be located that improves on both the accountability and autonomy agendas of the public and nonprofit sectors.

What might this fourth option entail? How can government meet its need for control, uniformity, and accountability while giving nonprofits the freedom they need to design and implement innovative programs? One answer lies in the move away from process measures inherent in traditional fee-for-service arrangements and toward a system geared to outcomes (Behn and Kant, 1999; Volkmann, 1999). In their contractual relations with nonprofit organizations, government agencies have traditionally focused on outputs, not client outcomes or actual results (Cline, 2000; Cohen and Eimicke, 1998; Osborne and Gaebler, 1992).

Inputs, outputs, and outcomes in the nonprofit sector (United Way of America 1995:3) can be defined as follows:

- **Inputs** are resources dedicated to a particular program (e.g., money, staff, facilities, volunteers, equipment and supplies, regulations, and funders' requirements).
- **Outputs** are the direct products of program activities (e.g., literature distributed, participants serviced, classes taught, counseling sessions, and hours of service delivered).
- **Outcomes** are the benefits for participants of program activities (e.g., new knowledge, increased skills, changed attitudes, improved conditions, modified behavior, altered status).

Under the standard fee-for-service method of contracting, nonprofit organizations often are rewarded regardless of the outcomes of their efforts. Government simply pays out money to nonprofits based on contracts keyed to the delivery of units of service. Thus, if a social service agency provides 1,000 hours of counseling services at $35 an hour, a state funder would write a check for $35,000 upon presentation of an invoice. Under fee-for-service arrangements, ultimate client results or outcomes are rarely tracked, because they are not the basis on which the performance is measured or rewarded. The consequences of this system reveal that there are rarely positive results when outcomes are not measured (Osborne and Gaebler, 1992).

As pressure for greater efficiency in the public sector has mounted over time, interest in changing the terms of government contracting rose. A new system was needed, one that tracked the use of inputs, measured the outputs produced, and—most importantly—tracked the final outcomes (see Figure 5.2). By the early 1990s, the shift to performance-based contracting

Figure 5.2: Outcomes and Nonprofit Program Autonomy

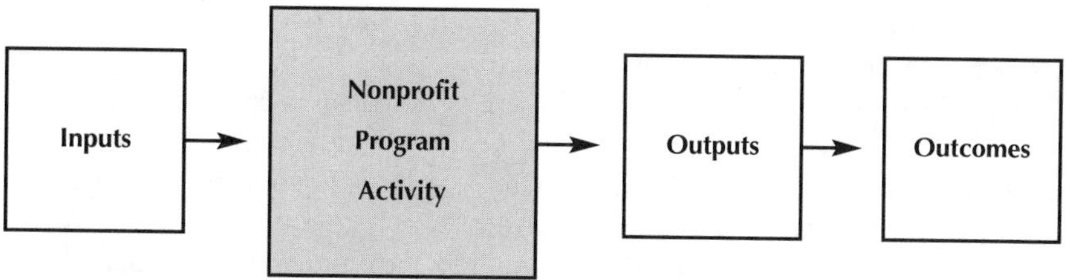

(PBC) began. The driving rationale behind PBC was the simple idea that public agencies need a way to ensure that they get impact for every public dollar spent and thereby ensure public support for government action (Zak Figura, 1999). Also driving the move to PBC was the sense that government could and should learn about management from businesses. The private sector has traditionally used a system of rewards to encourage certain actions and activities. When organizations are funded according to outcomes, however, they focus on performance and devote themselves to improving it (Osborne and Gaebler, 1992). The Government Performance and Results Act of 1993 (GPRA, 1993) standardized this new and different approach. It required organizations that received federal money to create specific goals and then post their advancement towards these ends (Buckmaster, 1999).

While much of the impetus to measure outcomes came from accountability concerns, the shift has had ripple effects on public management (Buckmaster, 1999). This new mind-set created the need to rethink the structure of performance measurement. When the focus is placed on performance and on paying nonprofits only upon demonstration of results and client outcomes, accurate assessment and performance measurement become critical (Herman and Heimovics, 1994; Murray and Tassie, 1994; Osborne, 1994; and Osborne and Tricker, 1995). Outcome measurement requires new skills, including participative planning, negotiated rules, quantitative and qualitative yardsticks, valid and reliable data collection, and a system for feeding information back into strategic planning systems. An entire field can be enhanced when outcome contracting is performed correctly and when best practices are shared (Buckmaster, 1999).

While outcome measurement procedures have been advocated as a means of eliciting better accountability and more effective program evaluation of nonprofit organizations, doubts about the efficacy of this approach persist. Five broad problems and concerns have surfaced in the literature. First, many managers resist the measurement of outcomes because they have previously seen it fail (Osborne and Gaebler, 1992). One well-known example of how an outcomes-based system can go awry is the Job Training Partnership Act of 1982. Providers were encouraged to target and train individuals who were most likely to succeed in a job, because their rewards were based upon the number of individuals that had secured job placements (Barnow, 2000). Sadly, the incentives of this program encouraged providers to select and assist people who were likely to succeed but who may not have been most in need of the services (Osborne and Gaebler, 1992). This phenomenon, often referred to as "creaming," occurs when organizations receive payments even when they follow the path of least resistance and avoid clients who are most in need of assistance.

A second concern with keying program payment to outcomes is related to the possible gaming of such systems (Gibbons, 1998; Lu, 1999). Defined as taking actions that increase payouts from incentive contracts without actually improving performance (Baker, 1992:600), gaming is a serious problem because it effectively negates the performance basis on which outcome funding rests. When nonprofits and their activities are not being tracked closely, it is easy for organizations to engage in activities that may call for payment, but that may not represent the fulfillment of the contract's real intentions. By taking advantage of the letter of a contract, nonprofits can undermine the spirit of a program (Brooks, 2000; Lawler, 1971, 1990; Hamner, 1975; Beer et al., 1984).

Third, some worry that a shift from traditional fee-for-service contracting to performance-based contracting will create conflicts within many mission-driven nonprofit organizations. These conflicts can challenge an organization's culture and identity. For some organizations, moving from fee-for-service to outcome funding raises deep questions of control and internal priorities (Williams, Webb, and Phillips, 1991). All aspects of nonprofit operation have the potential to be affected, from the location at which services are offered to the number of clients that are served (Smith and Lipsky, 1993). Some nonprofits find the shift to outcomes stressful because it brings with it a commitment not just to results, but also to programmatic scale and expansion. If outcome funding specifies both a rate of payment for a given set of outcomes and a minimum number of outcomes, nonprofits can be left scrambling to build the capacity to deliver services.

To make these adaptations harder, many nonprofits have organizational cultures that are grounded in the belief that performance targets are not appropriate for many of the human services (Light, 2000). Frequently, nonprofits have missions that are rooted in values and beliefs, and aim toward such broad outcomes as empowerment, improved quality of life, and community well-being. The fulfillment of these missions is often very difficult to measure (Brower, Abolafia, and Carr, 2000; Kanter, 1979; Drucker, 1992; Thompson and McEwan, 1958; Milofsky, 1988; DiMaggio, 1988; Drucker, 1990; Salipante, 1995; Buckmaster, 1999). Resistance to keying programs to outcomes may be strong if the chosen performance measures are seen as being detached from the broad social objectives of an organization (Stone and Gershenfield, 1996).

Fourth, there is some worry associated with outcome funding that nonprofits will not be able to focus on the quality of their services, but instead become engrossed with the number of outcomes produced. If reward systems are keyed to the achievement of results, there is the possibility that nonprofits will be forced to abandon their traditional systems of delivering services in favor of lower cost and lower quality methods. The threat to quality is particularly acute in markets where multiple nonprofits are competing for contracts and where programs appear comparable. In such cases, cost—not quality—may become the deciding factor by which organizations receive contracts for the provision of services.

Fifth, outcome funding can place personnel and human resource demands on nonprofits. As nonprofits grow and change to meet new accountability standards, employees need to acquire the knowledge and skills that will enable them to successfully meet the challenges of their newly defined roles. Program and technical staff may need special training to adapt to the new systems. Also, as these organizations continue to expand and develop, there is a concern that there will not be enough money available to attract and hire much needed, well-trained staff (Blacksell and Phillips, 1994). In organizations that traditionally depend on volunteers, the push to organize and professionalize may lead these nonprofits to bring in paid staff (Billis, 1989). The human resource challenge is rendered more acute when nonprofits are forced to compete with business firms for outcome contracts. In the field of welfare-to-work services (Pavetti et al., 1997; Jennings, 2000), where major corporations such as Lockheed and EDS actively pursue outcome-based contracts with states, nonprofits are struggling to attract and retain the best people in their organizations, especially when business can and will pay higher salaries (Frumkin and Andre-Clark, 2000).

While the debate over the strengths and weaknesses of outcome funding rages on, public managers need to define for themselves *in practice* how they can best structure their relationship with nonprofit service providers. As they develop contracting relations with nonprofit service providers, public managers will need to seek answers to the following question: How can the need for accountability be balanced with the need to give nonprofits freedom in program design and implementation? Instead of ignoring this question and the emerging tensions created by contracting, a new perspective on public-nonprofit relations is needed—one that preserves some of the boundaries between sectors, that gives nonprofits as much freedom as possible, and that makes broad, multi-dimensional appraisals of their performance easier. Rather than see the nonprofit sector as the servant of the public sector that obediently executes programs, public managers must begin to take more seriously the unique visions, values, and commitments that animate the nonprofit sector itself and that lead to programmatic innovations. Moving public management to a point where the values of public accountability and nonprofit autonomy can coexist will require the development of new strategies for managing public-nonprofit relations. An experiment in Oklahoma provides a glimpse of what a well-functioning, outcome-based system might look like (Rosegrant, 1998).

The Oklahoma Milestone Payment System

Preparing people with mental and developmental disabilities to live and work independently in society has long been a dilemma for public policy. Over the last several decades, many of the old solutions, including institutionalization as well as a variety of physical therapies, have been abandoned in favor of more humane measures that aim to assimilate the disabled into the broader community. Beginning in the 1970s, the federal government mandated that the public schools educate disabled children in regular classrooms alongside other children and prepare them to go to work after graduation. These changes did much to improve the prospects for many mentally and physically disabled young adults. However, for those such as the profoundly disabled, who needed more help, there was no place to go after graduation from high school. For a long time, putting the profoundly disabled to work was not thought to be feasible, and it thus took some time for the adult social service system to catch up with the education system. Finally, in 1986, in response to pressure from a variety of advocacy groups, the federal government passed legislation that authorized the delivery of vocational services (referred to as "Supported Employment") to people with "the most severe disabilities."

After the legislation was passed, 10 states began receiving funding to start programs to train the severely disabled. However, many other states were hesitant because they had not worked with the severely disabled before and thus required further impetus before they would respond. In 1987, in response to a lawsuit brought by the parents of children who had been residents of Oklahoma's largest institution for the developmentally disabled, Oklahoma began planning a program to train disabled adults to work in integrated jobs in their communities. In 1988, the Oklahoma Department of Rehabilitation Services (DRS) began providing employment assessment and training services for adults through community-based nonprofits (and a few selected government agencies).

Eligible individuals—primarily people with mental retardation or mental illness, though people with many other disabilities were also eligible—

are those for whom direct placement in a job in their community is the desired outcome. Typically, they would be paired with a job coach in order to assist them in locating and getting a job. Since they were providing a new service and did not really have any idea what it would cost, the state decided to structure the program as a traditional fee-for-service model that would reimburse the nonprofits at an hourly rate for all services provided.

Planning Change and Moving to Outcomes

By 1991, the program had expanded significantly, working with 20 nonprofits and serving nearly 500 clients. But Daniel O'Brien and Rebecca Cook, two administrators in the Community Rehabilitation Services Unit of the Department of Rehabilitation Services (referred to herein as "the agency"), concluded that the program was too expensive and that it was not doing a very good job of achieving its stated objective of training disabled people for integrated employment in their communities. For example, in 1991, it cost the agency more than $22,000 and took an average of 438 days to bring a single case to closure.

They concluded that the major cause of these problems was the agency's fee-for-service reimbursement structure, which created a distortion in the way the goal was pursued, putting too much emphasis on the process of providing the services—on ability and skills assessments, job training, and constant supervision once on the job (all of which would be billed on an hourly basis to the state)—at the expense of moving the clients as quickly as possible into stable jobs. They concluded that the system had created two competing goals: an implicit one, to maximize the number of hours spent on a particular client; and an explicit one, to get clients into employment. More often than not, the implicit goal took precedence. According to Cook, "the emphasis was not on the individual that they were serving.... It was on billing hours.... We've got everything askew here. We have a system in place, but it costs too much money and it's not doing what it ought to do."

What is a Milestone?

The Community Rehabilitation Services Unit of the Oklahoma Department of Rehabilitation Services created the Milestone Payment System, a reimbursement method based on incentive payments for service outcomes. DRS defines each milestone as a predefined checkpoint on the way to a desired outcome.

Cook and O'Brien aimed to devise a new way of paying for services that would, in the fairest and most efficient and cost-effective manner possible, put the emphasis back on the outcome. Their goal, according to O'Brien, was to create "an incentive for [the nonprofits] to find the inefficiencies in their system and to eliminate them. Within the hourly system, we created inefficiencies ... by the way we paid. There was no incentive for them to find the inefficiencies and we couldn't find them because we're external to their organization." The goal was thus to construct a system that would force everyone to compete with the most efficient and effective nonprofits.

After much deliberation, O'Brien and Cook designed a system, which they called the Milestone Payment System (MPS), that would reimburse nonprofits when clients reached each of a series of steps—the "milestones"—along the way to getting a job. (To qualify as a "job," federal guidelines require that the client work at least 20 hours a week and must earn at least minimum wage.) The milestones, designed to be easily observable, would involve looking at indicators such as job retention, wages, and employer and client satisfaction. The largest payment would be the final milestone, full employment for 17 weeks plus 90 days (known as "26 closure").[1] MPS would reimburse the nonprofit for the "average" cost of providing the outcome of the service rather than for the cost of staff time (as in fee-for-service). The structure of the milestones would differ slightly depending on whether the clients had mental or developmental disabilities, but looked roughly like this (see Figure 5.3):

- determination of need 10%
- vocational preparation 10%
- placement 10%
- four-week job training 10%
- 10-week job retention 15%
- stabilization 20%
- 26 closure 25%

In order to encourage the nonprofits to make good matches, the organization would be paid only once for each milestone. According to Cook, "It's very motivating to the vendor to make a good job match to begin with." In order to aid nonprofits in taking on more difficult clients, MPS also created a two-tiered system of payments through which service providers would be paid higher fees for serving people designated as "highly challenged." Cook notes, "We try to define who are the people who cost more money for the vendor to serve so that we can build a rate into the system that will help them say, 'It's OK to take a chance on this person because they are going to pay us more for him.'"

The agency solicits bids from primarily community-based nonprofits to care for a specified number of clients in the following year. To put together a bid, the nonprofit first must develop a budget that includes estimates for

Figure 5.3: Six Milestones

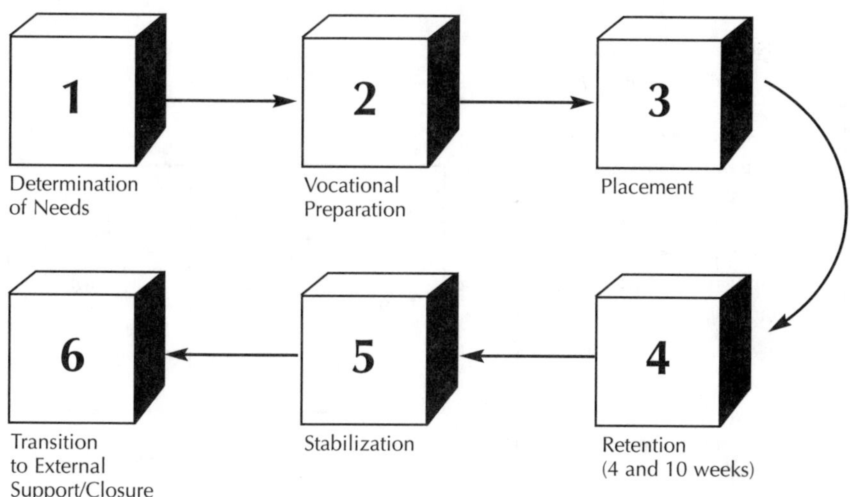

the number of clients they will serve and the number of staff they will need. Then they develop a bid based upon the average cost per closure from the previous year multiplied by the estimated number of closures for the contract year. Comparing the estimated number of clients to the estimated number of closures allows them to account, to some extent, for "dropouts," people who for whatever reason will not reach closure (and thus will deprive the nonprofit of the final, biggest payment). According to O'Brien, the bidding process forces all the service providers "to compete against the average, bringing down the high, the very inefficient providers, pressuring them to move towards the average."[2] Once the bids are received, DRS evaluates them—by looking in particular at the per-customer bid price and the average cost per closure, as well as past history and the geographical area served—and then negotiates with the nonprofit organizations to arrive at a reasonable bid. Required documentation at each stage ensures progress and triggers payment (see Figure 5.4).

Though the specific arrangements may differ some from one service organization to another, the process involves three key figures. First, counselors (something of a misnomer, since they do not actually "counsel" or work with clients), who are employed by the agency, authorize services to approved nonprofits. They oversee a number of different service providers and supervise the technical assistants. Second, technical assistants, who are also employed by the agency, train and oversee the job coaches. Third, job

Figure 5.4: The Milestone Bidding Process

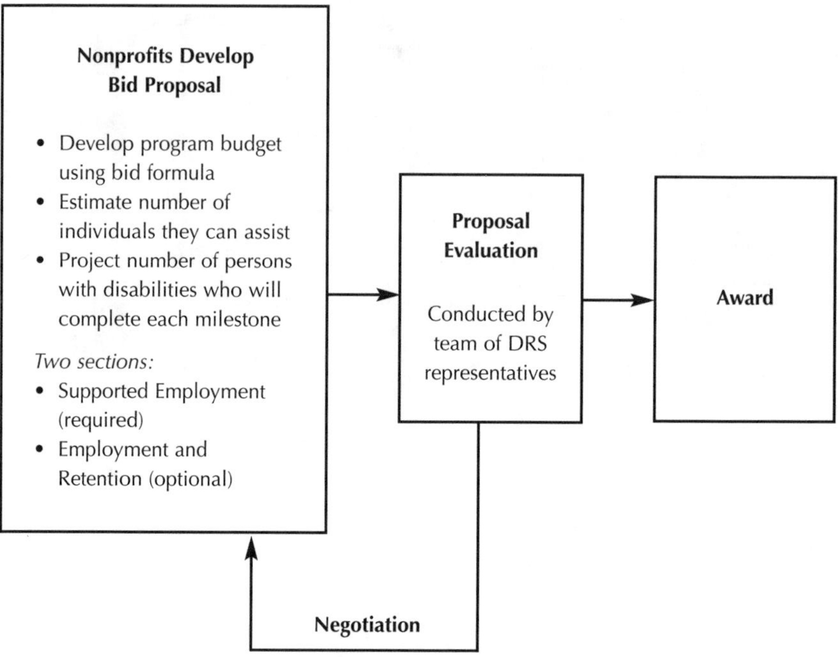

coaches, who are employed by the nonprofit, work directly with the client. They may work with anywhere from five to 12 (or sometimes more) clients at any one time. The job coaches try to find jobs in environments that will support the client. If a client has very restricted skills—most have at least three functional limitations—they will look for a job that requires only one or two of those skills, which usually means entry level positions at low wages. By all accounts, being a job coach is an enormously difficult and low-paying job. According to one estimate, regardless of training, it takes a job coach two years to become proficient.

Implementation and Expansion

The earliest Milestone's pilots—two nonprofits that served mentally ill individuals—were funded in October of 1992. Several other pilots followed over the next several years. In order to prepare the nonprofits to make the transition from fee-for-service to MPS with minimum confusion, the technical assistants from the agency held numerous training sessions and retreats with managers and job coaches so that they would understand how the bidding procedures worked and what would be expected of them in terms of outcomes once they received contracts. According to Cook, "We tried very hard from the very beginning of supported employment to bring vendors in as partners into the process of what we were trying to do ... they were accustomed to us calling them and saying, 'What do you think about this?'"

Still, in 1997, when the remaining programs from across the state that work with the agency were converted to MPS, they faced much trepidation on the part of the nonprofits. Many were concerned that they would be forced to spend less quality time with their clients, and others were worried that the nonprofits would be forced to select clients most likely to reach closure. The executive director of one MPS nonprofit, worrying that the quality of services would suffer, commented, "Will we really still be able to perform services in a similar manner to what we do now if it is purely outcome based?"

The changeover proved fairly painless for organizations that had been highly effective under fee-for-service. However, for many others, there were considerable growing pains. Looking back on the shift, 36 percent of nonprofits involved with the program said the overall transition to MPS was challenging. Despite all the preparation, getting used to the new bidding system simply took some time and adjustment. Many of the nonprofits had their bids rejected two or even three times before the agency determined that they were eligible for funding. For some, it was a struggle to shift the focus of their organization from "process" to outcomes.

It also became clear that many managers were not immediately up to the job of running effective outcome-focused organizations and that many job coaches simply did not have the skills and experience to work with profoundly disabled people. According to one technical assistant who spent a lot of time working with nonprofits during the transition, many of them "didn't have the skills for the job." A few nonprofits dropped out because they did not believe philosophically that employment should be the only outcome available to people in the program.

Finally, the clients with mental illness raised a host of additional complications. While the founders of MPS were convinced that integrated work in the community was just as important for the mentally ill as for the developmentally disabled, the directors of many of the nonprofits serving the mentally ill did not necessarily see employment in the community as an appropriate goal for their clients. According to Cook, "We had great difficulty getting mental health centers to see beyond [the view that] the person comes in for therapy, the person takes medication, the person sits and smokes and watches television all day, and getting them to see that work is part of the recovery process." Thus, it took a while for some organizations to come around, while many still have not and do not work with MPS.

Under a system like MPS, which trades some control for improved outcomes and programmatic freedom, how is success measured? Most obviously, the key measure is increased achievement of the core outcome, the placement of disabled people into stable jobs in their communities. The agency also looked at success in two other ways: the satisfaction of the consumers (meaning mainly the clients and the employers, but also the counselors and job coaches) and a reduction in the need for regulation and oversight. By these three measures, for the vast majority of those involved, MPS has been a dramatic success. The clients are receiving the kind of support that they need and are being placed in jobs in greater numbers and with far more success and satisfaction than before. The employers are getting well-trained employees who are often more dedicated to their jobs, and thus longer lasting, than non-disabled workers, which saves the employers additional funds in training costs.[3] The agency is getting greater impact because the system links funding with outcomes, which builds public support for the agency's mission. And the nonprofits are doing a much better job of achieving their explicit goal—and they are being rewarded for it.

According to a 1997 survey, 13 of 16 nonprofits that had converted had shown improvement in all areas. Time on waiting lists was reduced by half; time before job placement was reduced by 18 percent; the cost of assessments was reduced by 9 percent; paperwork decreased by 33 percent; data entry items were reduced by 98 percent; and the cost per closure dropped by 25 percent. To give a specific example, Goodwill of Tulsa has become twice as productive under MPS as it was under fee-for-service: They have been able to treat twice as many clients under Milestone with the same budget they had under fee-for-service. (See *Goodwill of Tulsa* in Appendix I.)

When asked what difference MPS has made, most nonprofits seem to agree that the new, less-onerous reporting requirements under MPS have freed the job coaches to spend more time with clients—not less, as had been feared by many nonprofits—and have freed the managers to spend more time supporting their job coaches and making sure their organizations are being run efficiently. One MPS participant says that his organization saves three months a year in employee time because of the reduction in paperwork. One nonprofit manager echoed these thoughts when she said, "Fee-for-service is a headache because there is so much paperwork involved." That alone—the more hours per week that they have to work with clients—may go a long way toward explaining why MPS has been so much more successful in achieving outcomes than the old fee-for-service system.

Most of those with experience under MPS seem to agree that its transparency—the idea that everyone understands their role in pursuing MPS's main goal—makes it much easier for them to do their jobs. The clients know, from the beginning, that they will have to follow a number of steps over a period of time and, at the end, they will have a job. The nonprofits know that they have to scout for jobs more aggressively, and are encouraged to spend more time marketing—themselves and their clients—which hadn't been a priority under fee-for-service. When a job coach focuses on making sure that a placement is suitable from the beginning of the process of working with a client, it often means that the first placement fits well, meaning that both the client and the employer are happy and that the placement is a success (see Figure 5.5).

In order to investigate this level of satisfaction further, a group of 20 nonprofits that participated in MPS was randomly selected and surveyed in the fall of 2000. Three quarters of the group had been with MPS for at least three years. The group was asked a variety of different questions. When nonprofits were asked about switching from their previous method of payment, 57 percent of the group said their transition to the MPS Payment System was easy. In response to follow-up questions about the design of MPS, 45 percent of the group said that the system afforded them a great deal of flexibility and 55 percent said they felt they had a lot of input in fine-tuning their contract with DRS.

The system also was perceived as being built on sound benchmarks: Almost half of the nonprofits polled said that Milestone was extremely accurate in measuring client progress. When the question of "creaming" was raised with nonprofits by asking if Milestone encouraged them to select clients who were more likely to succeed, 65 percent of the group answered no. When asked if the Milestone system increased their accountability to the state, 83 percent responded yes. When the nonprofit organizations were asked to choose the method of payment they preferred, 80 percent chose Milestone over fee-for-service.

At the end of the survey, 75 percent of the organizations rated their overall experience with Milestone as good or excellent. As one nonprofit manager said, "Milestone gives us a sense of accomplishment because the outcome is more clear." These responses are particularly impressive given the fact that in 2000 it cost the state $10,740 on average to bring a single case to closure, a substantial savings compared to an average cost in 1991 of $22,000. Milestone has thus created real savings for the taxpayers without alienating the nonprofit service providers.

Challenges and Concerns

Though reaction to MPS has been largely positive, the system does have its critics, and while most of them are managers with nonprofits that have performed poorly under MPS, some of their concerns are worth considering. From the outset, the two principal objections have been that the enhanced emphasis of the program on outcomes may potentially force the

Figure 5.5

Milestone	Documentation Needed
Determination of Needs	• Computerized Progress Report • Situational Assessment Reports and/or Vocational Assessment Forms • Summary Vocational Assessment Report or Vocational Profile Form
Vocational Preparation Services	• Dates and hours of attendance (attendance sheets submitted) • Consumer has completed program • Consumer has achieved 75% of predefined competencies
Job Placement	• Computerized Progress Report • Employment Verification Form signed by employer • Task Analysis Form • Job Analysis Form
Job Retention	• Employment Verification Form (verification of continued employment and hours **(four and 10 weeks)** worked per week will be required for payment) • Computerized Progress Report
Stabilization	Verification of the following: • The individual has been employed for a total of at least 17 weeks • A written Employer Evaluation has been submitted which indicates acceptable job performance during the most recent month • A current Client Job Satisfaction Questionnaire has been submitted which indicates client/family satisfaction • The individual has received support services defined in the IRP, including a minimum of two individual contacts and one employer contact per month • The individual has worked at least two entire shifts without job coach support in one week, as verified in the employer evaluation (This may be waived by the DRS Counselor if the consumer meets criteria for Highly Challenged) • The individual has met the weekly work goal in the IRP
Closure	• Current employer Evaluation Form • Current Computerized Progress Report • Current Client Job Satisfaction Questionnaire

nonprofits to provide a lesser quality service and that outcomes will lead nonprofits to screen their clients more carefully for those who are most likely to succeed. The concerns voiced by nonprofits in Oklahoma correspond fairly closely to the first and third reservations about outcome funding that we outlined in our summary of the public management and contracting literature bearing on outcome funding.

In the transition from fee-for-service to MPS, many providers worried that they would have less time to spend with clients and thus the quality of service would suffer. A technical assistant commented, in discussions with nonprofits before the transition, "Quality of services kept coming up time and time again." But MPS was designed explicitly to address this concern. One of the big problems of fee-for-service that MPS aimed to correct was that once providers got on the list of approved providers, they were almost never removed, no matter how ineffective they were at providing services. O'Brien and Cook felt that nonprofits who were not able to deliver effective services ought to lose their contracts. Given the nature of the clients seeking to achieve milestones, proper training and sensible placements are essential. MPS made nonprofit organizations, not the agency, responsible for outcomes, thus demanding of nonprofits that they provide quality services and penalizing them if they did not. Beyond putting the onus for quality services on nonprofits, MPS introduced careful monitoring of the end result of the service delivery system: The counselors under MPS have been vigilant about not approving placements unless the clients were sincerely happy on the job. This gives the service provider considerable incentive to focus on quality and to make sure the job is a good fit from the beginning.

The second concern, the selection problem of "creaming," is more serious. O'Brien has commented that creaming is the "Achilles' heel" of outcome-based payment systems. He notes, "It is something we have to be constantly vigilant about." One key measure to combat creaming was MPS's two-tiered structure of reimbursements that gives nonprofits a monetary incentive not to discriminate against harder-to-serve clients.[4] Clients are designated as either regular (though all of these clients had substantial problems) or as "highly challenged," and the nonprofits receive a larger payment—typically about $1,000 to $2,000 more than the regular payment—for taking on highly challenged clients. Despite these measures, as well as the fact that their budgets are supposed to include estimates of dropout costs, some agencies appear to be hesitant to work with difficult clients because of the perceived risk involved in failing to achieve closure. After all, the largest payment is the final one. And it has been suggested by some that the larger payment may not be large enough to make it worth assuming the risk of working with the most challenged clients.

What looks to some observers as creaming may in fact be a byproduct of some remaining confusion about the purpose of MPS, however. If MPS accomplished nothing else, it was able to alter the incentive structure in support of a very clear and enforceable goal. The concept of closure at the heart of this goal—integrated work for an extended period and a reasonable wage at a business in the community—reflects the conviction of its designers that everyone who is capable and wants to work should be able to do so, and that just about everyone can work if they get the right kind of assistance and support. O'Brien notes, "Work is part of what makes you feel part of the larger community. And staff people who think work is too difficult or demanding can increase the stress clients feel and contribute to low self-esteem, low expectations, and an inability to function fully in society." In addition, he comments, "We don't believe in sheltered employment.... We don't believe that it's good for people. It is institutionalizing.... The ideal is to put them in a normal environment, and what they start doing is acting like everyone else."

Further, O'Brien and Cook would suggest that the fact that no one got screened out in the old system was a flaw in *that* system. The reimbursement process under the old fee-for-service system encouraged nonprofit inefficiency by rewarding organizations for accepting people who could not work and then extending the service delivery process so their budgets could get padded. O'Brien comments, "It would take two or three years really to get to the point of saying, 'OK, you're not going to make it.'" The reason for this, O'Brien contends, is that the agency had all the risks. "There was absolutely no risk in taking somebody who would never get a job." Those people who will not be able to make it to closure or who may be excluded because of their inability to work are not without recourse. Other programs—at the state as well as federal level (e.g., programs such as Social Security, Title 16)—are available to help them with their needs. But Milestone is designed to encourage work and it ought to admit people who are capable of work.

Managing for Outcomes

Milestone contracting was designed to weed out ineffective or inefficient nonprofits and to give providers the opportunity to devise new interventions. Thus, it should not be surprising that not every program that made the transition to MPS has survived. But for those who have stayed and been successful, the key seems to involve two related factors—namely, strong management and effective job coaches. Organizations with strong managers made the transition to MPS with a fair amount of ease. And organizations with good job coaches have been able to make good assessments and to place their clients into suitable employment the first time out.

One of the biggest obstacles to the success of MPS was getting the nonprofits to change the way they approached their jobs, from a process-oriented mind-set to an outcome-oriented one. During the pilot phase, the agency spent a great deal of time working with the nonprofits in order to ensure that they knew what would be expected of them under MPS. And it seems to have worked. It is interesting to note that nonprofits commonly say that Milestone forced them to act in a more business-like fashion. Analogies like this often break down rather quickly if one looks too closely, but what it seems to mean in this case is that the nonprofits have been forced to treat potential employers as if they are customers. Nonprofits have had to learn to market themselves to those customers with a fair amount of sophistication. In order to ensure that the employer and the client are happy, they need to pay close attention to the needs of both so that they will make a good match.

But how they do so—e.g., whether they will need more or fewer staff members or what kind of training they will use—is completely up to them. According to Cook, "All we care about is: are you meeting the parameters of our contract in terms of outcomes? You figure out how you're going to do it." The additional risk they assume under MPS is balanced by the autonomy they have over how they will operate. As long as the nonprofits meet the conditions of their contract—that is, they make (or surpass) the amount of placements they promised—they have complete freedom in determining the best way to do it. MPS clearly affirms a fair amount of nonprofit autonomy by turning the service delivery process into an opaque, if not black, box from which outcomes are generated.

In such a situation, an organization without strong management may soon be out of business, because the freedom given to nonprofits can be used to innovate or it can be an excuse to flounder. Effective managers under MPS have to be well organized in order to deal with the many start-up issues that come up and, because of the nature of the contracting system, they must be particularly adept at managing money. Also, they have to know their "business" inside out so that they are able to recognize a good job coach from a bad one.

The job coach is really the linchpin of the whole process. One nonprofit manager noted, "The most important part in a client reaching closure is who the clients have as a job coach and how much that job coach is willing to help the client. Most people quit if there hasn't been substantial contact with the job coach."

It may be worth noting that the job coaches seemed to have a better understanding of what would be expected from them under the new system than the managers did. The amount of documentation and the rule-boundedness of the old system tended to frustrate job coaches. They were also frustrated by the eternally open-ended process, with nonprofits having little incentive to "fade" the job coach to allow the client to function independently. Under MPS, roles and goals were clarified and risk was distributed so that everyone had a stake in achieving better outcomes. One job coach observed, "We went from being caretakers to being coaches." They found it liberating. As another job coach noted, "I know if I have done my job well enough that this person is going to make it and we'll get our payments."

MPS still has a few wrinkles that need to be ironed out. High-performing nonprofits that place their clients too quickly into employment under one contract have no avenue for going back to MPS if they run out of money. According to O'Brien, "If you set up a system that has incentives for being productive, some people are going to go in and do that, and they're going to do it better than anybody else.... And if you don't have a way that they can grow their contract or grow their program, then, in effect, you're going to punish them for doing good." Under the current program design, they must either stop accepting new clients or operate for free until the new contract begins, neither of which is an attractive prospect. In several cases, the agency has been able to renew nonprofits' contracts early. This is hardly a permanent solution, however.[5] One possible solution that has been proposed is to institute open-ended contracts. The constant evaluation that MPS necessitates would seem to offer enough accountability to make such an arrangement possible. Others have suggested that MPS might be effective as a voucher system, allowing the clients (or their surrogates) to make their own decisions about the quality of services.

Whatever the value of these and other suggested improvements, it remains true that Milestone has been a remarkably successful innovation in public management. Fee-for-service has long been *the* chosen method for governments to pay for contracted services under the modern welfare state. But MPS has shown that there is a plausible alternative to fee-for-service, an alternative that exchanges the worst incentives of the old system—inefficiency, over-regulation, and poor performance—for the shared risk, greater accountability, heightened autonomy, and high performance of MPS.

A few key elements are worth some emphasis. The complexity of the change under Milestone necessitated extensive consultation on the part of the agency with the managers and job coaches or, it seems clear, it would have been a disaster. To combat creaming, the two-tiered reimbursement process gave the nonprofits incentives to take on difficult cases. The decision to set reimbursements at the average cost of a service was also crucial, giving the nonprofits incentives to root out inefficiencies within their organizations. The decision to offer a final payment only once per case gave the nonprofit an incentive to make sure that the initial placement would be the right one. Finally, by making the final payment the largest one and by making it apply only to real work in the community, MPS encouraged the nonprofits to not waste time on training and assessment and to place the clients in jobs they were suited for.

Perhaps the biggest obstacle to the success of MPS was changing the mind-set of the nonprofits. It was to be expected that the providers who were comfortable under fee-for-service would offer some resistance in the face of change. Managing the process under fee-for-service had been easy. Nonprofits simply needed to keep track and bill the agency for every minute of the workday, maximize enrollment, extend client assessment and training time, and stay on the job site with the client as long as possible. In the end, the dominance of this way of thinking distorted the process, causing inefficiency and poor performance. In sharp contrast, MPS offered the nonprofits an interesting bargain: If the nonprofits do a better job of putting their clients to work, the state will leave it to the nonprofits to figure out the best way to achieve this goal. Not all nonprofits were prepared to take the public sector up on this kind of bargain, but those who did have thrived. These nonprofits have risen to the challenge and their clients are far better off for it.

Lessons Learned

As nonprofit organizations consider the quality and impact of their relations with government, two fundamental concerns emerge that together constitute a strategic dilemma of significant proportions. On the one hand, nonprofits must be open and accountable to the public agencies that fund them. This usually entails complying with regulations and guidelines for the provision of contracted services, as well as completing evaluations and reports on the use of public funds. On the other hand, nonprofits must jealously guard their autonomy and independence. This often comes down to protecting their distinctive missions and values in the face of pressures from outside. For public managers, the stakes involved in working with nonprofits to strike the right balance could not be higher. As devolution and privatization push more and more government functions "down" to lower levels of government, and as privatization continues to push government function "out" to contractors, the task of working effectively with nonprofit service providers is becoming ever more pressing.

We identified at the outset the difficult tradeoff that nonprofit and public managers must strike between accountability and autonomy (see Figure 5.1). Finding ways to satisfy both nonprofit and public agencies is clearly a challenging task. Often, contracting relations prioritize accountability at the cost of nonprofit autonomy and end up supporting obedient, if uninspired, service providers who simply implement programs as instructed (point A in Figure 5.1 and cell A in Figure 5.6). Other times, contracting systems privilege the autonomy demands of nonprofits at the cost of sound oversight and create room for nonprofit renegades to take advantage (point B in Figure 5.1 and cell B in Figure 5.6). In some cases, neither value is optimized, and nonprofits simply perform poorly as unaccountable and unproductive vendors (point C in Figure 5.1 and cell C in Figure 5.6). The core challenge in public management is to promote both the values of accountability and autonomy at the same time and to allow nonprofits to act as responsive innovators (point D in Figure 5.1 and cell D in Figure 5.6). This appears to be happening in Oklahoma through the MPS system.

The MPS model is significant because it represents a clear attempt to move contracting to an optimal mix of accountability and autonomy. From the experience in Oklahoma, it is possible to draw some simple lessons for public managers on how to go about designing and implementing milestone contracts:

Design Stage

1. **Collaborate with nonprofits in the initial design of milestones.** Public managers should bring nonprofits into the process of designing milestones. One lesson that emerges from the Oklahoma experiment is that

Figure 5.6: The Four Identities of Nonprofit Organizations

Level of Autonomy Sought by Nonprofit Organization	Level of Nonprofit Accountability to Public Sector Agencies: HIGH	LOW
HIGH	**The Responsive Innovator** (D)	The Renegade Experimenter (B)
LOW	The Obedient Implementer (A)	The Detached Vendor (C)

good communication between public and nonprofit managers early in the contracting design process is essential. Many nonprofit organizations are likely to be apprehensive of a major shift in the way public contracts are administered. Collaboration will go a long way toward both assuring nonprofit support for change and the selection of meaningful and appropriate measures of progress. Public managers need to work to ensure that nonprofits buy into outcomes that are chosen, and this means giving them a voice in the development of the contracting system.

2. **Use a small number of milestones and use simple reporting forms.** The Oklahoma experiment demonstrates that the number of milestones should be kept modest if the system is to work efficiently. When milestones become too numerous, the administrative oversight and reporting requirements become acute. By keeping the number of outcomes small and by placing special emphasis on the final outcome sought, public managers can create room for nonprofits to innovate by freeing them from heavy reporting requirements. While the number of appropriate milestones will vary considerably depending on the kind of service being delivered, public managers should err on the side of too few rather than too many milestones.
3. **Shape incentives to avoid creaming.** Worries about client creaming were present in Oklahoma. Rather than dismiss these concerns out of hand, it is useful to confront them directly and to reassure nonprofits that incentives will be established to encourage organizations to continue to tackle the most difficult cases. By paying more money for hard-to-serve cases and by allowing nonprofits to get paid based on the risks they assume, public managers can go a long way toward removing the incentives that some agencies might have to become selective in the clients they serve under a milestone payment system.

Implementation Stage

4. **Help nonprofits make the shift from fee-for-service systems to outcomes.** Shifting away from fee-for-service clearly creates stress for nonprofit organizations. It removes a long-held safety blanket from these organizations and introduces contingencies into their funding. This can be a source of cultural conflict within nonprofits, as long-standing priorities and practices must be revisited in light of changes in the funding environment. To the extent possible, public managers need to be sensitive to these stresses that changes in payment systems can create and to work directly with nonprofit organizations to explain milestone systems and the rationale for moving away from fee-for-service systems. Demonstrating that milestones have the potential to both reduce paper-

work and increase programmatic freedom may go a long way to ease nonprofits' concerns.

5. **Be flexible and revisit milestones once a system is in operation.** Flexibility is a virtue in outcome funding. Although milestones allow the state to treat all nonprofits fairly, there is room to accommodate some variation in the system. Public managers need to be ready to accommodate special cases, especially when nonprofits work with special populations or when the system is first being implemented. Once a milestone system is in place, it is important to revisit the selection of milestones to ensure that the right outcomes have been selected. This can be done in consultation with nonprofit organizations after they have had some experience with milestone funding.
6. **Study effective programs and disseminate best practices for achieving outcomes.** Outcome funding is still in its infancy in nonprofit human services. A critical task for public managers is building knowledge about effective performance-based contracting systems. A critical step in this process is documenting and disseminating best practices so that others can learn and the field can continue to develop. Public managers should also be open to the possibility that outcomes may work better in some fields of social service activity than in others. Understanding exactly when, where, and why outcome funding is likely to be most helpful in improving performance needs to be illuminated through experimentation and analysis in the years ahead. Public managers should take a lead role in this work.

By breaking down some traditional boundaries and by challenging long-standing operating principles, public and nonprofit managers can work together to deliver effective programs. The Milestone system in Oklahoma represents a potent tool for advancing the shared interests of public and nonprofit sectors. By holding nonprofits accountable for producing results and by giving nonprofits substantial freedom in the design and implementation of interventions, Oklahoma has gone a long way toward defining a model that others can apply and develop even further.

Endnotes

1. Sheltered workshop environments do not count toward the final payment. Group placements count for partial payment. To receive the full payment, they must place the person in an integrated, competitive job in the community.

2. The term "competition" overstates the practice somewhat, because, in some parts of the state, especially rural areas, there may be only one nonprofit to choose from, and thus there isn't any real competition. Those nonprofits' bids are evaluated using averages and qualitative factors.

3. Client and employer satisfaction are verified using formal surveys that must be filled out before the final milestone is paid.

4. O'Brien and Cook discussed adding more levels—an Australian program that is modeled after Milestones has more levels of payments—but felt that the only thing they would really gain was more complexity.

5. It's worth noting that this is a problem not just of Milestones but also of all contract-based programs.

Bibliography

Baker, G. P. 1992. "Incentive Contracts and Performance Measurement." *Journal of Political Economy* 100: 598-614.

Barnow, B.S. 2000. "Exploring the Relationship Between Performance Management and Program Impact: A Case Study of the Job Training Partnership Act." *Journal of Policy Analysis and Management* 19: 118-141.

Beer, M., B. Spector, P.R. Lawrence, D.Q. Mills, and R.E.Walton. 1984. *Managing Human Assets*. New York: Free Press.

Behn, R.D. and P.A. Kant. 1999. "Strategies for Avoiding the Pitfalls of Performance Contracting." *Public Productivity and Management Review* 22: 470-489.

Billis, D. 1989. "A Theory of the Voluntary Sector," Working Paper 5. Centre for Voluntary Organization, London School of Economics, London.

Blacksell, S. and D. Phillips. 1994. *Paid to Volunteer: The Extent of Paying Volunteers in the 1990s*. London: The Volunteer Centre, UK.

Boris, E.T., and C. E. Steuerle, eds. 1999. *Nonprofits & Government: Collaboration and Conflict*. Washington, D.C.: The Urban Institute Press.

Brody, E. 1998. "Of Sovereignty and Subsidy: Conceptualizing the Charity Tax Exemption." *The Journal of Corporation Law* 23: 586-629.

Brooks, A.C. 2000. "The Use and Misuse of Adjusted Performance Measures." *Journal of Policy Analysis and Management* 19: 323-334.

Brower, R.S., M.Y. Abolafia, and J.B. Carr. 2000. "On Improving Qualitative Methods in Public Administration Research." *Administration & Society* 32: 363-397.

Buckmaster, N. 1999. "Associations Between Outcome Measurement, Accountability, and Learning for Non-Profit Organizations." *The International Journal of Public Sector Management* 12: 186-197.

Cline, K. D. 2000. "Defining the Implementation Problem: Organizational Management Versus Cooperation." *Journal of Public Administration Research and Theory* 10: 551-571.

Cohen, S. and W. Eimicke. 1998. *Tools for Innovators: Creative Strategies for Managing Public Sector Organizations*. San Francisco: Jossey-Bass Publishers.

DeHoog, R. H. 1984. *Contracting Out for Human Services: Economic, Political, and Organizational Perspectives*. Albany: SUNY.

DiMaggio, P. 1988. "Non-profit Managers in Different Fields of Service: Managerial Tasks and Management Training." In *Educating Managers of Nonprofit Organizations*, eds. O'Neill, M. and D. Young, 51-69. New York: Praeger.

Drucker, P. F. 1990. *Managing the Nonprofit Organization*. London: Butterworth Heinemann.

Drucker, P. F. 1992. *Managing the Nonprofit Organization: Principles and Practices*. New York: Harper.

Frumkin, P. and A. Andre-Clark. 2000. "When Missions, Markets, and Politics Collide: Values and Strategy in the Nonprofit Human Services." *Nonprofit and Voluntary Sector Quarterly* 29: 141-163.

Gibbons, R. 1998. "Incentives in Organizations." *Journal of Economic Perspectives* 12: 115-132.

Gooden, V. 1998. "Contracting and Negotiation: Effective Practices of Successful Human Service Contract Managers." *Public Administration Review* 58: 499-509.

Government Performance and Results Act of 1993 (US), Pub. Lno. 103/62, 107 Stat. 285.

Hamner, W. C. 1975. "How To Ruin Motivation with Pay." *Compensation Review*. 3:17-27.

Herman, R. and R. Heimovics. 1994. "Cross National Study of a Method for Researching Nonprofit Organizational Effectiveness." *Voluntas* 5: 59-85.

Jennings Jr., E. T. 2000. "Welfare Reform at the Millennium: Personal Responsibility, Race, Paternalism, and the Quest for Solutions." *American Review of Public Administration* 30: 334.

Kanter, M.K. 1979. "The Measurement of Organizational Effectiveness Productivity, Performance and Success," Program on Nonprofit Organizations, Yale University.

Kearns, K. P. *Managing for Accountability: Preserving the Public Trust in Public and Nonprofit Organizations*. 1996. San Francisco: Jossey-Bass Publishers.

Lawler III, E. E. 1971. *Pay and Organizational Effectiveness: A Psychological View*. New York: McGraw-Hill.

_____. 1990. *Strategic Pay: Aligning Organizations and Pay Systems*. San Francisco: Jossey Bass Publishers.

Light, P. 2000. *Making Nonprofits Work*. Washington, D.C.: Brookings Institution.

Lu, M.S. 1999. "Separating the True Effect from Gaming in Incentive-Based Contracts in Health Care." *Journal of Economics & Management Strategy* 8: 383-431.

Milofsky, C. 1988. *Community Organizations: Studies in Resource Mobilisation and Exchange*. New York: Oxford University Press.

Murray, V. and B. Tassie. 1994. "Evaluating the Effectiveness of Non-Profit Organizations." In Herman R.D. (Eds), *The Jossey-Bass Handbook of Non-profit Leadership and Management*. San Francisco: Jossey-Bass.

Osborne, D. and T. Gaebler. 1992. *Reinventing Government: How The Entrepreneurial Spirit Is Transforming The Public Sector*. New York: Penguin Group.

Osborne, S.P. 1994. *The Role of Voluntary Organizations in Innovations in Social Welfare Services*, Joseph Rowntree Foundation Findings No. 46.

Osborne, S. and M. Tricker. 1995. "Researching Nonprofit Organizational Effectiveness: A Comment on Herman and Heimovics." *Voluntas* 6: 85-92.

Pavetti, L., K. Olson, D. Nightingale, A. Duke, and J. Isaacs.1997. *Welfare-to-Work Options for Families Facing Personal and Family Challenges*. Washington, D.C.: Urban Institute.

Rosegrant, S. "Oklahoma's Milestones Reimbursement System: Paying for What You Get." Harvard University, Kennedy School of Government, Case Program, Case C14-98-1477.0.

Salipante, P. 1995. "Managing Traditionality and Strategic Change in Nonprofit Organizations." *Nonprofit Management and Leadership* 6: 3-19.

Smith, S. R. and M. Lipsky. 1993. *Nonprofits For Hire: The Welfare State in the Age of Contracting*. Cambridge: Harvard University Press.

Stone, M. and S. Gershenfield. 1996. Challenges of Measuring Performance in Non-Profit Organizations, Independent Sector Conference, 5-6 September, Washington, D.C.

Thompson, J. and W. McEwan. 1958. "Organizational Goals and Environment." *American Sociological Review* 23: 23-31.

United Way of America. 1995. *Measuring Program Outcomes: A Practical Guide*, United Way of America, Washington, D.C.

Volkmann, R. 1999. "Outcomes Measurement: The New Accounting Standard for Service Organizations." *Fundraising Management* 30: 26-27.

Williams, H. S., A.Y. Webb, and W. J. Phillips. 1991. *Outcome Funding*. New York: The Rensselaerville Institute.

Zak Figura, S., 1999. "Progress Slow But Sure." *Government Executive* 31: 37-40.

Appendix I: Goodwill of Tulsa

When MPS first came on the horizon in the early 1990s, Goodwill was worried that it would alter their ability to provide high-quality services to the clients they had traditionally served. David Oliver, Goodwill's executive director, remembers wondering, "Will we really still be able to perform service in a similar manner... if it is purely outcome based?" Cindy Donathan, who directs Goodwill's Career Develop-ment Center, comments, "There was a lot of concern in our group about how we can continue to serve the people that we're supposed to be serving and also meet these Milestones' requirements." While they had considerable input with the agency while MPS was in the design process, they were nevertheless on pins and needles, wondering which of their suggestions would be taken and which would be ignored. In particular, they were worried that the additional money that was promised for working with "highly challenged" clients would not end up being enough to make it worth the risk.

In January of 1997, they finally switched over to MPS, and the results were surprising. In the first year under MPS, while the size of their contract remained the same, they found that they were able to place twice as many people as they had in any previous year. This meant, financially speaking, that they did much better—not worse, as had been feared—than they had ever before. Oliver says, "The most surprising thing to me about MPS was that we started out ... billing more per month than we had under the old contract. And that amount stayed relatively stable." The keys to success were that (1) they reorganized their management structure to clarify everyone's roles and to be more responsive to the employers, and (2) they spent a considerable amount of time retraining their job coaches to be more client- and outcome-focused.

Speaking to the ways that their management style changed, Oliver suggests, "It caused us to operate more like a business.... If we didn't sharpen our thinking, then we weren't going to have any revenue with which to pay our job coaches." Cheryl Slaton, who manages Goodwill's Supported Employment program, explains what this entailed: "I went through a lot of stuff in terms of just building organizational skills, re-programming the way we were going to think, and reorganizing how caseloads ran, how billings ran, getting things set up.... We found additional people that would fit into place." One crucial decision they made regarding the management structure was taking marketing—identifying potential jobs in the community—out of the hands of the job coaches and putting it in the hands of a marketing specialist—in Goodwill's case, the program manager. Most of the job coaches had social work backgrounds and thus were, for the most part, inept at marketing. This made life easier for the employers—their customers—who prefer not to hear from multiple contacts at the same agency.

Most importantly, these changes helped the job coaches clarify their role so that they could focus on what is important for them—being a good job coach. In the process of retraining the job coaches, they found that some of them weren't up to the task and replaced them with job coaches with more experience. Asked about how MPS has changed the way job coaches work, Slaton comments, "I don't know if I'd call it pressure. But there's definitely encouragement to make those placements work and to really focus on the right job match. We think about the individual, what are their needs, what is their way to get to and from work, what are their limitations on the job. And then we market specifically for that person."

Sharon Brice, a job coach, feels there was much more pressure under fee-for-service: "If you're focusing on showing output every minute of your day, it binds you up." In contrast, she found that she had much more freedom under MPS. Slaton concurs. When asked what she likes best about MPS, she says, "If I had to label something, it would probably be the freedom that the job coaches have, because it enables them to really make their own decisions as to what's best for the client rather than what's best to get the billings up.... They like it much better."

It has been alleged by some nonprofits that Goodwill has been so successful because it doesn't accept the most difficult clients. Slaton herself comments, "If we don't believe that this [client] is somebody that we can help to be successful, and help to be independent—and we don't want to set anybody up to fail—if we don't believe we can get them to be independent, we can't take them in the first place." But she denies that creaming is going on. "The only people I wouldn't take are the people that ... wouldn't meet the qualifications of the program. If they can't be independent on the job, then they need to be in a different program...."

The bottom line seems to be that Goodwill has excelled under MPS. The administrative details are important, but the crucial difference is that they spend more time working with and getting to know clients. Slaton observes that MPS has allowed them "to help people overcome barriers to employment, to give them a chance, and not only to be successful, but to give them a chance to fail. Why should they be in the workshop all of their life if they can do other things? They need to have a chance to decide if they like working in the outside world, and if they can do it."

Appendix II: A Conversation with Dan O'Brien, Program Field Representative, Oklahoma Department of Rehabilitation Services

Given your experience, what do you think is the ideal number of milestones?

I firmly believe that the number of milestones needs to be kept to less than 10. If you have too many milestones, at some point you have diminishing returns because the system becomes too complex without yielding significant benefits. Having said that, some states use three milestones, and I think three is too few. A small number of milestones means that the state agency is not accepting enough risk. The number and weighting of the milestones determines the amount of risk each party is willing to accept. It represents the risk sharing agreement between the funder and the service provider. Part of the value of this system is the acceptance of risk by the nonprofit as well as the state. Traditionally, the state has carried all the risk; some outcome-based systems reverse this and shortsightedly ask the vendor to carry all the risk. Either risk-dumping approach is a mistake, creating perverse incentives leading to unintended consequences. It is our belief that an equitable method of risk sharing is the right balance. This acceptance of risk makes the vendor, usually a nonprofit, more accountable, reducing the need for oversight and micromanagement by the funder. The service providers become more serious about creating the outcomes sought by the customers that are represented in the milestones. Usually, six to seven milestones represents an equitable risk sharing arrangement, a win-win situation.

Have any other agencies adopted the Milestone Payment System?

About 15 to 20 other states including Massachusetts, Texas, and New York are using the Milestone Payment System. The Human Resources administration in New York City uses this system with their welfare-to-work recipients. They are very successful, especially given that they are working on a much larger scale. They work with about 30,000 people every year whereas we work with about 1,000.

Have you tracked the progress of any nonprofits that have dropped out of the system?

So far, only a couple of nonprofits have dropped out. Generally speaking, the nonprofits that drop out are the organizations that do not want to do what we want them to do. For example, one nonprofit we used to work with ran a sheltered workshop. Their main goal was to keep clients in their workshop and not to encourage individuals to seek outside employment. It was only the rare occasion where this organization would place someone in a work situation outside of their workshop. This same nonprofit previously received $68,000 for one person who went to work for six months. With MPS, the most amount of money a nonprofit would receive for this person was $6,500. Using MPS was not a lucrative thing for them, so they left. This particular organization had distinct philosophical differences with our system.

Did you find that your concerns about creaming were ill founded?

When we created the Milestone Payment System, we built in two measures that effectively negated any tendency towards creaming. One of the countermeasures we incorporated was the increased rate of payment we gave vendors for taking on more difficult cases. We paid nonprofits 30 percent more for taking on clients that met the severe-needs criteria. The second measure we used was the bidding process, a process that used a stochastic probability model. This model is used to calculate the likely risk picture a nonprofit will face for the next three years. With this model, we built in payment for the amount of risk nonprofits figured they expected to face. We tried to make the risk more manageable so that nonprofits were not forced to cream.

Has any nonprofit you've worked with made outstanding progress?

The best success story belongs to Goodwill of Tulsa. When this organization switched from the traditional fee-for-service system to the MPS system, they made an incredible amount of progress. Goodwill related to me that before MPS, progress was measured by simply putting people in jobs until clients did not fail. More money was made this way. When Goodwill made the switch to MPS, they started asking clients what they actually wanted to be doing, what they wanted to get up and do every morning. This shift made a big difference in the quality of work experience for the customer.

Have you had any major disappointments?

Presenting MPS as a collaborative approach has been challenging. It is difficult to get across to individuals that work within the state government that MPS needs to be approached with a collaborative mind-set. I try to get people's attention by saying they have a choice between using the Soviet model of "command and control" or by using a business approach. In general, these individuals are used to dictating based on their concept of what was needed and not by what was needed by the market.

If you could make any changes to Milestone, what would they be?

Currently, we are in the process of creating a more fulsome array of incentives for quality results for customers. The incentives we are creating demonstrate how we are moving to a place where we are improving and adding to the definition of our product, the customer.

One of the incentives we are creating is providing incentive payments for service providers, mainly nonprofits that find career jobs with benefits for customers. Unfortunately, not all of the jobs nonprofits find include medical insurance or other benefits. By "incentivizing" better jobs, we are encouraging nonprofits to become more invested in the long-term progress of their customers.

Another incentive we aim to create is a voucher for customers. This voucher would go to customers and allow them to select a service agency of their own accord. We envision this voucher becoming a tool of empowerment for customers. The voucher will encourage customers to take a more proactive role in their overall experience. This selection process will force them to think harder about the type of employment opportunity they want. Along with the voucher, we are developing a report card. The report card would be developed by an independent evaluation contractor and given to the customer so that the customers can decide which service provider to spend their voucher with. We believe that empowering the customer with the choice will create competitive forces that will improve service quality.

Appendix III: List of Interviewees

Vera Cheek
Project Director, Francis Tuttle Vo-Tech Center, Oklahoma City, Oklahoma

Rebecca Cook
Program Field Representative, Department of Rehabilitation Services, Oklahoma

Teri Egner
Technical Assistant, Department of Rehabilitation Services, Oklahoma

Mary Howell
Technical Assistant, Department of Rehabilitation Services, Oklahoma

Dan O'Brien
Program Field Representative, Department of Rehabilitation Services, Oklahoma

Linda Shipley
Project Director, Community Development Support Association, Enid, Oklahoma

Vionette Torres-Miles
Director of Employment Services, Northcare Mental Health Center, Oklahoma City, Oklahoma

Brian Wadell
Chief Executive Officer, Employment Resources, Inc., Tulsa, Oklahoma

Lydia Zachary
Jim Taliaferro Community Mental Health Center, Lawton, Oklahoma

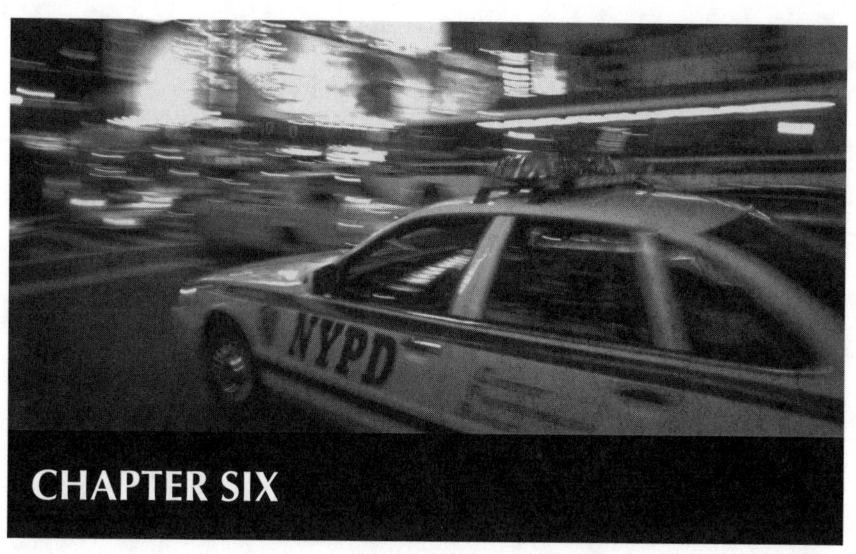

CHAPTER SIX

Using Performance Data for Accountability: The New York City Police Department's CompStat Model of Police Management

Paul E. O'Connell
Associate Professor
Department of Criminal Justice
Iona College

The New York City Police Department's CompStat Program

In 1994, the New York City Police Department (NYPD) began a carefully planned and well-executed redesign of its entire organizational structure. Under the leadership of Commissioner William Bratton, and with the backing of Mayor Rudolph Giuliani, the department employed a variety of corporate strategies designed to reengineer its business processes and create a "flatter" organizational structure based on geographic decentralization, teamwork, information sharing, and managerial accountability (Bratton, 1998). This rapid redesign of the department's organizational architecture was based upon the concept of continuous improvement of performance (benchmarking and the sharing of best practices) and the ability to manage and control change. In other words, the department was seeking to institutionalize the organizational learning process.

As a result of strategic policing initiatives, the overall rate of reported violent crime in New York City declined dramatically and far outpaced reported crime drops across the nation. From 1993 to 1998, New York City experienced a precipitous drop in the burglary rate (53 percent), a 54 percent drop in reported robberies, and an incredible 67 percent drop in the murder rate (Silverman, 1999). These extraordinary achievements were realized in large part due to the department's innovative model of police management, known as CompStat.

A Shift in Organizational Mind-set

Historically, the NYPD, like most police organizations, was addicted to formal rules and procedures and subject to an occupational culture that had proven itself to be particularly resistant to change. It was characterized by strict hierarchical structures, organizational rigidity, and a culture that was generally unreceptive to change (Silverman, 1999). Such organizational constraints are common within police organizations. As Maurice Punch explains:

> There is an overwhelming preference for regulatory supervision in policing—it is a natural and unavoidable consequence of some deeply ingrained assumptions regarding the nature of police work that are shared by the overwhelming majority of people inside and outside the police establishment (1983).

In accordance with classic bureaucratic structure, the overall orientation of managers within the department was downward rather than outward (toward the external environment) or upward. Precinct commanders "did not see crime reduction as their foremost responsibility" and were "essentially on their own in combating crime" (Silverman, 1999, p. 98). Commissioner Bratton quickly altered this mind-set by redefining the department's overall purpose and mission.

An emphasis was placed upon the realignment of organizational resources. An ambitious reengineering effort shifted the department from being a centralized, functional organization to a decentralized, geographic organization. A number of centralized, functional units were broken up, with their functions (and personnel) redistributed to new geographically decentralized units (precincts). Functional specialists were placed under the command of newly defined geographic managers, thereby moving decision making down the organizational hierarchy. This resulted in greater empowerment and participation in decision making, and more open, less hierarchical communications within the organization. The "information silos" through which managers had been able to hoard information and thereby suboptimize organizational performance were dismantled.

Bratton clearly described the direction in which he intended to move the organization, and highlighted with specificity the more particular pieces of managerial work that were strategically most important to achieve. To accomplish these goals, a variety of proactive crime-reduction strategies were developed and utilized. The instrument used to implement and monitor these strategies is known as CompStat.

CompStat

Upon taking office, Bratton immediately shocked his subordinates by establishing new, exacting standards of operational performance. He and his top aides recognized that data needed to be gathered and analyzed in a timely manner if effective crime-reduction strategies were to be implemented. Therefore, periodic meetings were scheduled at headquarters whereby precinct commanders were required to report and react to crime data generated from their areas of responsibility (i.e., their commands). Over time, these data-based informal discussions between department executives and field commanders developed into formal twice-weekly strategy meetings (known as CompStat meetings) whereby *all* levels of the department participate to identify precinct and citywide crime trends, deploy resources, and assess crime control strategies.

Bratton has credited CompStat with moving the department "from a micro-managed organization with very little strategic direction to a decentralized management style with strong strategic guidance at the top" (Bratton, 1995). New York City Mayor Rudolph Giuliani has praised CompStat's many

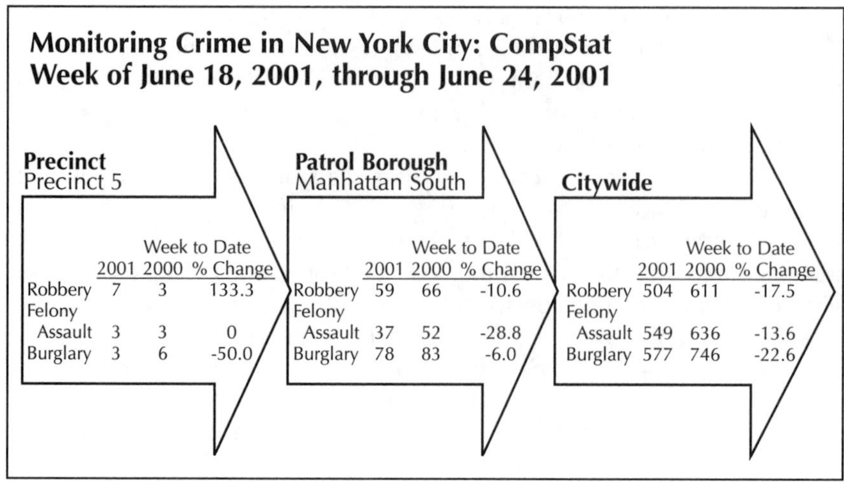

accomplishments, stating that it stands as one of the highlights of his administration that has contributed to the development of a "new urban paradigm" (Giuliani, 1999). By utilizing a system of internal benchmarking and the open transfer of best practices, CompStat has transformed the department into a learning organization that can "analyze, reflect, learn, and change based on experience" (O'Dell and Grayson, 1998).

Monitoring Crime in New York City: CompStat
Week of June 18, 2001, through June 24, 2001
Precinct
Precinct 5
Week to Date
2001 2000 % Change
Robbery 7 3 133.3
Felony
Assault 3 3 0
Burglary 3 6 -50.0
Patrol Borough
Manhattan South
Week to Date
2001 2000 % Change
Robbery 59 66 -10.6
Felony
Assault 37 52 -28.8
Burglary 78 83 -6.0
Citywide
Week to Date
2001 2000 % Change
Robbery 504 611 -17.5
Felony
Assault 549 636 -13.6
Burglary 577 746 -22.6

Today, CompStat has become synonymous with a more effective and proactive style of public management. Visitors from around the world travel to New York to participate in CompStat conferences or to sit in on the department's regularly scheduled CompStat meetings (Gootman, "A Police Department's Growing Allure: Crime Fighters From Around World Visit for Tips," *The New York Times*, October 24, 2000). CompStat has proliferated widely and has been replicated in a variety of public service venues. It has been reproduced in whole or in part by police agencies in the following jurisdictions: Abilene, Texas; Baltimore, Maryland; Charlotte, North Carolina; Durham, North Carolina; Indianapolis, Indiana; Los Angeles County, California; Mount Vernon, New York; New Orleans, Louisiana; New Rochelle, New York; Newark, New Jersey; Philadelphia, Pennsylvania; and Prince George's County, Maryland.

Perhaps most interestingly, the CompStat management model has now transcended the field of policing, and has been successfully implemented in a variety of other public sector organizations, such as New York City's Department of Correction (TEAMS), Department of Parks and Recreation ("ParkStat"), Traffic Division ("Trafficstat"), and Human Resources Administration ("JobStat") ("JobStat Works for Welfare," *Daily News*, October 4, 1999. p. 34). The city of Baltimore is presently using "CitiStat" to monitor many of its largest departments and agencies.

Mayor Rudolph Giuliani on CompStat

The CompStat program is … [a] program that has had a big impact on the level of crime. I used to be the associate attorney general. I was in charge of dissemination of national crime statistics. So, I've been involved in crime numbers for 20 years. And it seemed to me that we were doing something wrong in the way in which we measured police success. We were equating success with how many arrests were made. A police officer was regarded as a productive police officer if he made a lot of arrests. He would get promoted. A police commander in a precinct would be regarded as a really good police commander if his arrests were up this year. This wasn't the only measure of success, but it was the predominant one.

Arrests, however, are not the ultimate goal of police departments or what the public really wants from a police department. What the public wants from a police department is less crime. So it seemed to me that if we put our focus on crime reduction and measured it as clearly as we possibly could, everybody would start thinking about how we could reduce crime. And as a result, we started getting better solutions from precinct commanders.

We have 77 police precincts. Every single night they record all of the index crimes that have occurred in that precinct and a lot of other data. We record the number of civilian complaints. We record the number of arrests that are made for serious crimes and less serious crimes. It's all a part of CompStat, a computer-driven program that helps ensure executive accountability. And the purpose of it is to see if crime is up or down, not just citywide, but neighborhood by neighborhood. And if crime is going up, it lets you do something about it now—not a year and a half from now when the FBI puts out crime statistics. After all, when you find out that burglary went up last year, there's nothing a mayor can do about it because time has passed and the ripple of criminal activity has already become a crime wave.

Now we know about it today. And we can make strategic decisions accordingly. If auto theft is up in some parts of the city and down in others, then we can ask why. And that will drive decisions about the allocation of police officers, about the kinds of police officers.

This is one of the reasons why New York City has now become city #160 on the FBI's list for crime. Which is kind of astounding for the city that is the largest city in America. Think about the other 159 cities: Many of them have populations that are 300,000, 400,000, 500,000. And on a per capita basis, some of them have considerably more crime.

CompStat is an excellent system, but at the core of it is the principle of accountability. Holding the people who run the precincts accountable for achieving what the public wants them to do, which is to reduce crime.

(From "Rudolph W. Giuliani on Restoring Accountability to City Government," The Business of Government, *Summer 2000.)*

Public managers and academics alike have recognized CompStat's utility as a public management device. In 1996, CompStat was awarded the prestigious Innovations in American Government Award from the Ford Foundation and the John F. Kennedy School of Government at Harvard University.

The Essential Features of CompStat

The meeting: The term "CompStat," in its simplest form, generally refers to the strategic planning meetings that have been taking place within the NYPD every two weeks since early 1994. Precinct commanders are now regularly summoned to headquarters to respond to pointed questions posed by senior administrators about concrete operational issues that arise in the field. They stand at a podium facing a large dais, and engage in lively dialogue with individuals occupying the uppermost echelons of the organization. Large projection screens display real time data obtained from sophisticated geographic information system (GIS) software. These data relate to crime complaints, arrests, trends, and patterns. They enable all participants to "work off the same page" when reviewing organizational performance, allocating resources, and forecasting and reacting to a changing organizational environment. The CompStat Unit is chiefly responsible for gathering information from the field, analyzing it, and disseminating it back to field commanders and senior administrators so that it can be *used* effectively.

At first glance, one might be tempted to characterize these meetings as mere "staff meetings." Such a description would not only be inaccurate, but also would obscure one of the most significant features of the process. At CompStat meetings, *all levels of the organizational chart* are represented and actively participate. This is a significant distinction.

Drawing an example from the field of health care, one would properly characterize a meeting between a chief of surgery and the surgeons under his/her supervision as a "staff meeting." In other words, individuals with the same general job description and responsibilities would meet periodically to review their group's performance and to discuss issues of concern to them. By contrast, CompStat would call for physicians from *all* medical services (pediatrics, emergency medicine, etc.) to periodically meet with representatives from the nursing department, housekeeping, maintenance, security, and others, to address common issues, goals, and challenges that face the entire organization. In other words, a more comprehensive meeting would be necessary to view overall performance from the perspective of the larger organization, and to ensure open lines of communication and coordination of effort. During such meetings the hospital would in effect be talking to itself, thinking out loud, weighing options, and monitoring the overall performance of the entire organization. CompStat forces the organization to engage in a productive form of self-reflection that enables it to discern environmental changes and to react accordingly. In sum, CompStat provides a holistic approach to administration.

The NYPD has clearly benefited from the collaborative nature of these meetings. Today, if a discussion between a chief and a precinct commander happens to touch upon a legal issue, representatives from the department's Legal Bureau are present and available to participate and provide guidance and expertise. Similarly, if a problem relates to the department's information technology system, individuals with appropriate expertise are available at each meeting to narrow the issues, clarify them, and possibly rectify the condition.

CompStat has opened existing lines of communication within the organization but, perhaps more importantly, has also created new ones. People familiar with the hierarchical and bureaucratic nature of the department prior to CompStat were astounded in 1994 to see the chief of patrol (an administrator who is literally situated at the pinnacle of the organizational chart) engaging in lively and in-depth conversations with precinct anti-crime sergeants or detective squad commanders (individuals who rarely had direct access to upper-level managers at headquarters). Operational questions and concerns that typically required a flurry of memos from the field to headquarters, and back again, could now be addressed immediately via candid discussions between those at the top and bottom of the organizational chart.

CompStat has quite simply resulted in *more* communication taking place within the organization. While the NYPD formerly had many official reporting requirements and mandated notifications, these communications were typically the equivalent of a series of one-way streets running parallel to one another. Today, thanks to the CompStat meetings, these communication channels have been converted to two-way streets—broad two-way highways with several lanes of traffic running in many different directions at the same time.

The process: CompStat meetings are in fact the final stage of a detailed and collaborative process of data gathering and analysis. The "stat" process is predicated upon the gathering and intelligent use of timely and accurate information (see, generally, Maple, 1999). CompStat meetings would be virtually useless without a mechanism for assembling real-time data and an adaptive structure for data interpretation, strategic decision making, and prompt action. The CompStat model includes each of these features.

The NYPD's CompStat Unit is chiefly responsible for assembling and analyzing necessary data. It incorporates a sophisticated process of oversight, auditing, and inspections to ensure the accuracy of information that is generated and input from field commands. In an elaborate system of internal checks and balances, the department also requires a variety of other units

Monitoring Crime in New York City: CompStat
The Year 2001 (through June 24, 2001)

	Year to Date			2 Year	8 Year
Crime Complaints	**2001**	**2000**	**% Chg**	**% Chg**	**% Chg**
Murder	289	335	-13.7	-11.0	-67.6
Rape	934	986	-5.2	-7.1	-40.0
Robbery	12,547	14,890	-15.7	-23.5	-68.3
Felony Assault	10,951	11,950	-8.3	-11.0	-42.5
Burglary	14,572	17,661	-17.4	-26.4	-68.9
Grand Larceny	21,202	21,713	-2.3	-8.1	-45.7
G.L.A.	13,459	16,512	-18.4	-26.2	-74.8
TOTAL	**73,954**	**84,047**	**-12.01**	**-18.88**	**-63.17**

to conduct random inspections and audits of this information, as well as of the means by which it is obtained and compiled. The precincts themselves must also continually perform self-audits, in what sometimes appears to be a neurotic obsession with accuracy. This meticulous attention to detail is required, however, to allow senior administrators to *rely* on the information obtained. It allows them to view the relative progress of each of the component parts of the organization, which, in turn, provides them with an accurate and immediate assessment of the overall health of the organization.

Perhaps the most significant feature of CompStat is the fact that information is not just meticulously compiled, it is *used*. It is openly shared for the express purpose of collaboration and the development of effective new strategies. By analyzing the relative performance of each operational unit, upper-level managers can determine, relatively promptly and accurately, whether or not a planned course of action is succeeding. It informs their efforts with regard to strategic planning and problem solving and provides them with a direct and effective means of setting and communicating organizational goals, and then monitoring and evaluating performance vis-à-vis those objectives.

CompStat is therefore far more than an efficient performance monitoring system. It is a knowledge management device that enables the agency's chief decision makers to tap into and use the intellectual capital of the entire organization. This includes not only what is expressly known by the organization and its key administrators ("explicit" knowledge), but also what is known and understood intuitively or instinctually by the individuals who actually perform the work (Cook and Brown, 1999). CompStat is the perfect mechanism for the identification and harnessing of individual competencies, successful practices, skills, and routines. It is a particularly effective form of internal benchmarking that enables senior management to identify top performers, to analyze and pinpoint any significant distinctions that contribute to superior performance, and to communicate and/or adapt them to the entire organization.

CompStat also facilitates the transfer of knowledge among sub-units (by the sharing of best practices) and also corrects factors and/or structures that inhibit the transfer of knowledge. CompStat draws together otherwise disconnected groups and facilitates both the vertical and horizontal transfer of knowledge. It also confronts the powerful forces "that oppose productive dialogue and discussion" within the organization (Senge, 1990, p. 237). CompStat encourages teamwork and collaborative responses to problems and challenges.

The CompStat process enables administrators to take a holistic view of the entire organization. It views the organization as an open system and discourages "linear thinking." Rather than merely reacting to what is perceived as simplistic "cause and effect" chains, CompStat encourages administrators to continually search for the interrelationships of events and processes that hinder or facilitate peak performance. Senge (1990) refers to this as "systems thinking." Rather than basing one's managerial decisions on a series of random snapshots or glimpses of the performance of isolated parts, this management approach enables decision makers to keep the "big picture" in focus at all times.

CompStat also serves as a means of managing tension, strain, stress, and conflict within the organization. All organizations experience tension caused by the discrepancy between current reality and the desired state (vision) (see, generally, Fritz, 1996). CompStat enables an organization to *use* this tension to *redirect it* toward desired goals. It entails a continuous process of analysis, action, reevaluation, and adjustment that keeps the organization continually moving forward. Jack Maple, the NYPD official who is credited with creating CompStat, describes four basic principles that form the cornerstone of the CompStat process: accurate and timely intelligence/information; rapid deployment; effective tactics; and relentless follow-up and assessment (Maple, 1999, pp. 32-34). By proceeding in this manner, the organization learns, reacts, and gets smarter each time around.

The philosophy: Perhaps the most significant aspect of CompStat is the fact that it can change the overall orientation of the entire organization. CompStat is not merely a meeting or a process; it is a distinct management philosophy. It is based upon the need for continuous performance improvement and a general dissatisfaction with the status quo. CompStat is founded upon the belief that "things can always be done better."

This philosophical shift was accomplished within the NYPD by the decentralization of decision making and the wide distribution of authority and accountability. CompStat empowered field managers (i.e., precinct commanders) and encouraged them to sense and create opportunities. This sense of entrepreneurialism is quite distinguishable from the philosophies of traditional hierarchies (and of the NYPD in particular), which are often characterized by "timidity and caution on the part of subordinates who fear criticism from superiors and thus fear to pass unpleasant information up the line" (Perrow, 1979, p. 39).

CompStat released the creativity in NYPD managers by promoting innovation and experimentation. By pushing decisions down the organizational chart and distributing power more widely, it encouraged fresh thinking and expanded possibilities. Thinking "outside the box" quickly became the norm. In essence, each field command began to formulate and assess new methods and approaches to routine tasks, as well as unexpected challenges.

Although the overall direction of the organization was still monitored and controlled by senior administrators and policy makers at headquarters, CompStat enabled most "field decisions" to now be made "in the field." Field units began to perform functions that would ordinarily be reserved for a "research and development" section or a "skunkworks" unit. Commanders were encouraged and empowered to "try new things" and to take necessary steps to address the needs and challenges of their particular commands. The innovation, creativity, and experimentation that resulted yielded significant results in the form of rapidly dropping crime rates and enhanced organizational performance.

CompStat enabled the NYPD to manage change, but it also taught the organization to welcome, rather than fear, change. It also served to institutionalize a general dissatisfaction with the status quo and resulted in an organizational philosophy based upon the continuous search for "better," rather than "best," practices.

The Proliferation of the CompStat Model

The New Rochelle Police Department

The City of New Rochelle, New York, is a city of 70,000 that is situated approximately 25 miles north of Manhattan. Its current police commissioner, Patrick Carroll, is a seasoned police administrator who formerly commanded several New York City precincts as a member of the NYPD. When he was hired by New Rochelle in 1993, he continued to maintain many of his professional and personal contacts with the NYPD and its personnel. "I first heard of CompStat in late 1994," he states. "I heard they were holding these meetings and doing some very creative things." He believes he first learned of CompStat through "word of mouth," then began to read about its many accomplishments in the press and in professional publications.

Commissioner Carroll was invited to personally observe a CompStat session, and he attended the NYPD's first CompStat Conference, which was held in Manhattan. He not only brought a number of his staff with him to the conference, but even invited a number of other city commissioners to join them.

His first impressions of CompStat were quite positive. "This was something we all wanted to do, to get everyone on the same page," he recalls. He distinguishes what he observed from his own experiences within the NYPD. "We were held accountable for our commands, but often had little or no control over resources." CompStat struck him as an intelligent and useful approach to police management. He believed that field commanders could be held accountable for their command's performance only if they were provided with adequate resources and a certain degree of moral support.

He quickly decided that he wanted to replicate the CompStat model in his own agency. However, due to the dramatic contrast in overall size of the two agencies, several significant alterations had to be made.

First, since the 186-member police force pales in comparison to the NYPD (which currently has about 40,000 uniformed members of the service), the meetings held by the New Rochelle Police Department take place in a relatively modest conference room and are based upon the comparison of shifts or tours, rather than commands (i.e., precincts). This format lends a more "personal" flavor to the meetings and encourages a considerable amount of interpersonal interaction. The commissioner, who is seated at the head of the table, takes a leading role in these meetings and is intimately aware of virtually all significant issues and concerns of his agency. As with the NYPD, performance data are compiled, analyzed, and displayed on a projection screen. However, what differs most is the "comprehensive" nature of these discussions, the constant references to the "big picture," and the discussion of issues that face the entire organization. All discussions concern the same geographic area (the entire city), which is understood to be the shared responsibility of all individuals in the room. Rather than scrutinizing the operations of two or three precincts at a time in a city of 8 million people, New Rochelle's CompStat meetings always address citywide issues and trends.

Despite these adaptations, the New Rochelle Police Department's version of CompStat remains consistent with the NYPD model. New Rochelle has adopted and incorporated the underlying philosophy of CompStat. This is particularly true with regard to the issue of accountability. In many ways, Commissioner Carroll views this as the linchpin of the entire process:

> We let them [all members of the department] know what it is that we intended to accomplish. We then gave them the resources, showed them how to reach out to one another and how to get together, then monitored their performance and held them accountable for the results.
>
> It got them thinking. We said, "If you're having a problem, you think up the answers. Don't come looking for answers from above. You have the necessary resources. If you don't, come and ask for more."

Commissioner Carroll recalls that this new management philosophy "got them thinking" and facilitated a departmentwide approach to problem solving. The lines of communication were also opened, as tour commanders, patrol officers, and members of detective and specialty units all began to interact more openly with one another. The department also held classes to develop the problem-solving skills of both management and rank-and-file officers. Carroll believes that these efforts opened the door to more creative solutions for pervasive problems, and enabled the department to identify and react to problems more quickly and effectively. CompStat, he notes, can also help to coordinate crime prevention and community affairs efforts.

He explains:

> Say, for example, we notice that we are experiencing a spike in the number of cell phones stolen from autos, and we see that these larcenies seem to mostly occur in commuter parking lots by the train station. We can immediately do something about it, like sending our cops through the lots looking for phones left in cars. We can leave a note telling the owner to be more alert next time, and can actually prevent future problems.

Commissioner Carroll cautions that the information obtained through CompStat must be intelligently used. To do this, he believes that all members of the organization must continually keep the "big picture" in mind. Each CompStat meeting begins with a review of the department's overall goals and ongoing initiatives. This enables all members of the department to understand how all of their specific efforts are interconnected for the purpose of accomplishing several overriding goals (such as improving overall quality of life or reducing the overall rate of reported crime):

> We want everyone to be knowledgeable about all the problems we might have, all the key issues facing the department. From patrol cop, all the way up to the captains, they all need to understand what it is we're trying to do. They might only be officially responsible for one sector, but they need to see why their efforts are so important, if we are to accomplish our goals.

> They should also ask themselves, is there anything else I could do, should we be cooperating with other agencies? Maybe we should be working with the Fire Department or the Department of Buildings, in order to use their code enforcement capabilities to help us do our job. The CompStat philosophy encourages them to use all available resources, to look to other agencies, and even the public. We can then track their progress and share successful strategies with one another.

For CompStat to work, Commissioner Carroll believes that meetings must take place frequently. He feels that this "puts them on notice, it tells them we're going to meet regularly to discuss these issues, and that they'll be challenged...." He feels that CompStat forces his personnel to have a proactive, forward-looking perspective while performing their daily activities. He also believes that CompStat has significantly changed the way his people see themselves. "Today, they see themselves as managers, not just cops."

The New Rochelle experience indicates that the CompStat model can be successfully adapted in smaller police departments. Perhaps the most important lesson learned, however, is that an agency attempting to adopt this mechanism should accept the philosophy as well. Commissioner Carroll believes that the basic philosophy of CompStat is a simple but positive one. "Everything is doable," he states. "No problem is beyond solution. It's not overwhelming if we can just work together."

The New York City Correction Department (TEAMS)

At the same time that CompStat was being developed and implemented within the NYPD, a similar phenomenon was occurring in the New York City Correction Department. While police officials, with the express support of their mayor, were attempting to regain control of New York City streets, officials within the Correction Department were charged with regaining control of the city's jails. In January of 1995, Mayor Rudolph Giuliani appointed Michael Jacobson as commissioner and appointed Bernard Kerik as first deputy commissioner (by late 1997, Kerik took over the Correction Department and is currently serving as commissioner of the New York City Police Department). Both men critically examined the department's most fundamental practices and procedures in an effort to drive down inmate violence, improve employee morale, and enhance productivity in virtually all of the department's operations. They began with an extensive overhaul of the organization's management processes, with an eye toward creating a culture of continuous performance improvement and accountability. Quite naturally, they looked carefully at the CompStat management model and decided to adopt and modify it to meet their agency's own unique requirements. Their version is known today as TEAMS (which stands for Total Efficiency Accountability Management System).

The first TEAMS meetings took place as "division meetings" in May of 1996. These meetings were initially patterned after the CompStat model, insofar as the forum was similar (i.e., field commanders standing at a podium, responding to pointed questions from a dais comprised of the department's highest levels of management). Timely and accurate performance information was assembled, shared, and analyzed at these meetings, so that the department could set goals, act, and react as a cohesive whole. The meetings initially centered around the discussion and examination of 16 primary performance indicators, all of which related directly to the problem of inmate violence. These indicators included total number of slashings and stabbings, use of force by correction officers, overtime and manpower availability, etc.

Curbing inmate violence and reestablishing control of the jail system was the most immediate concern of department officials in 1996. Therefore, most (but not all) of the original indicators reviewed in these meetings related to the issue of violence. According to current Commissioner William Fraser, this was done in recognition of the fact that no proactive steps for improvement could (or should) be undertaken until such time as a safe and secure environment was re-established. Only then would the department be in a position to focus upon more proactive measures. The department's efforts paid off almost immediately. By 1998, departmentwide violence had dropped nearly 80 percent. Performance in a variety of other key areas improved as well during this period.

However, TEAMS was not designed solely as an effective violence reduction mechanism. From its very inception, the TEAMS process maintained an orientation that was considerably broader in focus than CompStat. This stems from the fact that the Correction Department has a particularly unique mission. Not only is the department charged with securing and providing for the physical safety of inmates, it must feed them, house them, transport them, provide medical treatment, etc. Therefore, the range of performance indicators that were monitored through 1996 was broad, and continued to grow rapidly. Today, the TEAMS Unit (the unit charged with assembling and analyzing all performance data) monitors nearly 600 indicators ranging from religious service attendance by inmates to the number of maintenance work orders completed in inmate housing units.

The diversity of information that is now available to and used by department officials is indeed remarkable. As Commissioner Fraser explains:

> I am always struck by the intimacy of knowledge [wardens and their staff] have. Now, when we ask a warden, "You had one serious food service

violation in October, what was it?" they'll give us the details; they have them at their disposal and you can tell they've been thinking about it, talking about it with their people, and working on it.

Today, wardens can talk to us about inmate council meetings, because they have to attend them. They will tell us what the inmates are talking about, how many gangs are in their facility, who the members are, who the leaders are, and which housing area they live in.

Commissioner Fraser credits TEAMS with opening old lines of communication within his department and creating new ones. Rather than waiting for a quarterly or monthly report to indicate a problem in performance, managers can now observe "spikes" of aberrations in their daily numbers and immediately begin asking questions and taking corrective action. The commissioner praises this ability to access real-time data and contrasts it to the time before TEAMS, when headquarters would often only find out about a significant operational problem in the field several days after it had occurred.

Commissioner Fraser also explains that the expansion of the number of indicators has occurred naturally, in response to particular demands:

Often, the presentations themselves would lead to the creation of new indicators, for purposes of explanation and clarification. For example, when [presenting wardens] started to explain their overtime numbers to us, they did so in terms of people who were actually available to them. Due to long-term illness or some other factor, an officer might be carried on the official table of organization as "available" when he or she really is not. We saw the need to differentiate these cases from personnel actually available for assignment, so we created new categories.

Similarly, when we examined the number of searches conducted in our facilities, we saw that some facilities reported very few. When we questioned our personnel, however, we found that "scheduled" searches might have been down a bit, but that the units were conducting a lot of unscheduled searches, or canine searches, instead. It really was just an issue of interpretation, so we began to record theses types of searches as well. Once we broke it down, everybody began to record it the same way. The information actually broke itself down, so that it could be made more understandable.

Unlike CompStat, TEAMS does not rely upon GIS software. This is because the Correction Department needs only to identify locations within its various facilities, and this can be displayed adequately on TEAMS' data spreadsheets. The NYPD, on the other hand, had an obvious need to track criminal incidents across a broader geographic landscape (i.e., precincts and boroughs throughout the entire city). Such capabilities are therefore critical for them, but not for Commissioner Fraser's department.

Like CompStat, the TEAMS meetings are actually the culmination of a very tedious and thorough process of record keeping and analysis. As Commissioner Fraser states, "The accuracy of the numbers is paramount; we always have to ensure the integrity and accuracy of our information." To do so, the department has designed a complicated system of checks and balances—several levels of auditing and inspections ensure that information is being gathered and input properly. At the core of the TEAMS philosophy is a fundamental belief that performance can always be improved.

The TEAMS process continues to evolve. Each month, the department adds, subtracts, or refines indicators as necessary. Recently, a new indicator was designed to track the performance of personnel who had been subjected to the department's new "civility tests." These tests are random inquiries that are made to check the professionalism of personnel who respond to inquiries or civilian complaints. Wardens are now reviewed according to how well their personnel performed on these tests. Important new programs or initiatives can easily be tracked in this manner.

TEAMS is used to reinforce organizational goals and to ensure that managers are in fact working toward them. It allows the highest levels of the organization to interact with wardens and their staffs and to publicly praise or reprimand them. It helps to identify the department's future leaders. To assist newly appointed managers, the department created the "Leadership Institute." This executive development program is designed to provide managers with the requisite skill set and prepare them for their future responsibilities. "Mini" TEAMS meetings are also held for training purposes.

TEAMS performs additional functions. As Commissioner Fraser explains, "In addition to being a management and training tool, it has helped us to document our use of resources and to explain our needs. For example, just recently we knew we were short maintenance staff, but we documented that need. TEAMS helped us to do that. By tracking work orders, we were able to show OMB (the city's Office of Management and Budget) our data and they saw the need. They agreed with us and authorized the hiring of additional maintenance personnel."

Perhaps the most significant contribution of the TEAMS process has been the shift in organizational culture and philosophy that has taken place. Commissioner Fraser believes "... the key is really the way that it assists us in using proactive and creative management. It expands possibilities and gets more people involved in the decision-making process. Our people don't just think of themselves as corrections officers anymore. Now they see themselves as managers."

Commissioner Fraser agrees with Mayor Giuliani that the TEAMS process has now become "institutionalized." He expects the TEAMS process to endure for two very simple reasons: Most of the managers who have been promoted in the past several years are now quite familiar with the system; and, most importantly, the system works. Commissioner Fraser adds, "Anyone who comes into this agency and sits in my chair but doesn't continue this process would be very foolish. As long as they follow this model, we should continue to have considerable success."

The New York City Department of Parks and Recreation (ParkStat)

The New York City Department of Parks and Recreation is currently responsible for the maintenance and operation of 28,287 acres of property within the five boroughs of New York City. Beginning in 1984, the department began to internally monitor its performance by means of the Parks Inspection Program (PIP). From 1984 through 1995, summary reports were produced three times per year and served as the primary mechanism for inspecting and auditing the department's most fundamental functions. In March of 1995, the system was changed to include 24 biweekly reporting periods per year. Today, each two-week "round" will include the review of 162 locations throughout the entire system that are randomly selected for inspection. These locations include ball fields, buildings, walking trails, etc., that are scattered across the city. Results of these on-site inspections are recorded in hand-held computers by inspectors in the field, and are later uploaded on the Operations and Management Planning ("OMP") database upon returning to the office (*Park Inspection Program Manual: Guide to the Parks Inspection Program & Official Inspection Standards*. Operations & Management Planning, City of New York Parks & Recreation, July 11, 2000). These data are analyzed and disseminated to top administrators and field staff for purposes of quality control and planning.

This pre-existing inspection program proved to be a natural fit with the "stat" process, when officials from the department visited the NYPD and personally observed the CompStat process in action. They concluded that CompStat meetings would be a valuable supplement to the PIP program and would enable them to "use" the information gathered in a more intelligent and efficient way. According to Derek Lombard, former director of OMP, "It was a natural fit. We wanted to supplement it, make it work better." Several "modifications" were made initially, but as Lombard describes, "it evolved on its own. We adopted CompStat's core design but modified it to our own purposes."

The first ParkStat meeting was held in March of 1997. At that time, only one district presented. By July of 1997, two districts attended each meeting and were required to discuss the results of their inspections and work with senior administrators to enhance performance.

Today, the department's upper management—represented by the director of OMP and the director of Field Operations—meet with District Maintenance and Operations (M&O) supervisors from the field to review their performance as reflected in their district's current "park ratings." Meetings are designed to focus analytical attention on what is occurring in the field (i.e., within the city's many public parks). ParkStat meetings are held each month and typically involve two districts (from two different boroughs). An effort is made to balance the number of times boroughs are called into ParkStat meetings (in other words, there is an informal rotation system in place to prevent one particular borough from being called in repeatedly). Initially, specific districts were invited to ParkStat meetings if their ratings were considered to be poor. Today, the system is designed so that every district cycles through the system. Year-to-date ratings are used to select districts for these meetings, and districts are typically informed of their selection three weeks in advance.

Districts are represented by their chief of operations, manager, PPS, and PSs. Junior-level personnel also attend, as necessary. Districts are brought in no more frequently than once every six months, and usually no more than once a year. Meetings take place at 7:30 a.m. in the Arsenal Building in Central Park, Manhattan. (*ParkStat*. City of New York/Parks & Recreation, Operations & Management Planning, July 3, 2000.)

Meetings typically last two hours, with approximately one hour devoted to each district. Data are displayed on a projection screen and form the basis of all discussion. Photographs of "unacceptable conditions" are also displayed (as PowerPoint presentations) and discussed. Photographs are taken as part of the routine inspections process. The discussions chiefly revolve around why these problems are occurring and what, if any, corrective actions may be taken. A chief concern is to correct localized problems before they can evolve into boroughwide, or citywide trends.

Presenters and their support staffs sit along one side of a large table, while the operations coordinator, the director of OMP, and a technical operator sit opposite them. Spreadsheets display specific ratings in the areas of overall condition and cleanliness of structural features such as benches, fences, sidewalks, play equipment, and landscape features such as trees, athletic fields, and water bodies. After the first district has completed its presentation and responded to all questions, there is a brief break. The second district then presents as the first one observes. At the conclusion of the second meeting, representatives from both districts are provided time to question one another.

Each meeting begins with a brief introduction of all individuals in attendance and a review of the overall purpose of ParkStat. At the beginning of one recent meeting, the director of OMP stated, "This serves as a good opportunity to review information and look for trends that have led to declines in performance." She indicated that the meeting was designed to "lend constructive conversation" and to "foster innovation."

There is a wrap-up period at the conclusion of each meeting. Follow-up memos are later forwarded to the districts concerning issues that arose during the meetings. Managers are given about 30 days to respond to these memos. The ParkStat team meets after each meeting to review the session, decide upon follow-up issues for the districts, and critique the process (i.e., the relative effectiveness of each session).

Specific discussions are "scripted" to the extent that specific questions are designed well in advance of each meeting and are often communicated in advance to presenting districts. This is done to ensure that presenters appear with intelligent explanations for their performance and are able to fully participate in all discussions (i.e., there should be very few real surprises at these meetings). The director of OMP and the operations coordinator typically lead the discussions, focusing on operational innovations and management strategies. Despite the "scripting," much spontaneous interaction takes place as a thoughtful and candid dialogue ensues. The director of OMP began one meeting by asking one district, "What do you think are your most problematic features?"

As with CompStat and TEAMS, an emphasis is placed upon pattern or trend identification. All performance data are viewed through three lenses, which look for districtwide trends, boroughwide comparisons and trends, and citywide comparisons and trends. The use of histograms (bar graphs) is extremely helpful in this regard. The department is currently working toward implementing a GIS mapping system to track performance even more carefully. These techniques help to visualize performance and to identify significant facts that could otherwise be missed by simply slogging through long sheets of statistics.

Once variations (increases or decreases) in performance are noted, they must be understood and explained. A threshold question seems to be, "Is this variation significant?" A secondary but nonetheless necessary question is, "What is causing it?" Once the answers to these questions are obtained, corrective action or steps to maintain positive trends, conditions, and practices can be taken. This facilitates strategic planning for field units, as well as the entire agency.

ParkStat serves many functions, not the least of which is the fostering of organizational learning. Senior administrators learn about what is occurring in the field at the same time that districts are learning from one another. Effective practices are openly shared and disseminated throughout the entire organization. For example, at a recent ParkStat meeting, a manager from one district indicated that he was having difficulty cleaning up ball fields due to heavy use by groups without appropriate field permits. He also indicated that many groups that did have properly issued permits were simply failing to clean up after themselves (and this, consequently, was affecting his district's performance rating). In response, the director of OMP stated, "I suggest you do what Flushing Meadow [Park] does, issue color-coded trash bags to groups with permits, see who is cleaning up after the games and who is not." This technique had apparently been quite successful for the other district. The suggestion was taken under advisement by the presenter, and was written down by several other people in attendance.

ParkStat also serves a more critical function. It can immediately communicate or reinforce directives that require immediate attention. For example, one photo displayed at a recent meeting showed a pool of standing water in one of the parks. Referring to this, the director OMP stated to the entire audience, "Because of West Nile [disease], I can't emphasize this enough, you've got to address this!" The clarity and concern conveyed in a personal communication of this type is difficult to reproduce in a memo.

ParkStat is the perfect mechanism for gathering necessary budget information, such as asking a manager, "How much would it take to correct that problem? Did you get an estimate?" It also facilitates resource allocation by ensuring that necessary resources are not only sent out to the field, but are actually used. For example, when discussing the photograph of a broken swing set, the director of OMP asked, "Do you need any additional tools?" The district manager responded that he had a "wish list" that included a cordless drill and vise grips for his crew. He explained their utility and described how work orders (like the swing set) could be processed more efficiently with them. His request was noted and taken under consideration by OMP.

The process does not focus upon minutiae, nor does it result in micromanagement. Rather, it is a collaborative learning process based on attention to detail. ParkStat fosters a constructive dialogue in which senior management communicates its requirements and expectations directly to the field, and field personnel explain their particular accomplishments, obstacles, or difficulties to personnel at headquarters. This dialogue is critical. It is important for senior management to understand how the job gets done. For example, at one meeting the director of OMP inquired, "Do you have a formal [grass-] cutting schedule, a rotation?" The presenter responded, "No. It depends on how much rain we get, what the supervisor sees when he inspects the area." This response seems reasonable enough and conveys a fundamental understanding of how work is being performed in the field. Clearly, for senior management to create reasonable performance standards and expectations, they need to have and understand this type of information.

The successful implementation of a process such as ParkStat cannot only improve the overall performance of the adopting agency, but also can benefit other neighboring agencies. For example, at one ParkStat meeting, a manager responded to a photo of graffiti by stating, "There's a gang moving into that section of the park." This particular manager knew the first name of the commanding officer of the local police precinct, and had worked with the police in the past to address criminal conditions. The manager stated, "We have to go back [and clean] every day" and explained that the police were attempting to "read the tags" [i.e., the content of the messages] in order to determine who was responsible. The manager described a boroughwide anti-graffiti task force that was available to assist in the cleanup and stated that he would avail himself of these additional resources.

During another ParkStat presentation, a photo of a damaged roadway was displayed. Apparently, this particular area was not the responsibility of the department or this particular manager. The manager explained, "I've reported this to DOT (the city's Department of Transportation)." Since this situation was a continuing condition, and since it was unknown whether or when DOT would be able to address it, he asked, "How can we put more pressure on DOT—what can be done at the higher level?" ParkStat enables field personnel to solicit the assistance of senior administrators whenever they encounter resistance from outside agencies. This type of support from above has a positive effect on morale and can facilitate field operations.

ParkStat is therefore a useful mechanism for the coordination of efforts between city agencies. Today, in-depth discussions about graffiti or gang activity in city parks are being held within the NYPD at CompStat meetings and in the Department of Parks and Recreation at ParkStat. Public managers in both agencies are being encouraged to seek out creative solutions for recurring problems. This often results in managers looking outside of their agencies for new ideas and support. The "stat" process has transformed both of these agencies and has provided an unprecedented opportunity for collaborative problem solving in the public sector.

The ParkStat program is continually developing. Indeed, the department recently renamed it "ParkStat Plus" and has expanded it to include a broader range of performance measures. The department now regularly monitors information relating to personnel, vehicle maintenance, resource allocation, and enforcement activity to ensure superior service delivery. ParkStat stands as an excellent example of how the CompStat model can be adapted and successfully implemented outside the field of criminal justice.

Utility as a Management Device for Citywide Initiatives (HealthStat)

In a speech delivered on June 16, 2000, Mayor Rudolph Giuliani announced his intent to have all eligible New Yorkers, particularly children, become enrolled in available state and federal health care programs. At that time, it was estimated that 1.8 million New Yorkers had no health care insurance. One quarter of those were believed to be children. ("A Healthy

Start for New Yorkers," *Daily News*, June 18, 2000.) The mayor made it a priority to enroll these people as quickly and efficiently as possible. To do so, he announced the development of "HealthStat," a citywide initiative that would draw upon the resources of more than 20 city agencies in a massive community outreach effort.

Under the plan, the city was divided into eight regions, each run by a manager. Within each area, a variety of city departments and agencies now work toward identifying and enrolling eligible individuals. (Bumiller, E., "Citing Own Cancer, Giuliani Offers Plan on Health Coverage," *The New York Times*, June 15, 2000.) Deputy Mayor Coles serves as moderator/supervisor of the process.

The most critical aspect of HealthStat is the outreach component. Simply identifying and graphing eligible populations does not address the underlying problem. The key is to make personal contact with these individuals, to inform them, and to steer them to such programs. HealthStat calls for placing outreach personnel in police stations, schools, and other points of contact between city employees and the public.

HealthStat was patterned after the TEAMS/CompStat model. It is distinguishable, however, in one essential aspect. It is the first time that the stat model has been used to coordinate the efforts of *several New York City agencies at once*. Representatives from the city's Department of Health, Housing Authority, Human Resource Administration, and Board of Education (to name just a few) now regularly meet to discuss their respective efforts at identifying and enrolling uninsured New Yorkers. Deputy Mayor Coles and Anne Heller, executive director of the Mayor's Office of Health Care Access, take leading roles in the questioning that takes place at HealthStat meetings and provide direction to all citywide outreach efforts.

By dividing the city into specific, geographically defined areas of responsibility, researchers could identify target areas with high numbers of eligible, but uninsured, individuals. School principals, police commanders, and other city officials assigned to those areas were then charged with developing innovative and effective outreach methods. Obviously, a large-scale initiative of this type progresses slowly, due in large part to the myriad difficulties associated with interagency cooperation. Interestingly, while various city agencies were charged with making such referrals, it was the Department of Correction that distinguished itself by making a particularly large number of referrals within the first weeks of the initiative. The progress made by the Department of Correction far outpaced the early progress of other city agencies.

Deputy Commissioner Kurtz attributes this to a very important fact: "We immediately included the number of enrollments or HealthStat contacts as one of our TEAMS performance indicators. The TEAMS infrastructure was already in place, so we simply began to monitor how effective a particular warden or facility was in identifying enrollment opportunities and following up on them." Arguably, if the TEAMS system had not been in place, the department's efforts might have lacked focus or might not have been perceived as a priority.

One would think that the amount of contact the Department of Correction has with the community at large would be minimal. On the contrary, Department of Correction officials immediately recognized that they were uniquely situated in relation to many of the individuals who were identified as the beneficiaries of HealthStat. As Deputy Commissioner Kurtz explains:

> Each day, large numbers of New Yorkers pass through the halls of Riker's Island [the city's principal jail facility] as they visit family members. Many times, these are the very same people who need to be reached. So additional Department of Correction personnel were trained and stationed at the visitor center at Riker's Island. They asked the visitors if they would like some information about the program. Immediately, we began to enroll large numbers of people, particularly children. We even offered additional visitation privileges if people would cooperate. It proved to be very effective.

The HealthStat initiative has been praised by local health care policy experts as an effective means of solving this serious problem "without creating a new, expensive health insurance program from scratch." (Bumiller, A1, June 15, 2000.) Experts describe this as a very complex and labor-intensive social problem, but note "a level of intensity in terms of signing up for public programs" that is not often seen. The Department of Correction has certainly taken a leading role in these efforts.

At a recent TEAMS meeting, Edward Galvin, the commanding officer of the Department of Correction's TEAMS and HealthStat Unit, described a variety of initiatives that had been established to facilitate his agency's outreach efforts. He cited numerous examples of collaborative efforts with the private sector, such as a number of "enrollment events" that were hosted and jointly sponsored by McDonald's restaurants. During these events, parents or children who enroll in HealthStat receive a free meal, courtesy of McDonald's. Several of these events were also jointly sponsored by the NYPD and the Housing Bureau. Other city departments and agencies are currently developing similar outreach efforts.

HealthStat marks a critical point in the development of the stat process. Not only has the stat process proven to be an efficient method of managing a large urban agency, it is now also being used as an effective means of coordinating and directing the efforts of many diverse agencies in a comprehensive citywide initiative.

The stat process continues to move within New York City government in a very collaborative fashion. Today, adopting agencies no longer need to rely solely upon the personal observations of key personnel to attempt to create their own version of CompStat. They can now draw upon the considerable expertise of individuals who have had great success using it in their own agencies. For example, at the direction of the Office of the Mayor, Deputy Correction Commissioner Deborah Kurtz has been working for the past two years with several other city agencies that wish to develop a management model similar to TEAMS. Her expertise has been critical to the development of the stat process in a variety of settings. In essence, Deputy Commissioner Kurtz serves as a mentor or consultant to these agencies to guide their efforts in reviewing organizational goals and strategies, selecting key performance indicators, and developing an appropriate monitoring system. The Office of the Mayor directs these efforts and coordinates interagency communication and planning.

Deputy Commissioner Kurtz has most recently been working with the New York City Department of Transportation, the New York City Fire Department, and the city's Probation Department. The TEAMS model has been successfully modified and adopted by DOT, which has developed a comprehensive system of management that now monitors such key performance indicators as: 1) the number of broken traffic signals; 2) average time required to respond to complaints of broken traffic signals; 3) percentage of operable parking meters; 4) total number of parking spaces available; 5) number of potholes; and 6) the results of periodic inspections. These indicators were compiled as a result of a series of in-depth discussions between representatives of DOT, personnel assigned to the Mayor's Office, and Deputy Commissioner Kurtz.

A recent *New York Times* article (Goodnough, April 22, 2001) describes the city's current efforts to institute the stat process into the Board of Education, an organization that has traditionally been criticized for a host of chronic "bureaupathologies." It describes Mayor Giuliani's intentions to "hold superintendents and principals accountable in the way that precinct commanders are under CompStat …" and describes the efforts of Deputy Mayor for Education Anthony Coles, who is working to develop what city hall aides call "LearnStat" (p. 35). The article quotes current Schools Chancellor Harold Levy as follows: "From my first day here, I have been focused relentlessly on getting better, more reliable data more frequently and using those measurements to improve the management of the system (p. 35)."

The feasibility of creating a stat process for the city's Board of Education remains to be seen, in light of the many deeply entrenched bureaucratic practices, policies, and procedures of the organization. What this effort does demonstrate, however, is the mayor's intention to implement the stat process into as many of the city's agencies and departments as possible prior to the end of his administration. He will be able to guide the stat process only so far, however, given the limited amount of time he has left in office.

The feasibility of a citywide stat system in New York is questionable, due to the enormous size of New York City government, but it is not out of the question. The considerable success of the Health-Stat initiative and the unprecedented level of interagency cooperation and collaboration associated with it suggest that it is at least possible that someday a citywide stat system might be developed for most, if not all, of the agencies and departments within the New York City government.

The City of Baltimore (CitiStat)

CitiStat marks another significant development in the evolution of the stat process. CitiStat represents the first time that a major American city has attempted to coordinate all of its major services and to formalize the process of interagency cooperation through the stat system.

Baltimore's current police commissioner, Edward Norris, is a former NYPD official who was chiefly responsible for coordinating that agency's CompStat meetings over the past several years. He brought the CompStat model with him to Baltimore, successfully implemented it, and has significantly improved the overall performance of his new agency. Perhaps the most significant result of his new approach to policing has been the reduction of Baltimore's homicide rate to a 10-year low. (Clines, "Baltimore Gladly Breaks 10-Year Homicide Streak." *The New York Times*, January 3, 2001.) Baltimore Mayor Martin O'Malley, the man who hired Norris, was apparently so impressed by Norris's use of CompStat that he has adopted it as the primary management tool for several other of his city's departments and agencies. Jack Maple, the former NYPD official who created the concept of CompStat, was retained as a consultant and charged with developing a program that would function on a citywide basis. This unprecedented move has yielded immediate results. Similar improvements have been noted in several of the other departments that are now monitored by CitiStat. For example, over an initial three-month period, Baltimore experienced a reported 25 percent drop in overtime in the Department of Public Works (DPW), Water and Waste Division. Unscheduled leave in that agency also fell by more than one-third during this period.

Today, CitiStat is used to evaluate performance and to coordinate efforts on a citywide basis. City supervisors are now summoned to appear before the mayor's cabinet every two weeks to discuss the overall performance of their departments. Previously, city managers met only quarterly to discuss goals that were established the year before. Now managers can plan, allocate resources, and engage in lively discussions with city hall based upon

The *New York Times* on CitiStat

Modeled on CompStat, the New York City Police Department's breakthrough computer program that tracks crime and management response street by street, Mayor O'Malley's CitiStat program is an 11-month-old effort to see if real-time tracking of the full range of urban problems can be a management tool reaching far more deeply into the warp and woof of a troubled city.

Already hailed by government specialists as a pioneering innovation in across-the-board, eye-on-the-sparrow management, CitiStat is attracting officials from other cities and counties to the sessions here in which municipal managers, harried or not, must return every two weeks for a fresh round of accountability.

"One of the best things about it is we can expect movement on a problem in those two weeks," said Mathew D. Gallagher, the program director, who previously worked in the Philadelphia municipal government. In the typical city hall, the severest scrutiny for change occurs only once a year at budget time, Mr. Gallagher said, while CitiStat does this twice a month, with memorandums on supervisors' commitments after each session.

(Francis X. Clines, "Baltimore Uses a Databank to Wake Up City Workers," New York Times, *June 10, 2001)*

"real time" information (obtained and analyzed by the CitiStat Unit). This has had a dramatic effect upon the organizational culture of the city's major departments. As Mayor O'Malley explains, it has served to "replace a culture of delay and avoidance with a culture of accountability and results—monitored by technology" (http://www.ci.baltimore.md.us/mayor/speeches/index.html).

CitiStat is now used to monitor such diverse social services as drug treatment, trash collection, vacant housing, and lead paint abatement. It closely resembles CompStat in that information is not just compiled and analyzed, it is *used*. During a recent budget address, the mayor stated:

> City governments collect an enormous amount of information. But it isn't used very much or very well. CitiStat will employ CompStat's principles to put that information to work. For the first time, the information we collect will become a blessing rather than a burden. (FY2001 Budget address, available at http://www.ci.baltimore.md.us/mayor /speeches/index.html.)

The forum is similar to CompStat in all essential details. Upon initially entering the room in which CitiStat meetings take place, one's eyes are immediately drawn to the large six-by-ten-foot projection screens on the

The Four Tenets of CitiStat

- Accurate and timely intelligence to ensure the most complete analysis possible
- Rapid deployment of resources to quickly address city problems
- Effective tactics and strategies to ensure proactive solutions
- Relentless follow-up and assessment to ensure that problems do not reoccur

wall, which serve as the centerpiece for detailed discussions. During CitiStat meetings, projectionists in a rear control room display graphs that track the performance of each department. A commercially available geographic information system software package allows senior administrators to access databases and obtain real-time statistics regarding agency performance. Performance data are displayed on these screens for all to see, and trends, both good and bad, are often quite easily identified. Histograms and global positioning system maps are used to make the data "come alive."

At the beginning each meeting, one screen displays and reinforces the "mayor's goals," which serve as an overriding mission statement for the entire city government. Another screen displays the four tenets of the CitiStat process, which are derived from the four basic principles of the CompStat model: accurate and timely intelligence; rapid deployment; effective strategies; and relentless follow-up. The logo chosen for the CitiStat process is quite appropriate—a magnifying glass. It suggests an enhanced level of scrutiny and attention to detail that might otherwise be unfamiliar to civil service agencies.

During CitiStat meetings, managers provide explanations and respond to pointed questions about operations and performance. They rely heavily upon their aides and support staff, who are often themselves called to the podium to provide more detailed responses to specific inquiries. Manager profiles are also projected on the screen during each presentation. These profiles provide information about each manager, such as the date of appointment, specific title, responsibilities, etc.

The fluidity of the process is quite apparent to even the casual observer. At the outset of one recent meeting, First Deputy Mayor Michael Enright suggested to the assembled group that the analysis of one particular agency should include a comparison of data obtained over four (rather than two) two-week periods. He explained that this would enable "better analysis."

Alterations such as this are apparently common. Once the data is assembled by the CitiStat Unit, it is relatively easy to look further back to gain a better appreciation of trends that might otherwise not be observed.

The following exchange illustrates how the standards for comparison can change as necessary:

> First Deputy Mayor Enright: I see overtime is up, why?
>
> Manager: Our personnel were engaged in a lot of weekend activities during this period.
>
> Enright: Do you have any idea as to where we were this time last year?
>
> Manager: No.
>
> Enright: Let's try to get that information and follow up on this.

It should be noted that positive trends, as well as negative ones, are identified and discussed. The CitiStat philosophy is premised on the belief that much can be learned from the in-depth analysis of positive performance:

> First Deputy Mayor Enright: How did we get that decrease (in one particular performance category)? That looks like a good trend. How did we manage to knock that down?

> Enright: I want to find out the story behind these numbers.

> Enright: Any ideas—any reason for this? We've discovered some interesting things in the past when we've looked into these things.

The potential training benefits of CitiStat are therefore obvious.

Another exchange during one particular meeting was also quite interesting, and led to an impromptu presentation by a woman who was seated in the audience. After noting that one particular unit's performance had been well above average for several periods, the first deputy mayor asked the supervisor, "What are some of the techniques you've used to keep such high productivity levels?" The supervisor began to respond, but eventually referred the question to the woman in the audience. She was apparently a senior inspector for DPW who had been requested to attend and observe the meeting. She explained in detail that it had been her practice to "personally assign" work to her inspectors and to use a "mentor system—to show inspectors how to make their stops" and to "emphasize teamwork." Her explanations clarified several issues for the audience and illustrated the potential training benefits of the CitiStat method.

CitiStat is premised upon a collaborative approach to public management, designed to break down the various information silos that are often quite common in city governments. Information is not hoarded by any one department or office. Rather, it is openly shared and made available to all interested parties. In other words, the inner workings of city management become quite transparent. CitiStat also enables administrators to draw upon the expertise of a broader array of professionals, who attend and actively participate in CitiStat meetings. For example, at one meeting, an issue arose concerning communications between one city agency and the private physician of an employee on sick leave (restricted duty). Upon learning of the need for such communication, the first deputy mayor was able to make a suggestion and have the commissioner of personnel verify that such a course of action was appropriate. These types of exchanges save time and are indicative of the impact CitiStat has had on the flow of information within the city government.

Members of the CitiStat Unit and others actively assist those who serve on the dais during these meetings. Indeed, at times the process seems quite similar to a congressional hearing, as aides whisper into the ear of a deputy mayor, or pass a note, during the course of a dialogue. Meetings progress in a methodical fashion, while retaining a spontaneous quality that encourages open dialogue and the search for creative solutions to pressing problems.

Some of the performance categories do appear at first blush to relate to minutiae and can oftentimes seem quite comical. Prolonged discussions at CitiStat meetings might relate to the number of "grass and weed" complaints that are received or the total number of baited traps set to catch vermin (such as rats). These indicators, however specific, are actually a necessary and reasonable way to operationalize the broad array of services delivered by a particular agency. These indicators describe the work that is actually being done in the field. They are the means to an end—the overall mission and goal of all city agencies being to create and maintain clean and safe neighborhoods.

As CitiStat develops and expands, city managers should become more comfortable with the process. Now that the process has become institutionalized, it appears that the stigma of being "called on the carpet" (to visit and respond to questions at city hall) is gone. CitiStat meetings, and the necessary process of data collection and analysis, are now an expected and ordinary part of doing business in Baltimore.

Perhaps the most interesting aspect of CitiStat is its potential for creating a positive synergy based upon interagency collaboration. As each department attempts to solve its own unique problems, managers will undoubtedly find themselves reaching out to other managers in different departments, in an attempt to craft innovative and effective solutions. This now appears more likely, as CitiStat has clearly opened new lines of communication within and between city agencies. During one meeting in which the DPW was presenting, an issue came up concerning a possible duplication of effort between DPW and Housing and Community Development (HCD) (the department that was scheduled to appear at that afternoon's CitiStat meeting). Noting an opportunity for correcting overlapping efforts and responsibilities, the first deputy mayor suggested, "We'd love you (a senior DPW official) to attend the next CitiStat meeting, to talk to HCD; it could save a lot of time, memos, and talking back and forth." His offer was taken up and an informal "side bar" was later observed in a back corner of the room. CitiStat also has great potential as an aid to communication between city government and the public. Mayor O'Malley has publicly stated his intention of making CitiStat meetings more "public" and of someday publishing CitiStat data on the city's official Internet website.

CitiStat appears to have institutionalized the organizational learning process. All meetings are well attended—by members of presenting departments, as well as others who anticipate being called at a later date. One presenter pointed to the audience and identified his colleagues, stating, "One of the reasons I brought my superintendents here today was that I want them to see what you're asking and what you are looking at." The spectator gallery in the CitiStat meeting room is typically filled with city employees from a variety of departments who are there to listen and learn. It is not unusual to see many of them taking notes. It seems as if every observer is generally interested, attentive, and willing to add their own insight or input if called upon to do so. This was graphically illustrated during a presentation at one recent meeting when a manager from DPW began his presentation by stating, "The list of ... ahh ..." As he briefly paused and attempted to collect his thoughts, three people in the audience finished the sentence for him by loudly shouting, "Eligibility!"

Interestingly, "mini" stat meetings are now being held in the field, prior to the official meetings. One supervisor noted, "We talked about this together last night [he and his subordinates], one particular case." Deputy Mayor Enright inquired, "Do you have pre-CitiStat meetings?" "Yes," the supervisor responded, "on what we anticipated your interest would be." Such informal meetings have recently become more routinized and have actually become part of the process.

Baltimore is continuing its efforts to gradually extend CitiStat and to include more city agencies and departments into the process in the future.

The success of CitiStat serves to highlight two important issues. First, that the stat process is a fungible concept that can successfully be replicated in other American cities. Secondly, and perhaps more importantly, it confirms that the stat process can be used to coordinate a particularly wide variety of government functions on a citywide level. CitiStat illustrates the very real potential for taking the stat process to the next level. If a number of city agencies can work collaboratively in this manner, the stat process might prove to be a viable alternative to more traditional methods of city administration.

Guidelines for Successful Implementation

Based upon many field observations and numerous interviews with administrators who have now successfully used the stat process to spur productivity, the following guidelines have been developed so that an adopting organization can create and sustain an effective version of the stat system.

Design Stage

1. Articulate organizational mission/vision and realign organizational structure to facilitate the meeting of goals and objectives.

To maximize effectiveness, the stat process must be pervasive. It must be the prevailing management philosophy throughout the entire organization. There could be a tendency to limit employee "buy-in" to those individuals and units working within the areas of auditing, inspections, and discipline. Every effort must be made to ensure a top-down buy-in by all members of the organization. This typically involves an emphasis on the transition process. Too rapid a shift in organizational philosophy and management approach could do more harm than good, particularly in a struggling organization. The actual length of time for transition depends upon a variety of factors, not the least of which is organizational culture. Proper implementation, therefore, entails knowing or anticipating how this change will affect your personnel.

Adopting agencies must be sure to utilize a sufficient number of motivated and creative administrators who are both students of, and believers in, the process. The success of both CompStat and TEAMS has been attributable, to a large extent, to a series of high-level personnel changeovers that provided continuity and strong leadership while also continuing to provide opportunities for creativity and innovation. To that end, the purpose and practices of the stat process should be incorporated into the current and future training curricula of all personnel. This would include training for new personnel at the time of appointment (initial hiring), as well as ongoing in-service training for current personnel. Additionally, an effort should be made to develop the public speaking and critical thinking skills of individuals who will be expected to present at stat meetings; this can be done by creating an executive development program or by engaging outside consultants to develop necessary skills for managers and administrators.

2. Have a modern organizational and information technology (IT) infrastructure in place prior to implementation.

GIS capabilities might not be necessary if analysis is not going to be based upon geographic comparison. Commercially available software packages with modern spreadsheet capabilities might be sufficient to produce the descriptive statistics, graphs, etc., that are required for meaningful analysis and comparisons. IT infrastructure would also include a sufficient number of well trained personnel, as well as a distinct auditing and inspections unit to ensure the timeliness and accuracy of the data.

Implementation Stage

1. Select performance indicators through a collaborative and fluid process.

There must be an open and authentic dialogue, otherwise administrators might yield to the temptation to merely "measure the measurable." As Senge (1990) explains, "focusing on what's easily measured leads to 'looking good without being good'" (p. 304). All performance measures must therefore be meaningful, and must address the core mission and basic goals of the organization.

When selecting indicators, it is important to address core business practices first, identifying the organization's most important functions and focusing on those first. The list of performance indicators can always be expanded and refined at a later date.

2. Identify equivalent units for comparison.

At the outset, it is important to identify "equivalent units" (e.g., caseloads, libraries, precincts, etc.) to have effective comparisons. There is always a need to compare apples to apples.

3. Review and refine indicators.

Performance indicators must also continually be reviewed and revised. It is imperative that all members of the organization understand the *meaning* of each of the indicators and that they use a common definition for each. For example, if a correctional facility records the number of inmate searches (and uses this as a performance indicator), it should be clear to everyone in the organization whether "unscheduled" or "random/spontaneous" searches should be included.

4. Compile timely and accurate data.

If the accuracy of the information relied upon is questionable or "stale," it gives presenters "wiggle room" to explain away poor performance (e.g., "Those numbers are not up-to-date; we're actually doing much better than that today!" or "We've already corrected that condition.).

5. Share all data and information compiled by the stat unit with field units well in advance of the stat meetings.

Preparation is the key. Comments, questions, and concerns from top administrators should be relayed to field units prior to the scheduled meetings. That is not to say, however, that everything will be scripted at the upcoming meeting. Only major issues (i.e., those that cause significant concern or are anticipated to take up some time at the meeting) will be communicated so that thoughtful responses can be formulated.

6. Hold "mini" CompStat meetings.

To prepare thoughtful responses, field units must engage in "mini" CompStats to organize their thoughts for the larger, more comprehensive meetings. Meeting with one another well in advance of the scheduled stat meeting allows field units to properly address anticipated areas of inquiry.

Meeting Stage

1. Hold stat meetings at a convenient time and place.

Meetings should be held at "headquarters," away from the many distractions that arise in the field. This serves a symbolic purpose, and also draws upon the additional resources (personnel, equipment) that are available at headquarters but rarely available in the field. Stat meetings should be scheduled early in the workday, preferably at 7:00 or 7:30 a.m., so that participants will not be distracted by other issues and matters.

2. Require key personnel to attend and participate.

At all meetings, the entire organizational chart must be present (i.e., have representation). There must be a competent and creative chief inquisitor —a top-level administrator who leads the discussions and questioning at all meetings. Failure to have such a focal point during meetings could lead to confusion. The dais will be made up of top-level managers, but must also include one or more "operational" people (i.e., individuals with extensive field experience and, hopefully, the respect of those in the field). Young, "corporate CPA types" with little or no operational background can be stonewalled or more easily misled. It is imperative to "know the job" first to properly monitor the work and move the organization forward. Also, non-presenting units or agencies should send a representative to attend stat meetings if it is anticipated that issues addressed by other agencies might be pertinent to them. Ideally, all stat meetings could be available online and made to be interactive so that the entire organization or city could observe and perhaps participate.

3. Schedule meetings frequently.

To maximize effectiveness, stat meetings must be scheduled frequently, based upon the needs of the specific organization. In many respects, the stat process is the equivalent of the organization checking its own pulse. Better organizational health depends upon proper monitoring. Hopefully, if the process is implemented and carried out properly, departments and sub-units should be obtaining useful information and direction, and should actually look forward to these meetings.

4. Record all meetings.

Meetings should be recorded (if not actually broadcast). Managers who make presentations and respond to pointed questions at stat meetings should be sent back with a tape or stenographic record of what exactly was said. This is necessary both for follow-up purposes and to critique one's own performance.

5. Prepare profiles for each presenting unit.

All presentations should include a profile of the department/unit, as of well as its highest ranking administrator. Typically, this information is projected on a screen for display during the meeting or is contained in the hard copy spreadsheets that are distributed to those in attendance. The profile would include the supervisor's date of appointment, geographic area(s) of responsibility, a brief description of the personnel and resources under that person's command, etc. This alleviates the need to have introductions at the beginning of all meetings. Introductions are often redundant, take time, and generally detract from the overall quality of the presentations. Profiles would obviously not be necessary, however, in smaller departments or agencies, such as the New Rochelle Police Department.

6. Maintain a professional and productive atmosphere.

It is critical that decorum be maintained throughout the entire meeting. A business-like atmosphere must always be maintained, characterized at all times by mutual respect. During these meetings, listening to one another is just as important (often far more important) than speaking at one another. Dais members should constantly be alert for personal attacks or unwarranted criticisms.

The stat process should not be viewed as a disciplinary tool—there is a need always to address successes as well as failures. A negative connotation for these meetings is bad for morale and counterproductive. Positive comments must be communicated with the same level of sincerity and concern as criticisms. Positive trends or increases in productivity must be sustained and thoroughly examined. It is also important to not only praise the presenters, but also the individuals who actually perform the work. The city of Baltimore actually gives out pairs of Orioles baseball tickets to presenters and their subordinates.

7. Engage in meaningful and constructive dialogue.

There must be an authentic and spontaneous dialogue during these meetings. It should take the form of a lively discussion, not an inquisition. The entire process is akin to the Socratic method of inquiry used today in most American law schools. It involves point, counterpoint, and thoughtful responses to insightful questions. The process should not be conducted like a deposition, where the respondent is grilled or battered with questions. Managing a stat meeting is an art as well as a skill. Competence develops over time.

8. Use the stat process to manage organizational knowledge.

The stat process is the organization thinking out loud. It allows the organization to detect and analyze information obtained from the internal and external work environments. The process enables the organization to weigh its options, reflect, and select the most rational and effective course of action available. The process draws upon all organizational resources, which include the practices and opinions of key personnel. The flow of information, therefore, must be in two directions. All participants teach and all can learn.

One of the greatest strengths of the stat process is the fact that it not only relies upon information that is compiled in the ordinary course of business, but also draws upon "tacit" knowledge within the organization. That is, information that is possessed by individuals in the field who work at the point of service delivery. This type of knowledge is more generally associated with skills or know-how (Cook and Brown, 1999). In every version of the stat process observed, presenters were often called upon to describe their standard operating procedures, to explain how they did things. Commissioners generally know and understand the ends (organizational goals) but not always the means (how things actually get done in the field). This process provides a perfect opportunity for bridging the knowledge gap between management and the rank and file. The stat process can therefore greatly enhance the body of useful knowledge available to the organization and "generate new knowledge and new ways of knowing" (Cook and Brown, 1999, p. 381).

9. Encourage active participation in the meetings by all members of the dais.

It is recommended that someone on the dais be chiefly responsible for recognizing instances of micro-management (i.e., detailed discussions that are not pertinent to the entire organization and that should be taken up in greater detail, at a later time, by the interested parties). Similarly, questioners should always be on the lookout for training opportunities (indeed, the director of training or his/her representative should be present at all stat meetings) to identify potential topics for additional in-service training. If a mistake is made by one manager, it is often likely that others will do the same. Negative trends can be stopped before they begin if administrators always have one eye on training.

Top-level administrators should also be aware not to get bogged down in retrospective analysis. Decision makers and planners need only to look as far back as necessary (to explain what's going on now and what can be expected in the future). Too much attention on the past will actually prevent progress. Participants also should always be on the lookout for collaboration opportunities with outside agencies, since they typically present themselves throughout the entire process.

10. Review and utilize *all information* compiled.

To be truly meaningful, *all* data must be reviewed by senior management (both positive and negative performance information). Managers should not view performance indicators in a vacuum. Numbers do not have a meaning unto themselves; they must be interpreted. Effective managers must at all times have a global perspective to truly understand the overall health and performance of each unit, as well as the health of the entire organization.

11. Understand organizational ends as well as means.

When measuring an agency's efficiency, a key question is, "Efficient for whom?" Administrators must have a thorough understanding of the needs of their end users and stakeholders (i.e., the public). It is important to understand that an efficiently performing public service organization can nonetheless be "inefficient" if it fails to meet the basic needs and expectations of the public.

12. Interpret data intelligently.

Top-level managers or individuals on their staff should have a working knowledge of statistics. They should know how to use and interpret basic comparative statistics (i.e., understand mean, median, and mode). They should also have a fundamental understanding of the phenomenon of regression toward the mean (i.e., the fact that performance improvements will slow over time; for example, a 20 percent drop followed by an 18 percent drop does not mean that the organization is "going backwards"). Similarly, they should be familiar with the terms *correlation* and *causation*, as well as the distinction between the two. For example, if numbers show that ice cream sales in the United States increase as the rate of drownings do, does this mean that ice cream causes drowning? Or that people consume large amounts of ice cream after a drowning occurs? Obviously not. We should always be on the lookout for what statisticians refer to as a "lurking" third variable, such as temperature, which in this case is the true cause of the variation in both variables, the real explanation. Data must be delved into and truly analyzed. There should be a constant search for statistically significant variations and possible correlations. Managers should carefully draw their own conclusions and be hesitant to accept simple explanations.

Managers should also understand that numbers can always be interpreted a number of different ways. For example, if sanitation trucks are completing their routes more quickly, one would assume that to be a good thing. Perhaps not. Maybe they are coming in too soon, not making all of their pickups. Sometimes quality is far better than quantity. It depends upon what is being measured. Managers need to always see the big picture and not focus on any one performance category. They need to use and understand the entire constellation of performance measures for the entire agency or city. That's where the true story is.

Managers should always be aware of similarities and distinctions between field units. Maybe a garbage route in a downtown area is inherently more difficult and slower than many others. It is unreasonable to assume that baselines will be the same for all units, although one would expect them to be substantially similar. Managers obviously need to know their own agency, the nature of the work, and their people. Once appropriate baselines are established (means, medians, and modes), they will have a proper frame of reference. Then they will be in a position to judge the overall performance of different units.

13. Engage in a continuous process of inquiry.

Top-level administrators must continually ask questions like: *How* did this happen?; *Why* did this happen? (What is causing it?); *When* did this happen (and how long has it been like that?); and *What* can we do to change (or sustain) it? Presenters should be dissuaded from responding with statements such as, "We're working on that," or "We'll take that under advisement." It is imperative that such platitudes be discouraged since this terminates the dialogue and is nonproductive. They should be told, "Please get back to us with an action plan that outlines the steps you will be taking to correct this situation." The burden is on upper management to keep the momentum moving in a positive direction. Follow-up questions should be encouraged, and used as necessary. For example, a stat meeting in one city resulted in the following exchange:

> Q: "What about working with the [adjacent] school personnel? Can't you work with them to come up with a creative solution?"
>
> A: "They don't help us at all."

Not being satisfied with this response, the supervisor asked, "Well, have you reached out to them at all? And if so, tell us how."

It also appears that there is a generic fiscal response that may be used by presenters to deflect criticism. This entails saying, "I'm aware of that [condition or deficiency], but I don't have the resources available to address that. I have more important issues to address." Such a response could stifle further discussion. In effect, it insulates the party from further criticism and justifies deficiencies in performance. Instead, budgetary constraints should be no surprise to any party. If a particular corrective measure cannot be undertaken for fiscal reasons, it should be discussed in detail, either during the stat meeting or at a later time, with interested parties in attendance.

14. Ensure accountability of field managers.

Managers who are being reviewed should be "geographically accountable." That is, they should have a proprietary interest or specific responsibility for the work being performed in a particular area or by a particular group of people. They need to have a stake in the work being performed if they are to be held accountable. Accountability only goes so far, however. There will always be instances where a crime wave spontaneously occurs despite the best efforts of the police, or where a school district's test scores will drop precipitously due to the rapid influx of immigrants. The stat process is based upon the creation and use of institutional memory. These otherwise unexplained events are explainable and understandable if we can see them in context and use the information provided by the stat process. Statisticians refer to these unforeseen situations as "outlyers." There will always be unusual situations that fall on the extreme ends of the bell curve. The key is to understand the uniqueness of these situations and to learn from them.

15. Conduct a review after each meeting.

One of the more obvious recommendations associated with the successful implementation of the stat process is to have a recap, "what we've learned today," at the conclusion of each meeting. This simple step performs an obvious training function and clearly articulates and records who is going to be following up with whom.

It should be understood that implementation is only the tip of the iceberg. A considerable amount of time and energy must be expended in connection with assuring that the mechanism survives. When properly developed and implemented, the stat process can be transferable to, and sustainable by, the next generation of administrators. Short-term success is simply not sufficient. As Robert Fritz (1996) puts it, "All organizations have success, but not all success succeeds in the end" (p.xv). The stat process should always be understood as being evolutionary. The process itself should never remain stagnant, but must constantly be modified and perfected. The entire philosophy and practice of the stat process is based upon the search for "better practices," not "best practices." There is always room for improvement.

Conclusion

The stat process has proven to be a fungible and malleable management process that holds great promise for public administrators. As New York City Deputy Mayor Joseph Lhota states, "It [the stat process] can be used in any area of government. The fact that it was developed in the public safety area does not mean that it has to stay there." The concept continues to spread to a variety of organizations. Most recently, it has made the leap into the area of federal service.

Beginning in 1998, Dr. Frank Straub, who was then special agent in charge of the Research and Analysis Unit within the Inspector General's Office of the U. S. Department of Justice, began to develop a version of the stat process that could be adapted to the unique requirements of an organization with nationwide responsibility. From its very inception, the system (known as "SACS") differed substantially from its predecessors. Thomas McLaughlin, current deputy assistant inspector general for investigations, explains:

> We use the system to monitor work being performed in our many field offices. Since they are located throughout the country, it was difficult to bring all of our managers to one central location for a meeting. Rather, we circulate key performance data for all offices, but have extended, office-by-office phone conversations in order to explore the relative performance of each.

McLaughlin personally traveled to New York and visited both CompStat and TEAMS meetings prior to the development of SACS. He believes in the utility of the SACS system and feels that it has proven to be quite effective for his organization. He describes the value of being able to assemble and understand a broad range of performance data, and to make meaningful comparisons:

> Once we assembled and interpreted our stream of numbers, we were able to identify certain areas that needed attention. We were then able to focus our attention and bring these areas down into a more normal range.

The potential benefits associated with the stat system are therefore not reserved exclusively for managers in local government. The philosophy and practices associated with the stat process are consistent with those outlined in the Government Performance and Results Act (1993). The stat process should therefore continue to be viewed as a viable option for all federal agencies looking to enhance productivity and ensure accountability.

Perhaps the most important lesson to be learned here is one of caution. The stat process is not a panacea. It is not a magical cure-all that will transform a poorly run and inefficient organization into a model of public service excellence. Rather, it is an additional tool that can be used by public administrators to enhance performance by means of careful measurement and planning, and effective allocation of resources. As these case studies show, it has been used with great success in a variety of venues and appears to hold great promise for the future.

Bibliography

Abrahamson, Eric and Lori Rosenkopf. "Institutional and Competitive Bandwagons: Using Mathematical Modeling as a Tool to Explore Innovation Diffusion." 18 *Academy of Management Review* no.3, (1993) pp. 487-517.

Bennis, Warren. *Changing Organizations: Essays on the Development and Evolution of Human Organization*. New York: McGraw-Hill (1966).

Bennis, Warren, Kenneth Benne, and Robert Chan. *The Planning of Change*. New York: Holt, Rinehart and Winston (1969).

Bratton, William J. *Great Expectations: How Higher Expectations for Police Departments Can Lead to a Decrease in Crime*. Paper presented at the National Institute of Justice Policing Research Institute Conference, Washington, D.C., November 28, 1995.

Cook, Scott D. N. and John Seely Brown. (1999). "Bridging Epistemologies: The Generative Dance Between Organizational Knowledge and Organizational Knowing." 10 *Organization Science* no. 4 (July/August), pp. 381-400.

Davenport, Thomas. *Process Innovation: Reengineering Work Through Information Technology*. Boston: Harvard Business School Press (1993).

Fritz, Robert. *Corporate Tides: The Inescapable Laws of Organizational Structure*. San Francisco: Berrett-Koehler (1996).

Giuliani, Rudolph W. Presentation at the Manhattan Institute Conference, June 21, 1999.

Goldstein, Herman. *Problem-Oriented Policing*. Philadelphia: Temple University Press (1990).

Goodnough, Abby. "For Schools in a Torpor, Shock Therapy." *The New York Times*, April 22, 2001), pp. 33, 35.

Gootman, Elissa. "A Police Department's Growing Allure: Crime Fighters From Around World Visit for Tips." *The New York Times*, October 24, 2000.

Ingraham, Patricia W. "Of Pigs and Policy Diffusion: Another Look at Pay-for-Performance." 53 *Public Performance* no. 4, pp. 348-356.

Kraatz, Matthew S. "The Role of Interorganizational Networks in Shaping Strategic Adaptation: Evidence From Liberal Arts Colleges." *Academy of Management*, Best Papers Proceedings, pp. 246-250.

McEwen,Tom. "NIJ's Locally Initiated Research Partnerships in Policing—Factors That Add Up to Success." *National Institute of Justice Journal*, January, 1999, pp. 2-10.

Moore, Mark. *Creating Public Value: Strategic Management in Government*. Cambridge, Mass: Harvard University Press (1995).

Moore, Mark H. and Robert C. Trojanowicz. "Corporate Strategies for Policing." 6 *Perspectives on Policing*, U.S. Department of Justice, National Institute of Justice (November, 1988).

O'Connell, Paul E. and Frank Straub. "Why the Jails Didn't Explode." 9 *City Journal* 2 (Spring 1999a), pp. 28-37.

O'Connell, Paul E. and Frank Straub. "Managing Jails with T.E.A.M.S." *American Jails* (March/April 1999b), pp. 48-54.

O'Connell, Paul E. and Frank Straub. "For Jail Management, CompStat's a Keeper." *Law Enforcement News*, September 30, 1999c, p. 9.

O'Dell, Carla and C. Jackson Grayson. "If Only We Knew What We Know: Identification and Transfer of Internal Best Practices." 40 *California Management Review* 3 (1998), pp. 154-163.

Perrow, Charles. *Complex Organizations: A Critical Essay*. Glenview Ill.: Scott, Foresman (1979).

Punch, Maurice. *Control in Police Organizations*. Cambridge, Mass: MIT Press (1983).

Rogers, E. *Diffusion of Innovations* (4th ed.) New York: The Free Press (1995).

Senge, Peter. *The Fifth Discipline: The Art and Practice of the Learning Organization*. New York: Doubleday (1990).

Silverman, Eli and Paul O'Connell. "Revolutionizing the Police: Fighting Crime in New York City," No. 9 *Security Journal* (1997), pp. 101-104

Silverman, Eli and Paul O'Connell. "Changing Decision-Making in the New York City Police Department," 22 *International Journal of Public Administration* 2 (1999), pp. 217-259.

Sparrow, Malcolm K., Mark H. Moore, and David Kennedy. *Beyond 911: A New Era for Policing*. New York: Basic Books (1992).

Straub, Frank and Paul O'Connell, "Managing With T.E.A.M.S.," *American Jails* (March/April 1999), pp. 48-54.

Straub, Frank and Paul O'Connell, "Why The Jails Didn't Explode," *City Journal* (Spring 1999), pp. 28-37 (reprinted in 17 *NarcOfficer* 3 (May/June 1999), pp. 18-26; excerpted in *The American Enterprise*, (September/October 1999), pp. 86-87.)

Terry, Larry D. "Administrative Leadership, Neo-managerialism, and the Public Management Movement." 58 *Public Administration Review* 3 (1998), pp. 194-213.

Appendix:
A Practical Model for Implementing CompStat

I. Review Organizational Mission/Vision

- Develop a new one or redefine the old
- Attempt to establish an adequate level of "buy-in," both at the top levels of management and throughout the entire organization

II. Adjust/Realign the Existing Organizational Structure (to accommodate the stat mechanism and utilize it properly)

- Institute a comprehensive training program to introduce employees to the concept
- Create a "CompStat Unit" or some equivalent that will be chiefly responsible for data collection, analysis, and distribution (make additional personnel shifts as necessary)
- Implement an appropriate information technology system

III. Select Performance Indicators

- Identify core business practices (determine "what exactly it is that you do")
- Identify specific (desired) goals, based upon organizational goals and mission
- "Operationalize" these goals (break them down into specific tasks and functions: what will need to be performed to accomplish these goals?)
- Develop a "preliminary" set of performance indicators for the organization (select the most important or fundamental functions first)
- Analyze (compare preliminary performance indicators to goals and overall mission of the organization to ensure consistency)

IV. Distribute Preliminary List of Indicators to All Stakeholders

- Provide list of performance indicators to all employees (including individuals in non-managerial positions, since their efforts will ultimately be monitored through this process)
- Provide preliminary list of indicators to external stakeholders (e.g., members of the public who will be provided services)

V. Solicit Feedback from All Stakeholders (authentic dialogue)

- Convene meetings with managers (or focus groups) to obtain feedback and recommendations
- Convene focus groups with stakeholders (i.e., members of the general public, public interest groups, members of other organizations, etc.) to obtain feedback and recommendations
- Revise indicators as necessary (obtain consensus/agreement of all stakeholders, both internal and external constituent groups and clients)
- Create new indicators (secondary, tertiary) as necessary

VI. Collect and Analyze Data

- Design a process for the collection and analysis of data
- Gather data (current, as well as historical, if available)
- Input data
- Analyze data (simple spreadsheet analysis might be sufficient)
- Set baselines for current performance
- Begin to examine historical data for trend analysis and long-term strategic planning
- Examine baselines and make comparisons of equivalent units
- Set reasonable (and obtainable) goals
- Identify significant distinctions in performance between units

VII. Distribute Data throughout Organization

- Disseminate results of initial analysis
- Solicit individual feedback from field units (i.e., their interpretation of the data and explanations for performance)

VIII. Prepare for Meeting

- "Mini" Compstat meetings take place in the field; each field command meets to discuss indicators and prepare for anticipated questions and comments at upcoming (organizationwide) Compstat meeting
- CompStat Unit meets to compile information and prepare questions for upcoming meeting

IX. Hold Meeting (to discuss data, trends, make inferences, and facilitate long-range strategic planning)

- Assemble top-level managers and representatives from all segments of organizational chart
- Presentations made by selected field units
- Questioning by dais, brainstorming for new ideas, techniques, etc.
- Decision making, long-and short-term strategic planning for field units as well as entire organization

X. Recapitulation

- Post-meeting re-cap (memorandum) to be communicated to entire organization, outlining future goals and strategies
- Conduct post-meeting follow-up with individual units as necessary
- Field units will conduct their own (internal) post-meeting assessment (and preparation for next scheduled stat meeting)
- Post-meeting review of list of indicators and performance baselines
- Revise or include additional indicators as necessary
- Training and follow-up for systemic problems or organizationwide recommendations for improvement

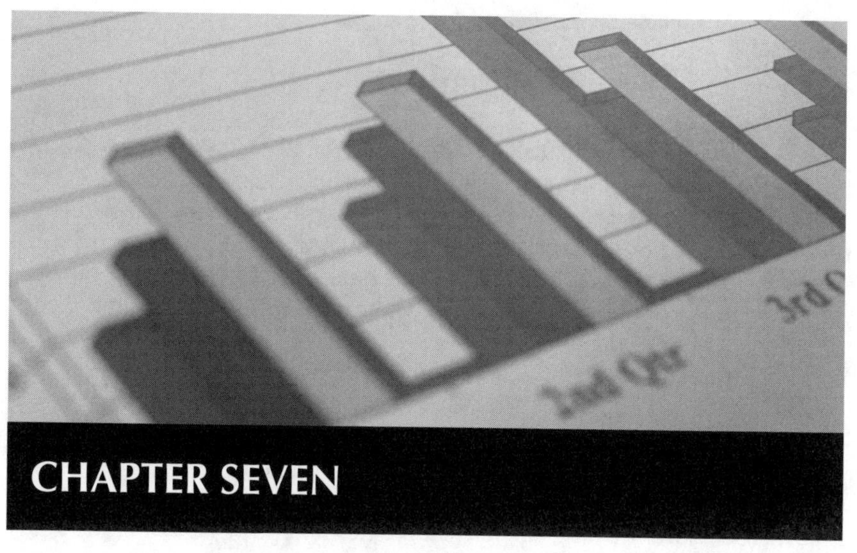

CHAPTER SEVEN

The Potential of the Government Performance and Results Act as a Tool to Manage Third-Party Government

David G. Frederickson
Doctoral Program
School of Public and Environmental Affairs
Indiana University

Introduction

The Government Performance and Results Act of 1993 (GPRA, or the Results Act) seeks to address the inefficiency and ineffectiveness of federal agencies. GPRA posits that these shortcomings are primarily managerial, specifically attributable to poorly articulated missions and inadequate performance information. Not only do these conditions breed poor performance, but they also lead to the public's low confidence in the government and hamper congressional decision making.

As a remedy for inefficiency and ineffectiveness, GPRA requires that federal agencies:

1. Establish strategic plans that provide broad descriptions of agency goals and objectives covering a period of three to five years;
2. Develop annual performance plans containing preferably quantifiable measures from which agencies can determine to what extent the goals and objectives (derived from strategic plans) are met; and
3. Report annually on agency performance according to these measures.

Although GPRA became law in 1993, government-wide implementation did not begin until September 30, 1997, when the first round of strategic plans was due. Since that time two other major GPRA implementation milestones have passed. In 1998, agencies prepared and submitted to the President and Congress performance plans for FY 1999. The culmination of the first round of GPRA implementation occurred on March 31, 2000, when agencies submitted their FY 2001 performance plans supplemented with data reporting on their success at meeting the goals found in their FY 1999 performance plans. Figure 7.1 provides a time frame for GPRA's requirements.

The law requires that agencies submit these performance plans/reports annually. The second round of GPRA implementation began on September 30, 2000, when agencies were required to submit revised strategic plans covering the years 2001 to 2005. Table 7.1 is an example of how the Centers for Medicare and Medicaid Services (CMS, formerly the Health Care Financing Administration, or HCFA) of the U.S. Department of Health and Human Services (HHS) has decided to measure their performance goal of decreasing the number of uninsured children in the United States as it appeared in CMS's FY 2001 performance plan/FY 1999 performance report.

Previous Federal Management Reforms

The history of large-scale efforts to reform the way the federal government conducts its business is much longer than it is distinguished. In most instances, the vehicle of reform has been changes in the process or format of the federal budget. Those who have worked for any length in the federal

Figure 7.1

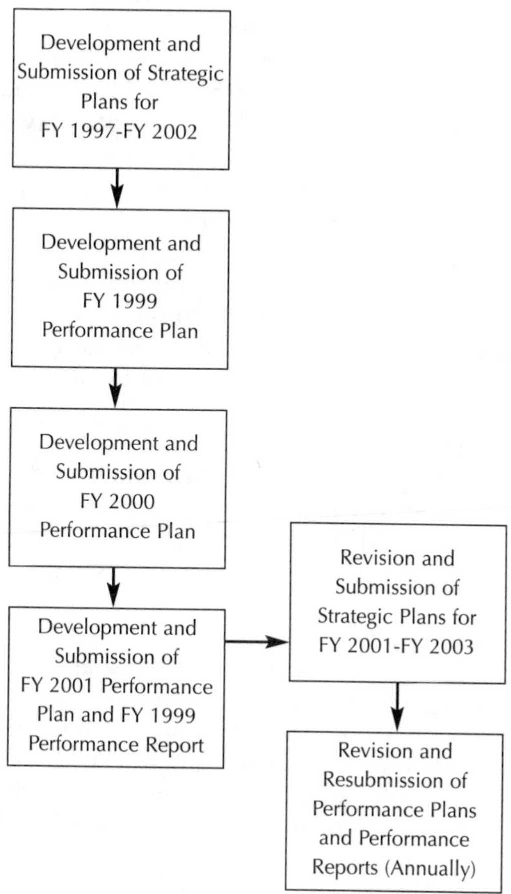

Table 7.1: CMS Performance Goal SCHIP1-01—Decrease the Number of Uninsured Children

Performance Goal	Targets
Decrease the number of uninsured children by working with states to implement SCHIP and by enrolling children in Medicaid. Increase the number of children enrolled in regular Medicaid or SCHIP.	FY 01: + 1 million over 2000. FY 00: + 1 million over 1999. FY 99: Develop goal; set baseline and targets.

Source: CMS's FY 2001 Performance Plan and FY 1999 Report

government will recognize the infamous acronyms and initials that have accompanied most of these reforms. They include performance budgeting, Planning-programming Budgeting System (PPBS or PPB), Zero-base Budgeting (ZBB), and Management by Objectives (MBO). The assumption that ties these budgetary reforms to each other is that if the federal budget were more logical and analytic, then the federal bureaucracy would in turn become more logical and analytic. The newest of these reform efforts, GPRA, shares not only the reformers' penchant for acronyms but also an intellectual heritage that ties bureaucratic reform to analysis.

There has been a considerable effort to examine previous attempts to implement performance measurement and performance budgeting in the public sector. A lengthy review of these efforts will not be provided here, as numerous such reviews are readily available. However, a summary of the recurring themes in this literature is helpful in framing the findings of this research.

These themes include:

- It is difficult to reach agreement on goals and to find adequate measures to determine the attainment of goals even if there is agreement on what those goals should be;
- Managers often turn to activity and output measures as proxies for outcome measures;
- Performance measurement and budgeting represent the superimposition of a managerial structure on a political process; and
- While performance information has not proven useful for appropriators, it has shown some promise for management decisions.

Given the previous attempts at reforms similar to GPRA, we might expect a similar fate. With the exception of the continued use of PPBS in the U.S. Department of Defense, each of these reforms lasted no more than a few years. There is one critical difference between GPRA and the previous efforts, however. While previous efforts originated from the executive branch, GPRA originated from Congress. The branch of government charged with oversight responsibilities now has a tool that is perceived to have potential to increase accountability. Further, GPRA carries the force of law. Despite any skepticism agencies might have about GPRA's long-term prospects, they are legally bound to comply with its requirements.

GPRA's Potential for Impact on Internal Management

The possible link between funding and performance and the difficulty of measuring the outcomes of public programs are the aspects of GPRA that seem to get the most attention. Perhaps the most lasting positive impact of GPRA, however, will be its potential to improve the internal management of federal agencies. Specifically, GPRA can lead to improvements in the relationship between federal agencies and the third parties they oversee or with whom they collaborate to produce public services. This study of the steps federal agencies have taken to implement GPRA has revealed some of the positive, yet not entirely intended, consequences of GPRA. The results orientation of GPRA coupled with the development of performance indicators to measure agencies' success in achieving these results have required a level of communication and coordination with third parties that did not exist in most agencies prior to GPRA's passage. This study will detail how the performance measurement process required by GPRA has served to improve internal management within federal agencies. The agencies studied for this chapter have developed new lines of results-oriented communication and improved their cooperation with the third parties they rely on to carry out their missions.

GPRA's primary implementation activities—goal development and goal measurement—are not uniform for all agencies, because federal agencies represent a diversity of policy instruments and therefore represent a diversity of implementation relationships. The term "policy instrument" refers to the primary activities federal government agencies engage in to achieve their objectives. The most prevalent examples include grants to state and local governments, direct service provision, contracted service provision, and regulation.

According to the law's text, the primary objectives of GPRA include increasing citizens' confidence in government, improving budget making, improving accountability, and improving the internal management of federal agencies. As with most legislative language, the connection between GPRA's requirements—goal setting, goal measurement, and performance reporting—and its stated objectives is not made explicit. It is hoped that through this chapter the connection between GPRA's requirements and its objectives of improved internal management and accountability will become clearer.

Agencies Studied

The agencies studied for this chapter, for example, were selected specifically because they represent a diversity of policy instruments. All of the agencies studied have different challenges measuring and meeting performance objectives depending on the policy instrument they use to achieve their policy objectives. These agencies are within the United States Department of Health and Human Services. They are the Food and Drug Administration (FDA), which is primarily a regulatory agency; the Centers for Medicare and Medicaid Services, which heavily relies on both contracted services in the Medicare program and grants to states in the Medicaid program; the Health Resources and Services Administration (HRSA), which is primarily a grant-making agency; the Indian Health Service (IHS), which provides grants to tribes and engages in the direct provision of health care and dental services to American Indians and Alaskan natives; and the National Institutes of Health (NIH), which produces scientific health-care-related research both intramurally (performed by NIH scientists) and extramurally (performed by grant recipients at hospitals, universities, and research institutions. Table 7.2 identifies and briefly describes the responsibilities of the HHS agencies studied for this chapter.

Table 7.2

Agency	Responsibilities
Food and Drug Administration (FDA)	Ensures that food, drugs, and medical devices on the market are safe and effective, and that these products reach the market in a timely way.
Centers for Medicare and Medicaid Services (CMS)*	Provides health insurance for over 74 million Americans through Medicare, Medicaid, and the State Children's Health Insurance Program (SCHIP).
Health Resources and Services Administration (HRSA)	Directs national health programs with the primary objective of assuring equitable access to health care services. These programs focus on providing primary health care to medically underserved people, including women, children, and persons with HIV/AIDS.
Indian Health Service (IHS)	Provides federal health services to American Indians and Alaska Natives who belong to approximately 550 federally recognized tribes in 35 states.
National Institutes of Health (NIH)	Oversees research and training aimed at acquiring new knowledge to help prevent, detect, diagnose, and treat disease and disability. The research and training funded by NIH is conducted intramurally (on the NIH campus) and extramurally (through grants and contracts to research institutes, universities, and hospitals).

* *formerly the Health Care Financing Administration (HCFA)*

While these agencies were selected to represent specific instruments, it should be noted they also use other policy instruments to achieve their objectives. CMS, for example, has a regulatory component in addition to its contracted services and grants, and HRSA uses loans and loan guarantees in addition to its extensive grant programs. The logic of selecting agencies that represent a diversity of the most common instruments is that complying with the goal setting, performance measurement, and performance reporting requirements of GPRA will play out differently in agencies that utilize different policy instruments or a different mix of policy instruments. While this diversity provides flexibility to HHS's efforts to improve America's health, it also adds extraordinary complexity to the implementation of a uniform goal-setting and performance-measurement system, such as GPRA.

Third-Party Government

Lester Salamon (1989) has used the apt metaphor of government by remote control to describe third-party government. Third-party government is government by remote control because the government authorizes policies and programs, but relies on other entities to carry out some or all of the implementation responsibilities. While there is nothing new about this phenomenon—governments have contracted out their services for years—there has been an increasing reliance on third parties to exercise discretion in matters such as goal making, financing, determining eligibility requirements, and developing and implementing accountability structures.

The advantages of third-party government include flexibility, competition, and avoidance of one-size-fits all solutions. These advantages are accompanied by immense accountability and management challenges. A central problem of third-party government, therefore, is how to achieve its advantages without creating public programs that are so complex and unwieldy that accountability becomes impossible. Some argue that the federal government's heavy reliance on third parties allows it to mask its true size (Light, 1999). To the extent that government's size is measured by the number of its employees, third-party service delivery is often accompanied by smaller agencies. A comparison of the size of the Social Security Administration (SSA) and CMS, the two largest (in budgetary terms) federal health and welfare agencies, is instructive. SSA, which directly provides its services, has approximately 63,000 employees. CMS, which provides its services primarily through third parties, has approximately 4,600 employees. One should not assume, however, that the bureaucratic apparatus supporting the Medicare and Medicaid programs is significantly smaller than the bureaucratic apparatus supporting Social Security. The critical difference is not the size of the bureaucracy, but that CMS has externalized much of its bureaucracy to insurance companies (Medicare) and states (Medicaid) while the SSA has not.

Third-Party Cooperation Needed

In addition to the differences in policy instruments, each of these agencies relies on third parties to help them achieve their policy objectives. Third-party responsibilities can include service delivery, administration, financing, goal setting, or any combination of these. Table 7.3 lists the primary third parties and policy instruments related to the agencies studied for this chapter.

Upon reading the text of the GPRA legislation and the documents produced through agency compliance, one is struck by the uniformity of reporting requirements. This uniformity exists despite the diversity of policy instruments used within the federal government and the individual challenges faced by agencies attempting to measure their performance. The only exception to these requirements is the option some agencies have to develop qualitative measures and report their performance in narrative form. The diversity of agencies selected for this research reveals the weaknesses inherent in GPRA's mostly uniform requirements. Each of these agencies represents a unique challenge to the goal setting, performance management, and performance budgeting required by GPRA. These challenges are not only related to what policy instrument an agency uses, but also the unique accountability relationships between agencies and the third parties they rely on to carry out their work.

Table 7.3

Agency	Instrument*	Third Parties*
Food and Drug Administration	Regulation	Regulated Industries
Centers for Medicare and Medicaid Services	Grants, Contracted Services	States, Insurance Companies
Health Resources and Services Administration	Grants	State Governments, Local Governments
Indian Health Service	Grants, Direct Service	Tribes
National Institutes of Health	Grants, Intramural Research	Hospitals, Universities, Research Institutes

* *Instruments and third parties listed in table represent the most significant (in terms of resources) activities of the agencies, but are by no means exhaustive.*

Implementing GPRA

As is the case with much federal legislation, knowledge of GPRA's text provides only limited guidance for those who are required to implement it. Aside from the methodological challenges inherent in measuring the outcomes of public services, one of the greatest challenges of implementing GPRA is reconciling the law's outcome measurement requirements with agency missions that are not focused entirely on policy outcomes.

Most federal agencies find themselves one, two, or several steps removed from the actual provision of public services. This is due to several factors. In agencies where programs are carried out through grants to state and municipal governments, the intent never was for the federal government to be ultimately responsible for policy outcomes. These programs benefit from the flexibility provided the grant recipients to determine the kind and level of services provided in addition to eligibility requirements. This allows grant recipients to cater public services to local preferences. Accompanying this flexibility, however, is great complexity in establishing performance measures and reporting performance information.

The example of the Medicaid program illustrates the complex challenge to federal performance measurement. Medicaid, like many federal programs, provides states with considerable latitude in establishing different levels and kinds of services, as well as eligibility requirements. The federal government establishes certain minimum service and eligibility requirements. Once those requirements are met, states are free to structure their Medicaid programs how they wish. While this provides flexibility, the absence of program uniformity also means the absence of goal uniformity.

Simply put, different states have different Medicaid goals. GPRA, however, requires that CMS establish goals for the entire Medicaid program, covering the different goals and objectives for all Medicaid grant recipients. One of the goals CMS has established for the Medicaid program is to increase the percentage of poor children receiving the recommended immunizations, which is a complex data challenge. Gathering the data necessary to measure performance requires extensive negotiations with third parties to assure that all 56 Medicaid "subcontractors" (50 of these being the states) measure, collect, and store data in compatible and comparable ways.

Observers of public sector performance measurement have long argued that the task's complexity leads administrators to measure data that are easily available and close at hand. A preliminary review of the FY 2001 performance plans/FY 1999 performance reports, with their emphasis on activity measures, confirms this argument. Are these measures adequate to evaluate the achievement of program objectives? Hardly. However, given the methodological and logistical problems associated with measuring public programs' performance, it is not difficult to understand why the majority of agencies' measures reflect inputs and activities. Much of the work of the five aforementioned agencies is carried out by third-party administrative and financing arrangements. While observing only five federal agencies is by no means representative of the entire federal government, the diversity of policy instruments and the use of a broad array of third parties can provide insight into the challenges agencies throughout the federal government face as they attempt to implement GPRA.

Third-Party Performance Measurement and Accountability Challenges

The necessity to coordinate with third parties to implement GPRA is not limited to intergovernmental programs, such as Medicaid. Virtually all federal programs work with third parties to carry out their policy objectives. The universe of third parties includes but is not limited to contractors, regulated industries, and public and private sector grant recipients. While GPRA's requirements are uniform for all federal agencies, agencies' roles in the production and delivery of public services are highly varied. For most agencies a significant portion of their work entails the management and oversight of third-party activities. There are two important aspects of GPRA implementation challenges that relate to this variety of third parties:

1. Different third parties have various kinds and levels of responsibilities in the delivery of public services; and
2. Different third parties have various levels of autonomy.

While these differences are critical to implementing GPRA, they have gone virtually unnoticed in the extensive discussion surrounding GPRA, from scholars to consultants. Federal managers, however, have an important story to tell with regard to the third-party coordination required to accomplish policy and program objectives and to implement the mission clarification, performance measurement, and performance reporting requirements of GPRA.

Over the last 20 years, research on the challenges introduced by the inclusion of third parties in the delivery of public services has been a major focus of public management scholarship. The addition of third parties adds layers of complexity to policy implementation. The terms "hollow state," "government by proxy," and "shadow state" are all used to connote a separation between the financing of government services and the provision of services. Research indicates that the skills required to manage in multi-organizational network settings are different from those required to manage in a direct service provision environment (Agranoff & McGuire, 1998). These networked service provision arrangements fragment power, obscure who is doing what, and sever the lines of control (Salamon, 1987). The research on implementing performance measurement systems in an intergovernmental administrative environment is scant but growing. However, given the reality of increasingly devolved federal programs to state and local governments, the rapid increase in contracting out, and the passage of GPRA, such research should take on a tone of urgency.

The difficulties in establishing performance measures for public health care programs are similar to those found in all indirect management situations. Indirect management can be characterized by the following conditions: (1) fragmented accountability; (2) differing opinions on policy purposes and objectives; (3) ongoing management relationships; and (4) shared information across formal boundaries (Rosenthal, 1984). Each of these conditions adds complexity to the design of performance measures and the collection of performance data. Adding to the difficulty of measuring performance in the federal system is the fear of state and local governments that performance measurement will be used as another form of federal mandate. States, counties, and cities fear that they will be underrepresented in the development of these measures and that they will be punished for not meeting the performance standards regardless of individual situations.

The heavy reliance on third parties has implications for two of GPRA's primary objectives: performance measurement and performance budgeting. The problems with performance measurement are discussed above. The implications for third-party government associated with performance budgeting relate to the connection between agency performance and appropriation. If agency appropriations are tied in any way to program performance, the added variable of third parties will complicate these decisions. This is not to suggest that federal agencies should not be accountable for failures of third parties, especially when contractors are used. In this new era of third-party government, managers in these agencies are as responsible for making "smart-buying" decisions (Kettl, 1993) and/or establishing thorough incentive structures and monitoring systems. Managers in previous eras, by comparison, were responsible for the competent administration of agencies with direct service provision responsibilities.

All Third Parties Are Not Alike

GPRA presents the opportunity to face the challenges of managing federal programs through a complex array of third-party partnerships. This complexity is not only a function of the numbers of those collaborating to deliver federal services, but also the diversity they represent in terms of their level of authority, their financial involvement, and the extent of their goal-making responsibility. Why is this a problem? It is a problem because GPRA requires agencies to set goals at the federal level for programs for which they do not have the final authority in many crucial areas.

When more authority is given to third parties it is accompanied by more complexity in the development of performance goals and measures. One example of this is the discrepancy between the number of goals for Medicaid compared to the number of goals for Medicare found in CMS's GPRA performance plan. Both programs are operated through third parties—Medicaid through the states, and Medicare through contractors. However, with Medicaid, the third parties share goal making and financing responsibilities with the federal government. Of CMS's performance plan goals specifically related to program performance, only three are intended to assess Medicaid program performance alone, while 20 of these goals are intended to assess Medicare performance alone.

This discrepancy is tied to the challenges associated with the vast differences among states' Medicaid services and the immense coordination and negotiation that would be required to establish even a rudimentary set of uniform Medicaid goals. Indeed, one of CMS's FY 1999 developmental performance plan goals was to work with states to develop Medicaid performance goals for inclusion in subsequent performance plans. This goal was met with the inclusion of goals relating to childhood immunization and the number of uninsured children. There are differences not only in the number of goals between the Medicare and Medicaid programs, but also in the kinds of goals. Some of the Medicare goals reflect a desire on the part of CMS to increase the satisfaction of Medicare customers. These goals include:

1. Improve the effectiveness of the dissemination of Medicare information to beneficiaries;
2. Improve beneficiary telephone customer service;
3. Sustain Medicare payment timeliness; and
4. Improve the satisfaction of Medicare beneficiaries with the health care services they receive.

The fact that no such customer satisfaction goals exist for the Medicaid program is arguably due, in large part, to the limited control CMS can exert on states compared to the control it can exert on Medicare contractors.

Study Findings

The initial findings of this research are presented in the form of brief descriptions of the GPRA implementation challenges in the five selected health care agencies, with an accompanying discussion. This is followed by consideration of the theoretical and then the practical implications of these findings. Table 7.4 summarizes the study's findings.

Table 7.4: Summary of Study Findings

Agency	Instrument	Third Parties	Implementation Challenges
Centers for Medicare and Medicaid Services	Grants, Contracted Services	States, Insurance Companies	When contractors are used to perform adminis trative responsibilities, performance goals should be used not only to measure outcomes, but also to strengthen contractor monitoring and compliance.
Indian Health Service	Grants, Direct Service	Tribes	Leadership and persuasion skills needed to encourage participation in performance measurement and reporting where federal agencies have limited authority and leverage over grant recipients.
Health Resources and Services Administration	Grants	State Governments, Local Governments	Grant programs' performance measurement challenges can be overcome by coordination, negotiation, flexibility, and resources. Disparate agency goals and limited resources constrain performance measurement efforts.
Food and Drug Administration	Regulation	Regulated Industries	Political climate dictates selection and priority of performance measures.
National Institutes of Health	Grants, Intramural Research	Hospitals Universities, Research Institutes	An agency's institutional, political, and cultural values can greatly impact their performance measurement efforts. Basic research agencies encounter unique and considerable challenges measuring and reporting performance.

Centers for Medicare and Medicaid Services (CMS): Using GPRA to Better Monitor Contractor Behavior

The GPRA implementation challenge that CMS's Medicare program has to overcome is coordination with and oversight of the work performed by contractors. Such contracts are widely used in both the private and public sector to infuse competition in the delivery of public services. However, the CMS case demonstrates that public entities that provide services through contractors are often confined in their efforts to monitor contractor behavior, calling into question the efficiency gains that are supposed to accompany contracting. This demonstrates that although CMS can establish Medicare performance goals, as GPRA requires, their ability to meet these goals is only partially under their control.

The contractor monitoring and enforcement mechanisms available to CMS are constrained by Medicare's authorizing legislation and its regulations. One major constraint is a provision within the authorizing legislation that does not allow CMS to contract with any intermediary it wishes. Instead, claims-processing intermediaries are selected by professional associations of hospitals and certain other institutional providers on behalf of their members. Another constraint is found in CMS's own regulations, which stipulate that the contractors who serve Medicare beneficiaries as carriers must be insurance companies, and that they must serve the full range of beneficiary needs. The regulations do not allow functional contracts for specific services—to respond to beneficiary questions, for example—even if other entities could provide the services more efficiently. Under the authorizing legislation, the final constraint is that CMS can contract only on a cost basis, which does not allow for fixed-price or performance-based contracts. Because these constraints limit the number of companies that qualify and want to contract with Medicare, the leverage that CMS is able to use to enforce contract terms is limited (GAO, 1999).

A recent example is found in CMS's attempts to assure that its Medicare contractors are Y2K compliant. One of CMS's performance goals was to "ensure millennium compliance (readiness) of CMS computer systems." Depending on how narrowly "CMS computer systems" is defined—taking into account only CMS's computer systems versus taking into account both CMS's and its contractor's computer systems—it could be argued that CMS met this goal well before December 1999. In practical terms, however, many "mission critical" Medicare computer systems are operated by contractors. Of Medicare's 99 mission critical computer systems, 24 are managed internally by CMS and the remaining 75 are managed by third parties (medical carriers and intermediaries). CMS's Y2K compliance difficulties stemmed not from their internally managed systems, but from the computer systems managed by their contracts. Many of CMS's Y2K compliance challenges resulted from constraints found in CMS's contracts with the medical carriers. As she attempted to find ways to address the agency's unique Y2K compliance challenges, Nancy-Ann Min DeParle, CMS's administrator during the second Clinton administration, looked to the contracts themselves. To her surprise, she found that the contracts' renewal were self-executing annually. Notwithstanding some debate about her ability to require contractors to be Y2K compliant, Min DeParle convened with many of the contractors' chief executive officers to encourage their compliance. She helped them to understand that the contractors could not afford system failure. In the end, CMS's systems (those managed internally and externally) operated through January 1, 2000, without any major disruptions (National Academy of Public Administration, 2000).

The difficulty of achieving Y2K compliance is only one example of CMS's contract monitoring challenges. Medicare fraud has plagued CMS for years, costing the agency billions of dollars. Medicare contractors, who pay claims to beneficiaries and are charged with monitoring and reducing Medicare fraud, are the culprits of much of the fraud. Ironically, these contractors are hired to carry out CMS's fraud reduction monitoring responsibilities. The recent behavior of these monitors, however, raises the critical question: Who is monitoring the monitors? Since mid-1997, 44 of these contractors have pleaded guilty to schemes to defraud the Medicare program, and they have paid more than $275 million to settle charges filed against them (Pear, 1999; GAO, 1999).

CMS's inadequate capacity to monitor the compliance of their contractors results from the previously mentioned constraints in Medicare's authorizing legislation and the agency's inability to "regularly check contractors' internal management controls, management and financial data, and key program safeguards to prevent payment errors" (GAO, 5, 1999). CMS's inability to adequately monitor contractor activities is highlighted by the fact that the fraudulent behavior of contractors is almost never detected by CMS but by whistle-blowers. In these instances, contractor employees brought the illegal activities to CMS's attention (Pear, 1999).

CMS's extensive focus on contractors' customer service activities might come at the expense of fraud detection. When CMS discovered that Blue Cross and Blue Shield of Michigan was providing inadequate service to Michigan's Medicare beneficiaries (from a customer service standpoint), CMS hired Blue Cross and Blue Shield of Illinois, based on its solid customer service reputation, to replace Blue Cross and Blue Shield of Michigan. Last year Blue Cross and Blue Shield of Illinois was ordered to pay $4 million in criminal charges and $140 million in civil charges based on their fraudulent Medicare activities (ibid.). CMS's hands were tied because their regulations do not permit functional contracts. Functional contracts would have allowed Blue Cross and Blue Shield of Michigan to continue its sound performance with regard to fiscal obligations, and let a separate contract for customer service related services.

While it is important for CMS to have goals related to both customer service and health care outcomes, CMS's primary responsibilities with regard to Medicare are financial and fiduciary. It should come as no shock to anyone that CMS employees do not provide health care services nor do they process claims for Medicare beneficiaries. In every instance CMS employees are at least one step removed from customer service and several steps removed from patient care. Although CMS has struggled with this relationship in the past, goals relating to monitoring their third parties are found in the agency's current performance plan. In this way CMS's leaders can use GPRA to better manage these relationships. Until changes are made to Medicare regulations and its authorizing legislation, contractor-monitoring efforts will have only limited success.

Indian Health Service

The nature of the accountability relationship between the IHS and its primary third party presents an entirely different coordination problem. Traditionally, the IHS was a direct service provision agency that hired health care workers or directly contracted with health care workers to provide basic health care and dental services to American Indians and native Alaskans. These services were provided at IHS service units located in hospitals and clinics. The portion of the IHS budget still dedicated to direct service provision or direct contracting presents few logistical problems for GPRA implementation. However, the Indian Self-Determination and Education Assistance Act (ISDEA, P.L. 93-638) of 1975 and its subsequent amendments have sought to provide tribes with the resources needed to act as sovereign nations.

From a practical standpoint for IHS, this means that tribes receive IHS monies directly so that they can contract on their own with health care providers. While other federal agencies have some leverage in their coordination and information collection—whether state and local governments, contractors, nonprofits, or other federal entities—IHS cannot require tribal leaders to submit performance information. In 1994, the year after GPRA was passed, an amendment to the ISDEA (P.L. 103-413) made it even less likely that tribal leaders will comply with GPRA's reporting requirements. The express purpose of these amendments was to allow tribal leaders to redesign IHS and other federal Indian programs and prioritize spending according to tribal discretion. They also provided tribes with the opportunity to get out from under the dominance of federal agencies and to transfer funds, including those intended to support federal oversight requirements, to the local tribal level.

The request for performance-related data to fulfill GPRA requirements is viewed by some tribal leaders as an unfunded mandate, or more accurately an unfunded request, as there is no obligation to provide this data. This reveals the lack of authority and weakness of IHS in their efforts to coordinate and gather performance information. Absent the ability to back incentives with threats and sanctions, IHS administrators have responded by explaining the details of GPRA to tribal leaders and demonstrating to them that faithful compliance allows tribes to speak in a more unified voice and could result in better information to support budget requests.

One innovative approach the IHS took was to hire a contractor to "sell" GPRA to tribal leaders. This contractor previously served in a prominent tribal leadership position in a self-governing tribe. He is a well-respected opinion leader among his peers. As a result of these efforts, and despite the absence of requirements, many tribal programs are not only participating (submitting the GPRA data needed by IHS), but also encouraging other tribal programs to participate. Some tribal leaders are concerned that funds spent on GPRA compliance are funds not spent directly on patient care. The respected contractor will continue working with tribal leaders to strengthen their support and encourage active participation in the development of performance goals and the submitting of necessary GPRA data.

Health Resources and Services Administration

HRSA provides an array of health care services that are targeted primarily to underserved, vulnerable, and special-needs populations. The majority of the programs operate through grants to states and localities. The Maternal and Child Health Bureau (MCHB) provides block grants to states to help improve the health of mothers, children, and adolescents, with an emphasis on those with low incomes. The response of MCHB administrators to the performance management problems inherent in block grant programs represents a unique and innovative approach to aligning third-party objectives and incentives.

One concern with block grant programs is that grant recipients might take advantage of the flexibility to aim resources and efforts at objectives different from those deemed important by Congress and the granting agency. The desire to avoid this must be balanced with the ability of state and local governments to design policies and programs their citizens need and demand. These are not easy values to balance. GPRA requires that federal agencies engage in a number of performance-related activities to increase accountability. By design, many of the programs these agencies oversee are under only limited federal control. Is there a way to implement GPRA in a manner that provides greater results accountability while not detracting from the flexibility of block grants? The MCHB has made a valiant effort to balance the competing values of results accountability and flexibility.

After GPRA became law, HRSA administrators met with representatives from all the states' Maternal and Child Health programs, interest groups, public health experts, and health data and data systems experts. After a 16-month process of input and negotiation, the Maternal and Child Health Performance Partnership developed a core of 18 measures to determine the overall performance of the state block grant program. Each state maternal and child health representative agreed to the core measures and agreed to report using such measures. To reduce the states' costs associated with monitoring states' performance on these GPRA goals, HRSA developed a uniform data collection and reporting format and provided an additional $100,000 annual grant to each state.

What about the flexibility that is supposed to accompany block grants? Were the MCHB's set of goals limited to the 18 agreed upon by all the states, the flexibility benefits of block grants would have been stymied. MCHB's implementation accommodates the priorities of states' citizens by requiring that states establish an additional set of 10 individualized goals. To create efficiencies, where a state's individualized goals coincide with other states' goals MCHB has established a uniform measurement and reporting protocol. One final impediment to activating MCHB's goal measurement and reporting system was the Paperwork Reduction Act of 1995, which is intended to limit the paperwork burden imposed by the federal government on state and local governments. Ironically, the MCHB's efforts to meet the requirements of one law were frustrated by the requirements of another law. MCHB negotiated with the U.S. Office of Management and Budget to obtain waivers in order to achieve compliance with the Paperwork Reduction Act.

Another unit within HRSA, the Office of Rural Health Policy (ORHP), faces more daunting impediments to establishing goals and measuring performance. The ORHP promotes better health care service in rural America. In this capacity, the office works with third parties in both the public and private sectors, including associations, foundations, health care providers and community leaders. Much of ORHP's mission is carried out through five grant programs. These grant programs face a myriad of difficulties measuring performance, including:

- *Diversity of grants.* Grants fund such a diversity of rural health activities—from training Emergency Medical Technicians (EMTs) to providing primary and preventive care to migrant farm workers—that it is difficult to select a sample of performance measures that are representative of the program's activities. Unlike other units within HRSA, ORHP does not consist of one program, nor is it governed by a single act of legislation.

- *Limited resources.* Most ORHP grants are awarded specifically to rural areas that lack crucial medical resources. Many of these health care facilities are staffed by one doctor, one nurse, and a part-time clerk. In these facilities, all available resources are directed toward patient care. There are few resources to devote to GPRA-related reporting. Indeed, many ORHP grants go to help rural health care clinics meet the quality assurance reporting demands of Medicare.
- *Misdirected resources.* One of ORHP's programs, the Rural Healthcare Network Development grant program, provides $80 million annually to support the establishment of managed care networks in rural areas. Because lack of funds is not the primary impediment to having managed care networks function in rural areas, recipients of these grants spend the monies on other health care activities.

GPRA's uniformity seems ill suited for programs such as those funded by ORHP. Further, OHRP will unlikely be able to take advantage of GPRA's requirements to further their coordination efforts with third parties, or grant recipients. The purposes of these grants are too diverse and the resources of the grant recipients are too limited to make complying with GPRA requirements anything but a waste of resources.

Food and Drug Administration

The FDA provides an interesting case study of the unique challenges faced by regulatory agencies in measuring performance and of the role national political dynamics play in the difficulties of implementing GPRA. With the passage of the Food and Drug Administration Modernization Act of 1997 (FDAMA), the FDA fundamentally altered its obligations with regard to the public's health. The act includes a congressionally mandated mission statement that adds to the FDA's traditional role of protecting consumer health by dictating that the agency will also promote consumer health. In practical terms, the promotion of consumer health translates into prompt review of clinical research and timely, appropriate action on the marketing of regulated products. As a symbol of the importance Congress places on prompt clinical reviews and action, the promotion of the public health component of the mission statement is put first, ahead of the protection of public health component. The consequences of the emphasis on health promotion are more than symbolic, however, as the allocation of FDA's budget has been directed toward pre-approval drug inspections (to get drugs on the market quickly) and away from post-approval inspections and other consumer protection activities.

In accordance with the Prescription Drug User Fee Act (PDUFA) of 1992, FDA collects user fees from the pharmaceutical industry. The law dictates that these funds may be used only to expedite the pre-market review of new drugs and biologics. As the revenues have increased they have accounted for a greater proportion of FDA's budget. As a result, the proportion and number of FDA employees dedicated to meeting FDA's other goals and objectives have decreased. Since PDUFA passed, these user fees have paid for 840 FDA employees who work exclusively to bring pharmaceuticals to the market more rapidly. During the same period, however, the number of FDA employees increased from 8,868 to 8,908 full-time equivalents (FTEs), an increase of only .5 percent. In the seven years since PDUFA's passage, employees whose salaries were paid from these user fees went from zero to just under 10 percent of the agency's workforce. In other words, given the slight increase of 40 FTEs during the same period, the PDUFA-purchased employees do not represent new FTEs, but resources redirected from other FDA activities, namely consumer protection.

An interesting challenge associated with GPRA implementation at FDA is the transition of responsibility for seafood inspection from the FDA to the industry itself. The program is called the Hazard Analysis Critical Control Point System, or HACCP, which is a system of process controls to ensure food safety. The implementation of HACCP represents a move away from traditional FDA inspection as a means of detecting food-borne hazards and toward industry self-regulation coupled with a system of FDA audits for monitoring purposes. The problem, however, is that the HACCP auditing portion of the FDA budget is chronically underfunded.

While Congress demands greater accountability on the one hand, on the other it is pressuring the FDA to radically reduce its ability to monitor and assure industry compliance with FDA standards. With HACCP, the monitoring activities traditionally performed by FDA have been entrusted to the industry. What was a delicate relationship to begin with is now rife with conflicts of interest. The auditing would serve as a check to these interest conflicts, but only if funded adequately. It is unclear whether politics or mixed messages have led to low funding for HACCP auditing. What is clear is that the combination of shifting from FDA inspections to industry self-regulation and a chronically underfunded auditing system invites industry noncompliance with FDA regulations.

The FDA case also points to the inconsistencies between GPRA and Congress's demand for outcome accountability and statutory requirements that mandate certain output levels, with no specific attention to eventual outcomes. Such is the case for the FDA's statutory site inspection requirements. Congressional mandates direct FDA efforts explicitly toward attention to immediate outputs rather than long-term outcomes. To meet Food Safety Assurance statutory requirements, for example, the FDA has to inspect 80 percent of sites semiannually. Alternatively, the agency's strategy puts an emphasis on visits to the most risky sites rather than on broader site coverage stipulated by statutory requirements. Because the risky sites take longer to inspect, attention to them comes at the expense of broader site coverage. Indeed, the FDA would certainly meet its statutory requirements for the Food Safety Assurance program only if it were to ignore the more risky, time-consuming sites. This puts agency leadership in a dilemma that pits congressional requirements against actual outcome performance.

Despite the unique challenges of implementing GPRA in a regulatory agency with intense political pressures, the FDA has done an admirable job both implementing GPRA and meeting the performance requirements established by Congress. For example, under an accelerated approval program, the FDA took only 5.8 months to approve Ziagen, a drug used in the treatment of HIV-1 infection in adults and children. Additionally, the median approval time for generic drugs has been reduced from an average of 19.6 months in 1997 to 17.3 months in 1999. Finally, the FDA set a goal to review 90 percent of priority new drug applications within six months.

National Institutes of Health

Of the five agencies studied, NIH's task to implement GPRA is the most daunting. The fundamental challenge that confronts NIH is its primary mission of basic research. Basic research activities do not lend themselves to easy quantitative measurement, nor is it easy to identify specific scientific advances taking place over as brief a period as a year. For five of the seven NIH performance plan goals that relate to its research program, NIH has selected qualitative measurements to assess their performance. The first of these goals is representative of the difficulties associated with the measurement of basic science research. This goal is to "add to the body of knowledge about normal and abnormal biological functions."

There are institutional, political, and cultural values within NIH that make performance measurement and the possibility of performance budgeting difficult to implement and analyze. The first thing to remember while considering NIH's implementation of GPRA is the notion of performance budgeting—some link between productivity, or even mere GPRA compliance, and appropriations. Even those who do not feel performance budgeting is unrealistic would find it difficult to create a rational link between performance and appropriations for NIH. NIH is popular with members of Congress on both sides of the aisle. This support is based on a number of considerations of which annually measured performance would likely rank low. First, it is a distributive agency. In FY 1999 NIH grants were awarded in all 50 states and many more congressional districts. Many members of Congress have been personally affected by some disease for which NIH is seen to have a critical role in its research. It is not unusual for the most fiscally conservative members of Congress to support NIH research.

A second factor complicating GPRA implementation at NIH is the great respect NIH has for its grant recipients. The solid reputation NIH enjoys results, in large part, from the stature and accomplishments of its grant recipients. This makes attempts to achieve accountability more delicate than in other grant situations. One NIH employee I interviewed indicated that if any of the grant recipients are aware of the goals within NIH's performance plan, it is by accident rather than design. NIH officials do not share agency goals with grant recipients, nor do they intend to do so. The justification for not sharing GPRA goals with grant recipients is straight-forward: NIH wants to avoid even the suggestion that its grant-supported research could be biased so as to satisfy performance expectations. While other agencies can exploit GPRA's requirements to coordinate with third parties and orient all activities toward outcomes, NIH is unable to use GPRA in this way.

A third factor complicating GPRA implementation is that the NIH is actually many semi-autonomous institutions. The plural "Institutes" in the agency's name refers to the numerous (about 25) subunits comprising the NIH, most of which are research institutes and centers. Further, the institutes do not conduct most of the research themselves; it is done extramurally through grants to hospitals and universities. This makes for an extremely decentralized agency, complicating monitoring and oversight of the grants. Finally, the basic research mission of NIH provides all the classic methodological concerns of many public sector activities, only worse. Many advances from current research will not be realized in practical applications for many years. This minimizes the usefulness of annual performance reporting.

Given these constraints, the NIH had to develop a series of goals that 1) would allow for a valid assessment of outcomes that are inherently difficult to measure, 2) would not be intrusive or create an environment that might bias grant recipient research, and 3) would be simple enough to allow compilation of data from all 25 centers and institutes. To meet these criteria, NIH devised an assessment system highlighting the research supported by NIH grants that appears in peer-reviewed science journals; the role NIH-supported research has played in advancements in specific fields of health such as cancer, spinal chord injuries, and diabetes; and the science awards and honors received by NIH grant recipients for their grant-supported research. Once the data were collected, a group of distinguished scientists and science advocates reviewed the materials to determine if NIH met their research-related performance plan goals.

A central concern of NIH leadership is to avoid the impression that the assessment working group serves merely as a rubber stamp instead of honestly and thoroughly reviewing NIH's success in achieving its goals. It is hard to imagine that such a combination of science expertise and advocacy can divorce itself from self-interest to the extent that it could provide an honest assessment of NIH's success in achieving its GPRA goals.

Conclusion

A recent GAO report (2001) based on interviews with nearly 4,000 federal managers reveals that managers in only four of the largest 28 federal agencies, did at least two-thirds of managers interviewed perceive a strong commitment to achieving results from their agencies' executives. In 11 of these 28 agencies, less that half of the managers interviewed perceived such a commitment for achieving results. This chapter also revealed that in only one of these 28 agencies did the managers interviewed feel that they have, to a "great" or "very great" extent, the decision-making authority they need to help their agency accomplish its strategic goals. It is unlikely that the poor support for achieving results in these agencies reflects negligence on the part of the agencies' leaders. Rather, it is likely a reflection of the reality that federal agencies have only partial control over the results for which they are held accountable. HRSA does not provide health care to underserved populations; it provides grants to states, counties, and private sector entities to provide health care to underserved populations. It is this disjunct that likely frustrates agency leaders' attempts to manage for results in a way that GPRA requires, focusing on goals and objectives.

This frustration will be reduced and GPRA will become a more useful tool for developing agency strategies and managing performance when it is used to assist agency executives in managing and monitoring their relationships with third parties. Whether GPRA compliance efforts are located within agencies' budget offices—which they often are—or with substantive policy experts, the skills that are required for contract monitoring and/or negotiation and coordination are seriously lacking. GPRA should be exploited by agencies to pay greater attention to contract bidding and monitoring. Monitoring activities should not be limited to agency relationships with contractors. Instead, GPRA can be the vehicle through which federal agencies expand their monitoring activities to include the universe of third-party relationships.

With the sophistication of program evaluation and organizational scorecards, the absence of a bottom line or the methodological and measurement difficulties should no longer be seen as the primary impediment to performance management at the federal level. If there is one lesson from the long history of management and budget reforms, it is that the information produced by these reforms was ultimately more useful for program managers than for legislators. This will likely be the case for GPRA, too. In this vein, as agencies attempt to implement GPRA, attention should turn to overcoming the logistical challenges and managing the wide range of accountability relationships with the various third parties that partner with federal agencies to deliver public services. To accomplish this, as agencies implement GPRA, greater attention needs to be paid to agencies' immediate responsibilities.

Even the names of some agencies connote their primary role as the delivery of public services. It is no coincidence that the Centers for Medicare and Medicaid Services is given that name. As mentioned previously, CMS's primary responsibilities with regard to the programs it oversees, Medicare and Medicaid, are financial and fiduciary. Some of this attention will come at the expense of the attention currently given to broad programmatic and policy objectives. While many of these agencies are one, two, or several steps removed from actual service provision, they are still ultimately responsible for meeting policy goals and objectives. To meet these responsibilities, agencies should have goals in their performance plans that pertain to their monitoring and supervisory obligations over third parties.

These goals should be guided by the nature of the relationship between the agency and the third parties. On one end of the spectrum are contractual relationships, such as those between CMS and the companies hired to handle Medicare claims. In this example CMS has substantial leverage, as it can terminate contracts when there is inadequate performance. In a pure contractual situation there is much to be learned from private sector experience in the area of contractor oversight. On the other end of the spectrum, the Indian Health Service has little to no leverage over tribal health care programs. In this instance the only instrument available to agency managers is persuasion. Somewhere between these two extremes exist federal agencies whose primary responsibilities are to provide grants to state and local governments. It is in these agencies where GPRA implementation presents the greatest frustration and the greatest opportunity for federal agencies to strengthen their capacity to manage intergovernmental programs. The challenge is to discover the appropriate combination of leverage and persuasion to exercise in their performance management. These accountability relationships are highlighted in Table 7.5.

What the appropriate combination of leverage and persuasion is should ultimately be determined by the extent to which grant recipients are charged with program financing and goal-making responsibilities versus the extent to which these responsibilities are retained by the federal agency. In each of these instances, agencies should develop performance plan goals that reflect the agencies' actual function in the provision or production of public services. Discovering the right combination of leverage and persuasion is difficult in light of the many and sometimes contradictory messages sent by Congress to federal agencies. On one hand, through GPRA, federal agencies are to be held accountable for their results or for demonstrating

Table 7.5

Instrument	Third Party	Obligations	Nature of Relationship
Categorical Grants	State and Local Governments	Varied: Financing, Very Limited Goal Making, Administrative	Persuasion, Authoritative
Block Grants	State and Local Governments	Varied: Financing, Goal Making, Administrative	Cooperation, Persuasion, Midly Authoritative
Regulation	Regulated Industries	Financing, Administrative	Coercion, Some Collaboration
Contracts	Contractors	Administrative	Coercion

the impact of their programs. On the other hand, there is a constant push to devolve more responsibilities to lower levels of government or administer them through private entities. It is just this sort of arrangement for which GPRA is well suited—helping federal agencies manage accountability relationships with third parties, while keeping their eye continually focused on achieving the objectives for which the federal programs were created.

Finally, an important practical lesson from the five agencies studied is that their GPRA-driven reform efforts can accomplish reform only to the extent that they do not conflict with authorizing law and all other existing laws. All of the case agencies have been impeded in their efforts to achieve their goals and collect data to determine the level of goal achievement by existing law. Sound policy implementation is hindered by contradictory sets of rules and constrained by authorizing legislation. Because the GPRA law does not have language that would allow its provisions to supercede any existing laws pertaining to the departments, agencies, and programs it intends to reform, GPRA's reach can extend only so far. There are many instances in the agencies studied here that illustrate how existing law either prevented thorough implementation of GPRA or had to be amended to accommodate its implementation. Some of the main impediments that inhibit agencies' GPRA implementation include the Paperwork Reduction Act of 1995, agency authorizing legislation, and an agency's own regulations. Although Congress's role is generally assumed to enabling and delegation legislation, the power of the purse, and oversight, laws that either constrain or increase agencies' ability to engage in monitoring activities make Congress a de facto partner in the management of federal programs (Gilmour & Halley, 1994).

Recommendations

Based on this chapter's findings the following recommendations about GPRA implementation are made:

Recommendations for Agencies

In developing their performance goals, each agency should make clear their role in the delivery of public services. Specifically, in addition to outcome measures, agencies that give grants to third parties should develop goals relating management and oversight of grantees' performance in achieving outcomes.

This chapter has identified the discrepancy between the demand for outcome performance measures and the actual work of many federal agencies. Direction in the development of these goals and their alignment with the actual work of agencies should come from the agencies' senior management. This is the only way that agencies will be able to use their performance plans and reports as a tool to devise management strategies that reflect their position, function, and capacity in the implementation of federal programs.

As the number of third parties that agencies must work with to implement federal programs increases, so too does the complexity of service delivery. As a general rule, more third parties in a given program means less leverage for the agency charged with its implementation. This fact is not an excuse for agency executives to shirk responsibility for results of programs for which they have only limited control. Whenever third parties are involved in service delivery, agencies become players in a partnership for delivering services. Agencies should use their GPRA strategic and performance plans to coordinate, measure, and oversee the activities of third parties to assure that all are working toward the goals established in GPRA strategic and performance plans.

Agencies should use GPRA not only as a means to communicate their performance, but also to communicate constraints that inhibit their performance.

GPRA provides critical information to decision makers within the agencies and in Congress. The release of the first two performance reports and the subsequent congressional and public response to each indicate that an agency's performance report will be judged on its own merits and not based on public or congressional perception of the agency. One agency that has received much praise for the quality of its performance report has been the U.S. Agency for International Development (USAID). What is particularly praiseworthy about USAID's report? According to the Mercatus Center at George Mason University, USAID's report "contains thorough discussion of management challenges." Additionally, the Mercatus analysts found that the "agency does not hesitate to criticize its own initiatives and discuss failures."

Some agencies have expressed concern that the performance information in GPRA reports will serve as additional ammunition for members of Congress to use during appropriations and oversight hearings. Aggressive congressional scrutiny existed prior to GPRA and will continue regardless of GPRA's ultimate fate. Agency executives can strengthen their hand in these discussions by using GPRA as a tool to systematically discuss agencies' management challenges. In many instances, members of Congress will discover or be reminded that many of the factors inhibiting performance are not under agencies' immediate control. In addition to the extensive use of third parties in the delivery of federal services, the rules set forth in authorizing legislation impede performance. In this way, agencies can frame the debate about their performance and even make recommendations to Congress about what it can do to help agencies meet their performance targets.

Recommendation for OMB

The U.S. Office of Management and Budget's Circular A-11, which includes a section on what information should be included in performance plans and reports, should require that agencies include information on third party collaboration in the development of performance goals and measures. Further, the A-11 should require that agencies' strategic plans include sections on the strategies that agencies have to manage third-party relationships to help achieve their performance goals.

As a general rule, agencies should collaborate with third parties in the development of performance goals. Because third parties play such a crucial role in the delivery of public services, it is a serious error to exclude their participation in the development of performance goals and the measurements used to assess their attainment. Complicating this effort is the fact that federal agencies' leverage over third parties ranges from very strong to very weak. Leadership—the ability to persuade, encourage, influence, and obtain commitment—plays a crucial role in gaining third-party cooperation in the development and achievement of performance goals.

Agency executives should take the lead in assuring that third parties participate in the GPRA performance management process. Evidence of third party participation in GPRA should appear throughout the strategic and performance plans required by GPRA. Particularly, the narrative section that accompanies each performance goal should clearly discuss the role third parties play in the goal's attainment and specific actions the agency is taking to work with the third parties to improve performance related to the goal.

The agencies studied for this chapter used leadership skills to persuade third party participation in GPRA. The IHS gained the cooperation of tribal leaders to participate in performance reporting even when tribes were under no legal obligation to do so. MCHB achieved consensus from state maternal and child health representatives from all 50 states to report on a set of 18 core measures. CMS was able to assure Y2K compliance from its contractors, even when its ability to legally require contractors to do so was in question. The lesson learned from these examples is that agency executives used leadership and creativity to align third-party interests with agency interests to help reach agreement on broad outcomes. Additionally, agency executives in these instances have helped third parties realize that the development and achievement of performance goals can hold advantages for them, too.

Recommendation for OPM

The U.S. Office of Personnel Management should take the lead in developing strategies to help agencies engage in an extensive effort to train and hire employees to manage all activities relating to third parties.

The federal workforce is ill-prepared to operate in the complex environment that results from managing programs and policies through third parties. There is much talk of the looming human capital crisis facing the federal government. Most of the attention of this discussion focuses on the large number of soon-to-be retiring federal managers and hiring, motivating, and training highly skilled employees to replace them. Much less attention, however, is given to the unique and specific skill mix required to manage and provide oversight to the third parties currently providing the bulk of federal services. There is much talk of the need to align employee skills with agency needs.

Unfortunately, talk of skill alignment often remains in the abstract. Even tools designed to analyze workforce skills needs (OPM, 2001a) and models to plan workforce needs (OPM, 2001b) deal mostly with generic skills. Neither of them include, nor do they discuss, skills related to managing third parties through grants or contracts.

The Department of Defense (DoD) recognized its own shortcomings in this area more than a decade ago. DoD leaders had the foresight to establish the Defense Acquisition University (DAU) in 1990. Through 12 DoD educational institutions and contractors, DAU trains the DoD acquisition workforce to work competently in the various fields of acquisition. Many of the courses provided through DAU relate specifically to achieving accountability when programs are delivered through third parties. Courses such as Contract Auditing, Contracting Basics, Management for Contracting Supervisors, and Grants Management prepare DoD managers to operate in the complex network of agencies and third parties that epitomizes contemporary federal management.

GPRA provides a means through which agencies can aim toward policy outcomes by coordinating and overseeing the efforts of the various third parties with whom they partner to deliver public services. Many agencies do not currently have the expertise or the capacity to manage these accountability relationships. OPM should take the lead in helping agencies recognize the importance of specific expertise in achieving results through third parties. There is a little known and widely ignored section of the GPRA legislation that provides for flexibility in personnel and staffing restrictions, limitations on compensation, and restrictions on funding transfers among budget classifications. Agencies should explore the possibility of using this flexibility to hire and train employees who have skills that more closely match the contemporary federal management environment.

Recommendation for Congress

Agencies should request and Congress should appropriate money for agencies to engage in the coordination necessary to include third parties extensively in the development of performance goals and the measures used to assess their attainment.

Of the agencies studied for this chapter, the MCHB provided the best example of direct cooperation with third parties in the development of performance goals and measures. To secure the states' cooperation required $5 million. The states used this money to collect and report data in the agreed-upon, uniform method. While the $5 million figure appears minimal, it represents the costs required to adequately measure performance for only one program within a single bureau. There are dozens of such bureaus (or similar entities) within the U.S. Department of Health and Human Services alone. Despite the costs associated with third-party cooperation in performance goal and measurement development, it is an essential investment.

Bibliography

Agranoff, Robert, and Michael McGuire, "Multi-Network Management: Collaboration and the Hollow State in Local Economic Policy," *Journal of Public Administration Research and Theory*. Vol. 8, No. 1 (January 1998: 67-91).

Gilmour, Robert S., and Alex A. Halley, (Eds.). 1994. *Who Makes Public Policy?: The Struggle for Control between Congress and the Executive.* New York: Chatham House.

Kettl, Donald F. 1993. *Sharing Power: Public Governance and Private Markets.* Washington, D.C.: Brookings Institution.

Light, Paul C. 1999. *The True Size of Government.* Washington, D.C.: Brookings Institution.

Milward, H. Brinton. 1996. "Symposium on the Hollow State: Capacity, Control, and Performance in Interorganizational Settings," *Journal of Public Administration Research and Theory.* Vol. 6, No. 2 (April 1996: 193-195).

National Academy of Public Administration. Minutes of the Standing Panel on Executive Organization and Management. February 18, 2000.

Pear, Robert. "Fraud in Medicare Increasingly Tied to Claims Payers," *New York Times*. September 20, 1999.

Rosenthal, Stephen R., "New Directions for Evaluating Intergovernmental Programs," *Public Administration Review.* Vol. 44, No. 6 (November/December 1984: 469-76).

Salamon, Lester M., *Beyond Privatization: The Tools of Government Action.* Washington, D.C.: Urban Institute Press, 1989.

U.S. General Accounting Office. 1999. *Medicare Contractors: Despite Its Efforts, CMS Cannot Ensure Their Effectiveness or Integrity.* Washington: U.S. General Accounting Office.

U.S. General Accounting Office. 2001. *Managing for Results: Federal Managers' Views on Key Management Issues Vary Widely across Agencies.* Washington: U.S. General Accounting Office.

U.S. Office of Personnel Management. 2001a. Workforce Skills Analysis Tool for Supervisors, Managers, and Executives. http://www.opm.gov/workforceplanning/index.htm. Washington: U.S. Office of Personnel Management.

U.S. Office of Personnel Management. 2001b. Federal Government Workforce Planning: 5 Step Workforce Planning Model. http://www.opm.gov/workforceplanning/index.htm Washington: U.S. Office of Personnel Management.

About the Contributors

Mark A. Abramson is executive director of The PricewaterhouseCoopers Endowment for The Business of Government, a position he has held since July 1998. Prior to the Endowment, he was chairman of Leadership Inc. From 1983 to 1994, Mr. Abramson served as the first president of the Council for Excellence in Government. Previously, Mr. Abramson served as a senior program evaluator in the Office of the Assistant Secretary for Planning and Evaluation, U.S. Department of Health and Human Services

He is a Fellow of the National Academy of Public Administration. In 1995, he served as president of the National Capital Area Chapter of the American Society for Public Administration. Mr. Abramson has taught at George Mason University and the Federal Executive Institute in Charlottesville, Virginia.

Mr. Abramson is the co-editor, with Paul R. Lawrence, of *Transforming Organizations*. He also recently edited *Memos to the President: Management Advice from the Nation's Top Public Administrators* and *Toward a 21st Century Public Service: Reports from Four Forums*. He is also the co-editor (with Joseph S. Wholey and Christopher Bellavita) of *Performance and Credibility: Developing Excellence in Public and Nonprofit Organizations*, and the author of *The Federal Funding of Social Knowledge Production and Application*.

He received his Bachelor of Arts degree from Florida State University. He received a Master of Arts degree in history from New York University and a Master of Arts degree in political science from the Maxwell School of Citizenship and Public Affairs, Syracuse University.

Colin Campbell was born in Calgary, Alberta, in 1943. He was educated in that city and at Gonzaga University in Spokane, Washington, where he received his A.B. (Hons.) in political science in 1965. In 1966, he obtained his M.A. in political science at the University of Alberta. He completed his Ph.D. in political science at Duke University in Durham, North Carolina, in 1973.

From 1975 to 1983, Campbell taught at York University in Toronto, where he became professor of political science and coordinator of the Public Policy and Administration Program. At Georgetown, he is university professor of public policy. From 1990 to 1998, he directed the Georgetown Public Policy Institute. He has served as a guest scholar at the Brookings Institution in Washington, D.C., three times (1979, 1982-83 and 1998-99). During 1979-81, he served as president of the Canadian Study of Parliament Group. From 1984 to 1989, he was co-chairman of the International Political Science Association Research Committee on the Structure and Organization of Government. From 1987 to 1993 and 1996 to 1997, he was co-editor of *Governance: An International Journal of Policy and Administration* published by Basil Blackwell of Oxford. He has had fellowships at York University, University of Manchester and the Australian National University. He has been visiting professor at Meiji University in Tokyo, the University of Melbourne, the University of Sydney, and Fondation Nationale des Sciences Politiques (Paris). In 1993, he gave the Martin D'Arcy Lectures at Oxford University. He has consulted for Organisation for Economic Cooperation and Development, the World Bank, and Synergy, Inc. He is a Fellow at the National Academy of Public Administration.

Along with co-editing five collections and publishing numerous articles and chapters in scholarly journals and books, Campbell has published eight books: *The U.S. Presidency in Crisis* (1998), *The End of Whitehall?* (1995), *Political Leadership in an Age of Constraint: The Australian Experience* (1992), *Politics and Government in Europe Today* (1990, 1995), *Managing the Presidency: Carter, Reagan and the Search for Executive Harmony* (1987), *Governments Under Stress: Political Executives and Key Bureaucrats in Washington, London and Ottawa* (1983), *The Superbureaucrats: Structure and Behavior in Central Agencies* (1979), and *The Canadian Senate: A Lobby From Within* (1978). *Managing the Presidency* won two national awards—the 1987 American Political Science Association Neustadt Prize for the best book on the presidency and the 1986 Alpha Sigma Nu Prize for the best book in social or natural sciences published by a faculty member at one of the 28 Jesuit colleges and universities in the U.S. *The U.S. Presidency in Crisis* won the 1999 *Governance* and International Political Science Association Levine Prize for the best book in the areas of comparative policy and administration.

John Carnevale has over 14 years of federal government drug policy experience at the executive branch level. He served for 11 years at the White House Office of National Drug Control Policy (ONDCP), where he served as the director of the Office of Programs, Budget, Research, and Evaluation.

While there, he prepared the National Drug Control Strategy and the Federal Drug Control Budget to implement it. He also developed the Performance Measures of Effectiveness, which is the tool used by the federal government to evaluate whether the strategy is achieving its goals and objectives. He recently directed the presidential transition for drug policy for the George W. Bush administration.

Prior to ONDCP, Dr. Carnevale worked at the White House Office of Management and Budget, where one of his responsibilities was to monitor drug policy issues and to oversee the U.S. Customs Service budget account. In total, his experience spans three administrations and four drug czars.

Dr. Carnevale's other government experience includes working at the Department of Treasury, where he monitored the fiscal health of the state and local government sector. He also was responsible for monitoring the fiscal condition of New York City under the Federal New York City Loan Guarantee Program.

He received his Ph.D. in economics from the Maxwell School of Syracuse University. He is trained in public finance and has published articles on drug policy, budget, the fiscal impact on local budgets of federal grant programs, and the fiscal health of the state and local government sector.

Dr. Carnevale left federal service in January 2000. He is currently president of Carnevale Associates LLC, which he founded to provide leadership and guidance on the difficult policy and program challenges engendered by drug use and its damaging consequences. He works with all levels of government to provide strategic planning, resource management, accountability standards, and stakeholder involvement in all aspects of drug control policy and programming.

David G. Frederickson is a public affairs doctoral candidate at the Indiana University School of Public and Environmental Affairs (SPEA), with concentrations in public finance and public management. Mr. Frederickson is a graduate of Brigham Young University (1992, B.A. in political science) and of George Mason University (1995, Master of Public Administration).

Mr. Frederickson has taught courses in statistics/research methods, organizational behavior, and program evaluation. He has published in the areas of public sector reform efforts, public sector change management, and pay for performance. His current research is on the Government Performance and Results Act (GPRA) and principal-agent relationships between federal agencies and third parties.

Peter Frumkin is assistant professor of public policy at Harvard University's John F. Kennedy School of Government, where he is affiliated with the Hauser Center for Nonprofit Organizations. At the Kennedy School, he teaches courses on public and nonprofit management.

His recent research has examined compensation policies in nonprofit organizations, the impact of fundraising strategies on nonprofit revenue generation, the professionalization of private foundations, and the impact of public funding on nonprofit mission definition. He has published articles in the *American Review of Public Administration, Public Administration Review, Nonprofit and Voluntary Sector Quarterly, Nonprofit Management and Leadership Society,* and numerous other journals.

Frumkin's current research focuses on public policies shaping the nonprofit sector, the management of nonprofit organizations, and the performance of private philanthropic foundations.

Frumkin has been awarded both the Best Dissertation Prize and a Best Paper Prize from the Academy of Management's Public and Nonprofit Division.

Prior to coming to the Kennedy School, Frumkin worked as a foundation program officer and as a program evaluator in nonprofit and public agencies.

He is a graduate of Oberlin College (1984) and holds an M.P.P. (1989) from Georgetown University. He received his Ph.D. in sociology from the University of Chicago in 1997.

John M. Kamensky is director of the managing for results practice for PricewaterhouseCoopers LLP and senior research fellow for the Endowment for the Business of Government. During 24 years of public service, he played a key role in helping pioneer the federal government's performance and results orientation. He is passionate about creating a government that is results-oriented, performance-based, and customer-driven.

Prior to joining PricewaterhouseCoopers LLP in February 2001, Mr. Kamensky served for eight years as deputy director of Vice President Gore's National Partnership for Reinventing Government. Before that, he worked at the General Accounting Office for 16 years where he played a key role in the development and passage of the Government Performance and Results Act. Mr. Kamensky received a Masters in Public Affairs from the Lyndon B. Johnson School of Public Affairs, in Austin, Texas.

Patrick J. Murphy is an assistant professor of politics at the University of San Francisco, where he teaches courses in public policy, public administration, and American government.

Prior to teaching, he worked at the Office of Management and Budget coordinating drug policy issues and serving as the liaison with the Office of National Drug Control Policy. He also worked for the RAND Corporation and continues to serve as a research consultant with RAND. He has published several reports and articles on the economics of drug dealing, drug problems in the Washington, D.C., area, the coordination of drug policy, and drug budgets.

His current research is a collaboration with the Center for Reinventing Public Education at the University of Washington. It focuses on the dimensions of the shortage of teachers and strategies that school districts have used to address this problem.

Kathryn Newcomer is professor and chair in the Department of Public Administration at the George Washington University, where she teaches public and nonprofit program evaluation, research design, and applied statistics. She conducts research and training for federal and local government agencies on performance measurement and program evaluation, and has done consulting work for the governments of the United Kingdom, Ukraine, and Brazil on performance auditing. She is currently consulting with the Smithsonian Institution to design a performance measurement system.

Dr. Newcomer has published three books, *Improving Government Performance* (1989), *The Handbook of Practical Program Evaluation* (1994), and *Using Performance Measurement to Improve Public and Nonprofit Programs* (1997) (all published by Jossey-Bass), and numerous articles in journals including the *Public Administration Review*. Her current research focuses on the changing role of the Office of Inspector General (OIG) in the federal government, as she updates the OIG profiles she provided in 1992 and 1996. She currently serves on the Advisory Council on Auditing Standards for the General Accounting Office, and is a Fellow of the National Academy of Public Administration. Dr. Newcomer has won two awards for her teaching; in 1996 she was awarded the Peter Vail Excellence in Education Award, and in May 2000 she received the George Washington Award.

Dr. Newcomer earned a B.S. in education and an M.A. in political science from the University of Kansas, and her Ph.D. in political science from the University of Iowa.

Paul O'Connell is an associate professor and former chair of the Department of Criminal Justice at Iona College in New Rochelle, New York. He teaches undergraduate and graduate courses in law, criminal justice, and public administration.

His recent research has focused upon the areas of program evaluation, and police administration and training. He is currently engaged in a project entitled, "An Intellectual History of the CompStat Model of Police Management." He has published articles in the *International Journal of Public Administration*, *City Journal*, *American Jails*, *Law Enforcement News*, and a variety of other journals and publications.

Prior to joining Iona College he served as a New York City police officer, an NYPD Police Academy law instructor and curriculum coordinator, and a civil trial attorney for the firm of Cummings & Lockwood in Stamford, Connecticut.

He is a graduate of St. John's University (1981), and holds an M.P.A. and an M.Phil. from City University of New York, John Jay College (1984, 2000), and a J.D. from St. John's School of Law (1989). He is currently completing his doctoral dissertation in criminal justice.

Mary Ann Scheirer is an independent consultant in program evaluation and performance measurement, as well as a member of the adjunct faculty of the Department of Public Administration, George Washington University. She has more than 20 years of experience conducting program evaluations, with recent emphasis on developing performance measurement systems for government agencies, both in the United States and in several other countries. Her research on assessing program implementation has been published as several books, including *Program Implementation: The Organizational Context* (1981) and *A User's Guide to Program Templates: A New Tool for Evaluating Program Content* (1996), as well as in the *Handbook for Practical Program Evaluation* (1994), and in numerous journals.

Dr. Scheirer has worked with many government agencies, including the National Institutes of Health, the Department of Education, the General Accounting Office, the Substance Abuse and Mental Health Administration, and the Health Resources and Services Administration. She served as chair of the Evaluation Review Panel of the U.S. Public Health Service Review of Health Program Evaluations in 1994, 1995, and 1996. She was elected to the boards of directors of the American Evaluation Association and the Consumer Health Foundation, and as president and treasurer of the Washington Evaluators.

Dr. Scheirer's professional training is in applied sociology, including a Ph.D. in sociology and research methods from Cornell University, and a master's degree in public administration from the Graduate School of Public and International Affairs at the University of Pittsburgh.

About The PricewaterhouseCoopers Endowment for The Business of Government

Through grants for research, The PricewaterhouseCoopers Endowment for The Business of Government stimulates research and facilitates discussion of new approaches to improving the effectiveness of government at the federal, state, local, and international levels.

Research grants of $15,000 are awarded competitively to outstanding scholars in academic and nonprofit institutions across the United States. Each grantee is expected to produce a 30- to 40-page research report in one of the areas presented on pages 263-265. Grant reports will be published and disseminated by The Endowment. All the chapters presented in this book were originally prepared as grant reports to The Endowment.

Founded in 1998 by PricewaterhouseCoopers, The Endowment is one of the ways that PricewaterhouseCoopers seeks to advance knowledge on how to improve public sector effectiveness. The PricewaterhouseCoopers Endowment focuses on the future of the operations and management of the public sector.

Who is Eligible?

Individuals working in:

- Universities
- Nonprofit organizations

Description of Grant

Individuals receiving grants will be responsible for producing a 30- to 40-page research report in one of the areas presented on pages 263-265. The research paper should be completed within a six-month period from the start of the project. Grantees select the start and end dates of the research project.

Size of Grant

$15,000 for each research paper

Who Receives the Grant

Individuals will receive the grant, not the institution in which they are located.

Application Process

Interested individuals should submit:

- A three-page description of the proposed research
- A résumé, including list of publications

Application Deadlines

There are three funding cycles annually, with deadlines of:

- The last day of February
- The last day of June
- The last day of October

Applications must be postmarked or received online by the above dates.

Submitting Applications

Hard copy:

Mark A. Abramson
Executive Director
The PricewaterhouseCoopers Endowment for The Business of Government
1616 North Fort Myer Drive
Arlington, VA 22209

Online:

endowment.pwcglobal.com/apply

Program Areas

E-Government

The Endowment is seeking proposals that examine the implementation of e-government in the following areas: (1) Government to Business (G2B); (2) Government to Citizen (G2C); (3) Government to Employee (G2E); and (4) Government to Government (G2G). The Endowment is especially interested in innovative approaches to providing information so citizens can make their own choices, complete service transactions electronically, hold government more accountable for results, and offer feedback.

Examples of previous grants in this area:

- The Auction Model: How the Public Sector Can Leverage the Power of E-Commerce Through Dynamic Pricing *by David Wyld*
- Commerce Comes to Government on the Desktop: E-Commerce Applications in the Public Sector *by Genie N. L. Stowers*
- The Use of the Internet in Government Service Delivery *by Steven Cohen and William B. Eimicke*

Financial Management

The Endowment is seeking proposals that examine specific financial management issues, such as cost accounting and management, financial and resource analysis, financial risk management and modeling, internal controls, operational and systems risk management, financial auditing, contract management, reconciliation, and overpayment recovery. The Endowment is especially interested in full costs and budgeting approaches for support services and capital assets, retirement, and other employee benefits, and other nondirect costs associated with delivering program services.

Examples of previous grants in this area:

- Audited Financial Statements: Getting and Sustaining "Clean" Opinions *by Douglas A. Brook*
- Credit Scoring and Loan Scoring: Tools for Improved Management of Federal Credit Programs *by Thomas H. Stanton*
- Using Activity-Based Costing to Manage More Effectively *by Michael H. Granof, David E. Platt, and Igor Vaysman*

Human Capital

The Endowment is seeking proposals that examine human capital issues related to public service. Human capital consists of the knowledge, skills, abilities, attitudes, and experience required to accomplish an organization's mission. It also includes an organization's ability to recruit and retain employees, as well as to undertake workforce planning and analysis.

Examples of previous grants in this area:

- Leaders Growing Leaders: Preparing the Next Generation of Public Service Executives *by Ray Blunt*
- Reflections on Mobility: Case Studies of Six Federal Executives *by Michael D. Serlin*
- Winning the Best and Brightest: Increasing the Attraction of Public Service *by Carol Chetkovich*

Managing for Results

The Endowment is seeking proposals that examine how organizations align their processes—such as budgeting, workforce, and business processes—around their strategic goals. This area also focuses on how organizations use performance and results information to make policy, management, and resource allocation decisions. The Endowment is especially interested in how different organizations work collaboratively to achieve common outcomes. The Endowment is also interested in case studies of the use of balanced scorecards, including the measurement of customer service.

Examples of previous grants in this area:

- The Challenge of Developing Cross-Agency Measures: A Case Study of the Office of National Drug Control Policy *by Patrick Murphy and John Carnevale*
- Using Performance Data for Accountability: The New York City Police Department's CompStat Model of Police Management *by Paul O'Connell*
- Using Evaluation to Support Performance Management: A Guide for Federal Executives *by Kathryn E. Newcomer and Mary Ann Scheirer*

New Ways to Manage

The Endowment is seeking proposals that examine specific instances of new ways of delivering programs and services to the public, including contracting out, competition, outsourcing, privatization, and public-private partnerships. The Endowment is also interested in innovations in the way public organizations are managed.

Examples of previous grants in this area:

- Entrepreneurial Government: Bureaucrats as Businesspeople *by Anne Laurent*
- San Diego County's Innovation Program: Using Competition and a Whole Lot More to Improve Public Services *by William B. Eimicke*
- The Challenge of Innovating in Government *by Sandford Borins*

Transforming Organizations

The Endowment is seeking proposals that examine how specific public sector organizations have been transformed with new values, changed cultures, and enhanced performance. This area also includes studies of outstanding public sector leaders.

Examples of previous grants in this area:

- Transforming Government: The Renewal and Revitalization of the Federal Emergency Management Agency *by R. Steven Daniels and Carolyn L. Clark-Daniels*
- Transforming Government: The Revitalization of the Veterans Health Administration *by Gary J. Young*
- Transforming Government: Dan Goldin and the Remaking of NASA *by W. Henry Lambright*

For more information about The Endowment

Visit our website at: endowment.pwcglobal.com
Send an e-mail to: endowment@us.pwcglobal.com
Call: (703) 741-1077

About PricewaterhouseCoopers

The Management Consulting Services practice of PricewaterhouseCoopers helps clients maximize their business performance by integrating strategic change, performance improvement, and technology solutions. Through a worldwide network of skills and resources, consultants manage complex projects with global capabilities and local knowledge, from strategy through implementation. PricewaterhouseCoopers (www.pwcglobal.com) is the world's largest professional services organization. Drawing on the knowledge and skills of more than 150,000 people in 150 countries, the practice helps clients solve complex business problems and measurably enhance their ability to build value, manage risk, and improve performance in an Internet-enabled world. PricewaterhouseCoopers refers to the member firms of the worldwide PricewaterhouseCoopers organization.